✫ Forbes
TRAVEL GUIDE
Formerly Mobil Travel Guide

NORTHERN CALIFORNIA
2011

RO5011 97847

ACKNOWLEDGMENTS

We gratefully acknowledge the help of our representatives for their efficient and perceptive inspections of the lodgings listed. Forbes Travel Guide is also grateful to the talented writers who contributed to this book.

Front Cover image: ©iStockphoto.com
All maps: Mapping Specialists

ISBN: 9781936010899
Manufactured in the USA
10 9 8 7 6 5 4 3 2 1

CONTENTS

STAR ATTRACTIONS

If you've been a reader of Mobil Travel Guide, you will have heard that this historic brand partnered in 2009 with another storied media name, Forbes, to create a new entity, Forbes Travel Guide. For more than 50 years, Mobil Travel Guide assisted travelers in making smart decisions about where to stay and dine when traveling. With this new partnership, our mission has not changed: We're committed to the same rigorous inspections of hotels, restaurants and spas—the most comprehensive in the industry with more than 500 standards tested at each property we visit—to help you cut through the clutter and make easy and informed decisions on where to spend your time and travel budget. Our team of anonymous inspectors are constantly on the road, sleeping in hotels, eating in restaurants and making spa appointments, evaluating those exacting standards to determine a property's rating.

What kinds of standards are we looking for when we visit a property? We're looking for more than just high-thread count sheets, pristine spa treatment rooms and white linen-topped tables. We look for service that's attentive, individualized and unforgettable. We note how long it takes to be greeted when you sit down at your table, or to be served when you order room service, or whether the hotel staff can confidently help you when you've forgotten that one essential item that will make or break your trip. Unlike any other travel ratings entity, we visit each place we rate, testing hundreds of attributes to compile our ratings, and our ratings cannot be bought or influenced. The Forbes Five Star rating is the most prestigious achievement in hospitality—while we rate more than 5,000 properties in the U.S., Canada, Hong Kong, Macau and Beijing, for 2011, we have awarded Five Star designations to only 54 hotels, 23 restaurants and 20 spas. When you travel with Forbes, you can travel with confidence, knowing that you'll get the very best experience, no matter who you are.

We understand the importance of making the most of your time. That's why the most trusted name in travel is now Forbes Travel Guide.

STAR RATED HOTELS

Whether you're looking for the ultimate in luxury or the best value for your travel budget, we have a hotel recommendation for you. To help you pinpoint properties that meet your needs, Forbes Travel Guide classifies each lodging by type according to the following characteristics:

★★★★★These exceptional properties provide a memorable experience through virtually flawless service and the finest of amenities. Staff are intuitive, engaging and passionate, and eagerly deliver service above and beyond the guests' expectations. The hotel was designed with the guest's comfort in mind, with particular attention paid to craftsmanship and quality of product. A Five-Star property is a destination unto itself.

★★★★These properties provide a distinctive setting, and a guest will find many interesting and inviting elements to enjoy throughout the property. Attention to detail is prominent throughout the property, from design concept to quality of products provided. Staff are accommodating and take pride in catering to the guest's specific needs throughout their stay.

★★★These well-appointed establishments have enhanced amenities that provide travelers with a strong sense of location, whether for style or function. They may have a distinguishing style and ambience in both the public spaces and guest rooms; or they may be more focused on functionality, providing guests with easy access to local events, meetings or tourism highlights.

Recommended: These hotels are considered clean, comfortable and reliable establishments that have expanded amenities, such as full-service restaurants.

For every property, we also provide pricing information. All prices quoted are accurate at the time of publication; however, prices cannot be guaranteed. Because rates can fluctuate, we list a pricing range rather than specific prices.

STAR RATED RESTAURANTS

Every restaurant in this book has been visited by Forbes Travel Guide's team of experts and comes highly recommended as an outstanding dining experience.

★★★★★Forbes Five-Star restaurants deliver a truly unique and distinctive dining experience. A Five-Star restaurant consistently provides exceptional food, superlative service and elegant décor. An emphasis is placed on originality and personalized, attentive and discreet service. Every detail that surrounds the experience is attended to by a warm and gracious dining room team.

★★★★These are exciting restaurants with often well-known chefs that feature creative and complex foods and emphasize various culinary techniques and a focus on seasonality. A highly-trained dining room staff provides refined personal service and attention.

★★★Three Star restaurants offer skillfully prepared food with a focus on a specific style or cuisine. The dining room staff provides warm and professional service in a comfortable atmosphere. The décor is well-coordinated with quality fixtures and decorative items, and promotes a comfortable ambience.

Recommended: These restaurants serve fresh food in a clean setting with efficient service. Value is considered in this category, as is family friendliness.

Because menu prices can fluctuate, we list a pricing range rather than specific prices. The pricing ranges are per diner, and assume that you order an appetizer or dessert, an entrée and one drink.

STAR RATED SPAS

Forbes Travel Guide's spa ratings are based on objective evaluations of more than 450 attributes. About half of these criteria assess basic expectations, such as staff courtesy, the technical proficiency and skill of the employees and whether the facility is clean and maintained properly. Several standards address issues that impact a guest's physical comfort and convenience, as well as the staff's ability to impart a sense of personalized service. Additional criteria measure the spa's ability to create a completely calming ambience.

★★★★★ Stepping foot in a Five Star Spa will result in an exceptional experience with no detail overlooked. These properties wow their guests with extraordinary design and facilities, and uncompromising service. Expert staff cater to your every whim and pamper you with the most advanced treatments and skin care lines available. These spas often offer exclusive treatments and may emphasize local elements.

★★★★ Four Star spas provide a wonderful experience in an inviting and serene environment. A sense of personalized service is evident from the moment you check in and receive your robe and slippers. The guest's comfort is always of utmost concern to the well-trained staff.

★★★ These spas offer well-appointed facilities with a full complement of staff to ensure that guests' needs are met. The spa facil ties include clean and appealing treatment rooms, changing areas and a welcoming reception desk.

TOP HOTELS, RESTAURANTS AND SPAS

HOTELS

★★★★★FIVE STAR
Chateau du Sureau (*Oakhurst*)
Four Seasons Hotel San Francisco
(*San Francisco*)
The Ritz-Carlton, San Francisco
(*San Francisco*)
The St. Regis San Francisco
(*San Francisco*)

★★★★FOUR STAR
Bernardus Lodge (*Carmel Valley*)
Calistoga Ranch (*Calistoga*)
Casa Palmero at Pebble Beach
(*Pebble Beach*)
CordeValle, A Rosewood Resort
(*San Martin*)
Four Seasons Hotel Silicon Valley at East
Palo Alto (*Palo Alto*)
The Inn at Spanish Bay (*Pebble Beach*)
Les Mars (*Healdsburg*)
The Lodge at Pebble Beach
(*Pebble Beach*)
Mandarin Oriental, San Francisco
(*San Francisco*)
Meadowood Napa Valley (*St. Helena*)
Monterey Plaza Hotel & Spa (*Monterey*)
Post Ranch Inn (*Big Sur*)
The Ritz-Carlton, Half Moon Bay
(*Half Moon Bay*)
Rosewood Sand Hill (*Menlo Park*)

RESTAURANTS

★★★★★FIVE STAR
The Dining Room at the Ritz-Carlton
(*San Francisco*)
The French Laundry (*Yountville*)

RESTAURANTS

★★★★FOUR STAR
Auberge du Soleil (*St. Helena*)
Campton Place (*San Francisco*)
Cyrus (*Healdsburg*)
Erna's Elderberry House (*Oakhurst*)
Fleur de Lys (*San Francisco*)
Gary Danko (*San Francisco*)
La Folie (*San Francisco*)
Madera (*Menlo Park*)
Manresa (Los Gatos)
Masa's (*San Francisco*)
Marinus (*Carmel Valley*)
Quince (*San Francisco*)
The Restaurant at Meadowood
(*St. Helena*)
Sierra Mar (*Big Sur*)
Silks (*San Francisco*)
Spruce (*San Francisco*)
Terra (*St. Helena*)
The Village Pub (*Woodside*)

SPAS

★★★★FOUR STAR
Auberge Spa (*Rutherford*)
Post Ranch Spa (*Big Sur*)
Remède Spa (*San Francisco*)
The Ritz-Carlton Spa, Half Moon Bay
(*Half Moon Bay*)
Sense, A Rosewood Spa, CordeValle
(*San Martin*)
Sense, A Rosewood Spa at
Rosewood Sand Hill (*Menlo Park*)
The Spa at Bernardus Lodge
(*Carmel Valley*)
The Spa at Calistoga Ranch (*Calistoga*)
The Spa at the Carneros Inn (*Napa Valley*)
The Spa at Meadowood Napa Valley
(*St. Helena*)
The Spa at Pebble Beach (*Pebble Beach*)
Spa Du Sureau (*Pebble Beach*)

YOUR QUESTIONS ANSWERED

WHAT ARE SOME OF SAN FRANCISCO'S BEST EXPERIENCES?

There is so much to see and do in San Francisco that it's hard to single out a few attractions. However, some of the best experiences include a trip to Fisherman's Wharf. Locals might compain about it, but that doesn't stop it from being one of the city's top attractions. You have to see the lazy sea lions at least once and enjoy some clam chowder served in Boudin's sourdough bread bowls. Another must-see is Alcatraz. As part of the U.S. National Park Service, the well-maintained and fascinating site focuses on history—witness the superb audio tour, narrated by former guards and inmates—and on a foggy day, the tales you'll hear are bone-chilling indeed.

If you haven't held on to a cable car while it climbs to the top of a hill, you simply have not experienced San Francisco. Its system is the last manually operated one in the world, and watching the operators maneuver the lever to grip and release the cable is a great glimpse into the past. The iconic cars chug along three routes, merrily clanging as the humming cables pull them along. Angle for a seat on the outside for a breezy experience, and beat the interminable lines at the turnaround points by boarding at any stop designated by a brown and white sign.

WHEN IS THE BEST TIME TO VISIT NORTHERN CALIFORNIA?

Really, any time is a good time to visit spring-like Northern California. But unlike its Southern counterpart, Northern California doesn't have picture-perfect weather year round. Spring will deliver the best weather, with sunny skies, though fall sees the warmer temperatures. The rain usually comes in the late fall and early winter. Summers have cooler, windy weather and the fog hangs over the city in the mornings. The weather can change drastically, so be sure to pack layers, whichever season you decide to visit.

WELCOME TO NORTHERN CALIFORNIA

A DREAM OF GOLD EVEN BEFORE IT BECAME A STATE,

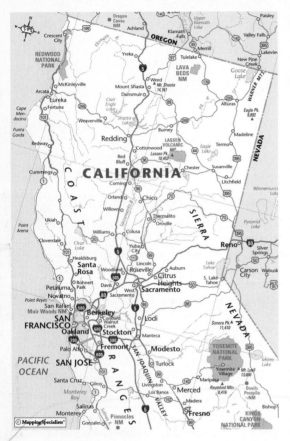

California has long enticed world travelers. Over land and across the Pacific Ocean, in sunshine and in fog, travelers keep coming to cruise along 1,200 miles of coastline and picnic among vineyards, lounge on beaches and play in the surf, climb mountains and ski snowy peaks, look down on the Golden Gate Bridge from the heights of San Francisco and gaze up at gargantuan redwoods.

With the oldest-known trees on Earth—a stand of bristlecone pines said to be more than 4,700 years old—and with the lowest and highest points in the continental United States—Death Valley and Mount Whitney—only 80 miles from one another, the Golden State does things in a big way.

Spaniards, Mexicans, English, Russians, Chinese and others helped write the state's rich history. Many streets and buildings in California bear the name of Juan Rodríguez Cabrillo, a Portuguese explorer and the first European to venture into California waters in 1542. English explorer Sir Francis Drake is believed to have landed just northwest of what is now San Francisco in 1579.

It took almost 200 years more, however, for the first towns to develop around Spanish missions, beginning in 1769. For five years, the Mexican flag flew over California after Mexico won independence from Spain. In 1826, American settlers revolted against Mexican authorities and formed the short-lived Bear Flag Republic (commemorated by the state flag). The 1848 Treaty of Guadalupe Hidalgo ended the Mexican-American War—during which the U.S. cut Mexico in half—and led to California becoming part of the developing coastal boundary of the United States.

The same year, a glimmer of gold in the American River set off a mass migration of a half-million California dreamers from around the world, whose arrival enlivened the drowsy countryside and split the Far West wide open. The 49ers who came for gold stayed to enjoy the geographic and agricultural splendors of what would become the most populous state in the union. Now it's your turn.

NORTH COAST

The rugged North Coast provides a beautiful backdrop with nature preserves and forests. And of course, there are the wineries that dot the region. There are a number of towns where you can take in the scenery and taste some local wines.

Bodega Bay is a gorgeous stretch of shoreline that's a favorite for day-tripping San Franciscans. Covering eight miles of coast, there are sandy beaches to swim, surf, windsurf and just enjoy the scenery. Bodega Bay is a great spot to go whale watching or horseback riding through the mountains, and it's close enough to Sonoma county wineries for some wine tasting. Another beachy area is Fort Ross State Historic Park, one of the oldest in the California state park system. It offers a beach, steep bluffs, a cove and plenty of forest to explore.

Famous for its wineries, Glen Ellen was home to writers Jack London and Hunter S. Thompson. Only 45 minutes from San Francisco, it is a popular destination for weekend getaways.

Minutes from more than 150 wineries, Santa Rosa is surrounded by vineyards and mountains. The rich soil and even climate of the Sonoma Valley lured famed horticulturist Luther Burbank here, where he lived and worked for 50 years, developing innumerable new and improved plant life. Many farm and ranch products originate from the area.

WHAT TO SEE

BODEGA BAY
DORAN REGIONAL PARK
201 Doran Beach Road, Bodega Bay, 707-875-3540; www.sonoma-county.org
Build a sandcastle on two miles of sandy beach or wander out onto a rock jetty at the harbor mouth for crabbing or fishing. You can also go surfing or hiking. And this is a lovely spot for a picnic. Dogs are permitted on a leash only.

BEST ATTRACTIONS

NORTHERN CALIFORNIA'S BEST ATTRACTIONS

CENTRAL COAST TOWNS
The High Sierra region encompasses some of Northern California's most beautiful scenic spots. From Big Sur to Carmel to Pebble Beach, you'll get more than an eyeful of breathtaking canyons, bluffs, waterfalls and ocean views.

NAPA
Visitors head to Napa Valley's tasting rooms to sniff, swirl and sip their way through this bucolic countryside, before retiring to one of the top-notch restaurants at night for even more wine and mouthwatering cuisine. There are plenty of small towns to explore.

SACRAMENTO
As California's capital, Sacramento is where all of the politicos conduct their deals. The city's also a good spot for tourists, with Old Sacramento, a downtown arts and entertainment corridor, museums and more.

SAN FRANCISCO
No city is more synonymous with Northern California than San Francisco. The city of hippies, artists and tech millionaires has great neighborhoods such as Haight-Ashbury, Chinatown and the Mission as well as countless museums, parks and other attractions.

SONOMA
The quieter sister to nearby Napa, Sonoma has plenty of top-notch wineries, luxurious inns and spas, and superlative dining, but without the crowds. The area includes the towns of Sonoma and Healdsburg, which are the most popular for touring wineries.

YOSEMITE NATIONAL PARK
The majestic Yosemite is one of the nation's most amazing parks. It's famous for its waterfalls, but outdoorsy types can head there to partake in biking, fishing, rock climbing, hiking and horseback riding.

FORT ROSS STATE HISTORIC PARK
FORT ROSS STATE HISTORIC PARK
19005 Coast Highway 1, Jenner, 707-847-3286; www.parks.ca.gov

The fort was once a distant outpost of the Russian empire and, for nearly three decades in the early 1800s, an important center for the sea otter trade set up by the Russian-American Company of Alaska. A Californian bought the land in 1841. Look for a reconstructed Russian Orthodox chapel, the original seven-sided and eight-sided blockhouses, the Commandant's house, officers' barracks and stockade walls. While on the beach or surrounding bluffs, you might see migrating grey whales and sea lions or harbor seals lounging in the sun.

KRUSE RHODODENDRON STATE RESERVE
Jenner, 707-847-3221; www.parks.ca.gov

Adjacent to Salt Point State Park, this 317-acre reserve is overflowing with flowers. Five miles of hiking trails lead past Douglas firs, grand firs, tanoaks and rhododendrons, which bloom in April and May.

SALT POINT STATE PARK
25050 Coast Highway 1, Jenner, 707-847-3221; www.parks.ca.gov

Sandstone from Salt Point was used to build the streets and structures of San Francisco in the 1800s. Fisk Mill Cove supplies an area for picnicking with tables and barbecues. One of the first underwater parks, the Gerstle Cove Marine Reserve, is located here and offers a good spot for scuba diving. There are also more than 20 miles of hiking and riding trails.

Visitor center: April-October, Saturday-Sunday 10 a.m.-3 p.m. Daily sunrise-sunset.

SONOMA COAST STATE BEACH
Jenner, 707-875-3483; www.parks.ca.gov

On 4,200 acres along the coastline, running from Bodega Bay to Jenner, these sandy beaches, rocky headlands and sand dunes provide a scenic place to play. The rocky headland forming the entrance to the Bodega Harbor is a popular crabbing area. Goat Rock has a sandy beach where seals congregate to sunbathe, while Shell Beach offers plenty of tide pools to explore. Dogs are prohibited on most beaches.

GLEN ELLEN
JACK LONDON STATE HISTORICAL PARK
2400 London Ranch Road, Glen Ellen, 707-938-5216; www.parks.sonoma.net.com

A memorial to the writer Jack London, this park is located on the site of his mansion, where he lived from 1905 until his death in 1916. The grounds include the gravesite of London and his wife, Charmian.

Daily 9:30 a.m.-5 p.m.

MENDOCINO
MENDOCINO ART CENTER
45200 Little Lake St., Mendocino, 707-937-5818; www.mendocinoartcenter.org

Overlooking the Pacific Ocean, the Mendocino Art Center was the focal point for the town's revitalization as an artistic community after its logging economy faltered. Exhibits by working artists at four galleries typically change monthly and several artists-in-residence open their studios to the public on a regular basis. Try to catch a show by the Mendocino Theatre Company, which also makes its home here.

Daily 10 a.m.-5 p.m.

THE PHILO APPLE FARM
18501 Greenwood Road, Philo, 707-895-2333; www.philoapplefarm.com

In early fall, stop by this nearly 2,000-tree orchard about 120 miles north of San Francisco to pick fresh apples from among 80 varieties. The apple stock is typically sold out by mid-November. At the season's height, take a peek into the busy kitchen, where apples become preserves, butters, syrups and cider, which you can purchase at the farm stand. If you're in San Francisco, you can also find the produce at the Farmers' Market on Saturday or inside the Ferry Building at Cowgirl Creamery where some of the farm's jams and chutneys are sold.

VAN DAMME STATE PARK
Highway 1, Mendocino, 707-937-5804; www.parks.ca.gov

The tiny, 6-inch to 8-foot venerable trees of the Pygmy Forest dominate the southeast part of this 2,190-acre park, where poor soil conditions inhibit tree growth. Some trees, nearly 200 years old, have trunks only an inch in diameter. Divers can head to a protected cove in the Little River and hikers can explore the fern canyons. Rent a kayak or take a kayak tour to see all the tide pools and sea caves. There are also camping and picnicking sites here.

MENLO PARK
FILOLI HOUSE AND GARDENS
86 Cañada Road, Woodside, 650-364-8300; www.filoli.org

This 654-acre estate holds a venerable Georgian-style residence, once featured in the television series *Dynasty*, and 16-acre Italian Renaissance-style gardens with terraces, lawns and pools.

House and garden; guided tours: mid-February-October, Tuesday-Saturday 10 a.m.-3:30 p.m., Sunday 11 a.m.-3:30 p.m.; reservations required. Self-guided tours: no reservations required.

SUNSET MAGAZINE GARDENS
80 Willow Road, Menlo Park, 650-321-3600; www.sunset.com

These attractive gardens are tended by the publishers of *Sunset* magazine and its namesake books.

Self-guided tour of gardens: Monday-Friday.

SANTA ROSA
LUTHER BURBANK HOME & GARDENS
Santa Rosa and Sonoma avenues, Santa Rosa, 707-524-5445; www.lutherburbank.org

This historic landmark is where the locally famous horticulturist Luther Burbank lived. His work is on display along with a greenhouse, gardens, a carriage house and exhibits.

April-October, Tuesday-Sunday 10 a.m.-3 p.m. Gardens: Daily 8 a.m.-sunset.

BEST ATTRACTIONS

WHAT ARE THE TOP THINGS TO DO IN THE NORTH COAST?

GET SOME SUN AT SONOMA COAST STATE BEACH

Along the beach's 4,200 acres, you can watch seals, explore tide pools, go swimming or just play on the dunes.

VISIT JACK LONDON STATE HISTORICAL PARK

If you are a fan of *Call of the Wild* or author Jack London, visit this state park, which is on the site of the writer's mansion. His grave can also be found on the grounds.

CHECK OUT FILOLI HOUSE AND GARDENS

This Georgian-style mansion might look familiar. That's because it's been featured in films such as *The Wedding Planner* and *The Joy Luck Club* and shows like *Dynasty*.

GO SKATING AT REDWOOD EMPIRE ICE ARENA

Dubbed Snoopy's Home Ice, this rink was built by *Peanuts* comics scribe Charles M. Schulz. After skating a few laps, head to the Schulz Museum next door.

SEE EXOTIC ANIMALS AT SAFARI WEST WILDLIFE PRESERVE

Who says you have to head to Africa to go on a safari? You can take a safari in the middle of wine country at this wildlife preserve with giraffes, zebras and more.

REDWOOD EMPIRE ICE ARENA

1667 W. Steele Lane, Santa Rosa, 707-546-7147; www.snoopyshomeice.com

Built by Charles M. Schulz, the creator of the *Peanuts* comic strip, this ice arena, known as Snoopy's Home Ice, is a great place to cool off on a hot summer day. The rink offers skate rentals, events and has a restaurant onsite. Next door is the Charles M. Schulz Museum, known as the Snoopy Gallery, which also contains a gift shop.

Hours vary; call or visit website. Snoopy's Gallery: Daily 10 a.m.-6 p.m.

SAFARI WEST WILDLIFE PRESERVE AND AFRICAN TENT CAMP
3115 Porter Creek Road, Santa Rosa, 707-579-2551, 800-616-2695; www.safariwest.com

Board a safari vehicle and head into the hills in search of the more than 600 exotic mammals and birds that call this place home. Animals include cheetahs, giraffes, antelopes, zebras and more.

Admission: adults $68, children 3-12 $30, children 1-2 $10. Monday-Thursday 9 a.m., 10 a.m., 1 p.m., 2 p.m.

WHERE TO STAY

BODEGA BAY
★★★BODEGA BAY LODGE
103 Coast Highway 1, Bodega Bay, 707-875-3525, 888-875-2250; www.bodegabaylodge.com

Just an hour north of San Francisco, this lodge overlooks the ocean, a nature preserve, Doran Beach State Park and the bluffs of Bodega Head. The comfortable guest rooms feature ocean views and most have fireplaces, private balconies, bathrobes, minibars, CD players and European-style bedding. After a day of pampering at the onsite spa, snag a table at the Duck Club, which overlooks the ocean and serves up seasonal local seafood, meats and regional ingredients.

84 rooms. Restaurant. Pool. Spa. $251-350

★★★THE INN AT THE TIDES
800 Coast Highway 1, Bodega Bay, 707-875-2751, 800-541-7788; www.innatthetides.com

From the bay and harbor views in the guest rooms to the staff's attentiveness, this resort is all about relaxation. Ask for a room with a wood-burning fireplace, along with views of the harbor or bay. Take a dip in the indoor/outdoor heated pool and detox in the Finnish sauna. Dine at one of two restaurants, the Tides Wharf or the Bay View, both of which feature views of either the bay or the harbor.

86 rooms. Restaurant, bar. Complimentary breakfast. Fitness center. Pool. $151-250

FORT ROSS STATE HISTORIC PARK
★★★TIMBER COVE INN
21780 N. Coast Highway 1, Jenner, 707-847-3231, 800-987-8319; www.timbercoveinn.com

A soaring cathedral ceiling, large stone fireplace and picture windows welcome guests to this lodge-like inn, located on the Sonoma Coast. The lobby is filled with leather couches, fresh flowers and a grand piano. Guest rooms are just as comfortable with spacious patios, which offer views of the ocean or the inn's quaint Japanese pond. There are 26 acres of trails and a half-mile of ocean frontage on the grounds.

50 rooms. Restaurant, bar. $151-250

GLEN ELLEN
★★★ST. ORRES
36601 Coast Highway 1, Gualala, 707-884-3303; www.saintorres.com

This inn is located three hours north of San Francisco on more than 50 acres of coastal sanctuary. Local craftsmen built the Russian dacha-like house, working with materials found in the area to form its distinct onion-domed towers, stained glass features and woodwork. Rooms have a rustic atmosphere and amenities such as wood-burning stoves, fireplaces, soaking tubs, French doors or decks. Most rooms provide an ocean view, and the restaurant offers a myriad of fine cuisine.

21 rooms. Complimentary breakfast. Restaurant, bar. $151-250

MENDOCINO

★★★ALBION RIVER INN

3790 N. Highway 1, Albion, 707-937-1919, 800-479-7944; www.albionriverinn.com

Set in a historic town on 10 secluded acres, this inn provides complimentary breakfast, wine, binoculars for whale watching and bathrobes. Rooms are spacious and simply decorated with modern furnishings. Many rooms feature private decks, whirlpool tubs and fireplaces. Enjoy the breathtaking views of the ocean bluffs and rugged north coast from your bathtub. The restaurant here provides beautiful views of the ocean while serving fresh local and regional seafood, meats and organic produce. Choose from a wine list that features more than 500 wines and more than 140 single malts.

22 rooms. Restaurant, bar. Complimentary breakfast. $151-250

★★★THE HARBOR HOUSE INN

5600 S. Highway 1, Elk, 707-877-3203, 800-720-7474; www.theharborhouseinn.com

Serene gardens surround this refurbished 1916 bed and breakfast featuring craftsmen style architecture. Six rooms are located in the main house, which has high ceilings and large windows that look out to the garden and ocean. Each room is decorated with antiques, luxury bedding, a large bath, a fireplace and sitting area. There are also four cottages, which have private bathrooms, fireplaces and private decks. A full breakfast and four-course dinner for two is included with each room and served daily.

10 rooms. Restaurant. Complimentary breakfast. No children under 16. $251-350

WHICH HOTELS HAVE THE BEST VIEWS?

Albion River Inn: Most of the rooms at this inn have private decks, but you can enjoy beautiful vistas of the ocean and rugged coast from your bathtub.

Bodega Bay Lodge and Spa: This lodge offers a slew of views; it overlooks the ocean, a nature preserve, Doran Beach State Park and Bodega Head.

Hill House Inn: The lovely water and garden views at this inn, which sits near the Pacific Ocean, have lured in famous guests such as Bette Davis.

★★★HILL HOUSE INN

10701 Palette Drive, Mendocino, 707-937-0554, 800-422-0554; www.hillhouseinn.com

This charming oceanside inn offers beautiful ocean views, lush gardens and a convenient location to all that Mendocino has to offer. The inn has had famous guests stay here over the years, including Bette Davis. If you're a fan, choose to stay in the Bette Davis Suite or check out the photo gallery in the lobby with signed photographs of her and other celebrities.

44 rooms. Restaurant, bar. $61-150

★★★MACCALLUM HOUSE INN

45020 Albion St., Mendocino, 707-937-0289, 800-609-0492;
www.maccallumhouse.com

This artfully landscaped, secluded inn is made up of several properties, including a hilltop mansion overlooking the Pacific Ocean and an 1882 mansion on Main Street. Inquire about rooms with fireplaces, claw-foot soaking tubs and picturesque ocean views. There are also seven cottages near the main house, most of which feature private decks and wood stoves. Thoughtful amenities include a complimentary gourmet breakfast served daily; in-house limousine service and wine tours; rental bikes; an outdoor hot tub; and croquet on the main lawn. The charming MacCallum House Restaurant serves up fresh organic cuisine, much of which is made and prepared in its own kitchen.

32 rooms. Restaurant. Complimentary breakfast. Pets accepted. Beach. $151-250

★★★THE STANFORD INN BY THE SEA

Highway 1 and Comptche Ukiah Road, Mendocino, 707-937-5615, 800-331-8884;
www.stanfordinn.com

This inn's organic gardens, farm and rugged coastal beauty complement the comfort of its tastefully decorated rooms, which include wood-burning fireplaces. The lobby, guest rooms and suites have pine and redwood paneling, which warm up rooms and provide rustic charm. The restaurant, Raven's, serves delicious organic vegetarian (and vegan at dinner) cuisine. The wine list features wines from certified organic vineyards. Canoes and kayaks are also available for rental to take out on the Big River.

33 rooms. Restaurant. Complimentary breakfast. Spa. Pets accepted. $351 and up

MENLO PARK

★★★★ROSEWOOD SAND HILL

2825 Sand Hill Road, Menlo Park, 650-561-1500; www.rosewoodhotels.com

This stylish resort, opened in 2009, fills a need for an upscale place to stay, dine and relax in Silicon Valley. The resort, tucked away against the hills off a busy main road in Menlo Park, feels more like it's in secluded wine country than suburban Menlo Park, with its rambling, low buildings, manicured landscaping and beautiful views. The contemporary décor is California casual, with an impressive art collection sourced from local galleries. The rooms are supplied with sprawling bathrooms, plush, pillowy mattresses topped with down duvets and Italian linens, flat-screen TVs and Nespresso coffee makers. The polished staff attends to every need with confidence, whether it's recommending a local bottle of wine to sip by the outdoor fire pits, or delivering extra thick towels to the poolside chaises. The onsite spa is an attractive, sybaritic space for indulging in a full menu of treatments.

123 rooms. Restaurant, bar. Fitness center. Spa. $351 and up

SANTA ROSA

★★★HILTON SONOMA WINE COUNTRY

3555 Round Barn Blvd., Santa Rosa, 707-523-7555, 800-445-8667; www.winecountryhilton.com

Located on top of a hill in the center of more than 140 world-class Sonoma County wineries, this hotel gives guests quick access to surrounding towns, as well as hiking, biking and sailing at nearby state parks. Rooms are spacious and some include private decks. The hotel offers plenty of amenities, including a large outdoor heated pool and jogging track. Nectar Restaurant and Lounge features seasonal regional ingredients.

250 rooms. Restaurant, bar. Business center. Fitness center. Pool. Spa. Pets accepted. $151-250

★★★HOTEL LA ROSE

308 Wilson St., Santa Rosa, 707-579-3200, 800-527-6738; www.hotellarose.com

Located in Santa Rosa's historic Railroad Square, this European-style boutique hotel is a short walk from downtown shops, restaurants and movie theaters, and is across the street from the visitor center in the old train station. The hotel's original building dates to 1907, with a more contemporary annex on an adjacent street. Guest rooms are equipped with armoires, duvets, lots of pillows and marble bathrooms. Visit Josef's, the hotel restaurant, for continental cuisine.

47 rooms. Restaurant, bar. Complimentary breakfast. $61-150

★★★HYATT VINEYARD CREEK HOTEL & SPA–SONOMA COUNTY

170 Railroad St., Santa Rosa, 707-284-1234, 800-633-7313; www.hyatt.com

From the guest rooms and suites to the outdoor sculpture garden, an artistic flair sets this hotel apart from others. At the spa, choose from a full menu of treatments, including seven types of massages and six types of facials. Several treatments use crushed grape seeds and olive oil to soften and smooth skin. Using Sonoma county ingredients, the hotel's restaurant, Seafood Brasserie, serves dishes that taste of French country cooking.

155 rooms. Restaurant, bar. Fitness center. Pool. Spa. $151-250

★★★KENWOOD INN & SPA

10400 Sonoma Highway, Kenwood, 707-833-1293, 800-353-6966; www.kenwoodinn.com

Set among 2,000 acres of vineyards, this Mediterranean villa recalls the Tuscan countryside. The cozy and charming rooms have striped fabric headboards, iron scroll work and terra-cotta tile floors that capture the romance of Italy. Most rooms have featherbeds, private jetted tubs, fireplaces and either patios or sitting areas. Amenities include two pools, fountains, landscaped gardens, a wine bar and a full-service spa. The Restaurant features traditional Italian dishes made with local ingredients. A private wine bar located within the courtyard offers rare wines and light fare.

29 rooms. Restaurant, bar. Complimentary breakfast. Pool. Spa. No children allowed. $351 and up

★★★VINTNERS INN
4350 Barnes Road, Santa Rosa, 707-575-7350, 800-421-2584; www.vintnersinn.com

On the grounds of a 92-acre vineyard, this Southwestern-style inn owned by winemakers Ferrari-Carano surrounds an attractive central courtyard with a fountain. Spacious guest rooms have beamed ceilings, bathrobes, featherbeds, honor bars, decks or patios and whirlpool tubs. All suites and upstairs fireplace rooms have wood-burning fireplaces. You can book an in-room massage or take advantage of the vineyard trail and go for a jog or walk. There's also a bocce ball court and a fitness room. A complimentary breakfast is provided and a bottle of wine is given as a welcome gift.

44 rooms. Restaurant, bar. Complimentary breakfast. Fitness center. $251-350

RECOMMENDED

GLEN ELLEN
GAIGE HOUSE INN
13540 Arnold Drive, Glen Ellen, 707-935-0237, 800-935-0237; www.gaige.com

At this woodsy yet luxurious resting spot, the guest rooms give the impression of outdoor living, with large windows looking out onto the countryside. Rooms are individually designed—some with fireplaces or private Japanese gardens. Four off-site cottages are even more secluded and ideal for longer visits.

23 rooms. Complimentary breakfast. Pool. Spa. No children under 12. $251-350

MENDOCINO
BREWERY GULCH INN
9401 N. Highway 1, Mendocino, 707-937-4752, 800-578-4454;
www.brewerygulchinn.com

With a mission to improve and enhance the ecosystem and regenerate the land, Brewery Gulch Inn is constructed of 150-year-old redwood timber, and rooms are painted with eco-spec paint and feature fluorescent lighting, gas-burning fireplaces, organic cotton towels and low-flow showerheads. The kitchen features organic and locally-sourced vegetables and herbs that come from the inn's garden. All rooms have ocean views, gas fireplaces, down comforters and pillows, feather beds, luxurious linens, organic towels and more.

10 rooms. Complimentary breakfast. No children under 12. $151-250

STEVENSWOOD SPA RESORT
8211 N. Highway 1, Little River, 707-937-2810, 800-421-2810; www.stevenswood.com

This secluded hotel offers rooms with wood-burning fireplaces, Italian espresso machines, bath butler service, Egyptian cotton linens, down comforters and more. At the Indigo Eco-Spa, you can receive a range of treatments from facials to massages, scrubs and reflexology.

7 rooms. Restaurant, bar. Complimentary breakfast. Fitness center. Spa. $251-350

WHERE TO EAT

BODEGA BAY
★★★THE DUCK CLUB RESTAURANT
Bodega Bay Lodge, 103 Coast Highway 1, Bodega Bay, 707-875-3525, 888-875-2250;
www.bodegabaylodge.com

Head out to the southern fringes of Bodega Bay for fine dining at the Bodega
Bay Lodge and Spa. The lodge's restaurant overlooks a bird sanctuary and
Doran Beach, with Bodega Head and the Pacific Ocean as a backdrop. Ask for
a seat on the dining room's western side for a sea view through large picture
windows. Chef Jeff Reilly's menu offers local, sustainable seafood, meats,
cheeses and produce. You'll find options such as crab cakes with tomato ginger
chutney, clam chowder, tenderloin carpaccio, oysters and pistachio-crusted
halibut with roasted bell peppers.
American. Breakfast, dinner. $36-85

MENDOCINO
★★★ALBION RIVER INN
3790 N. Highway 1, Albion, 707-937-1919, 800-479-7944; www.albionriverinn.com

Dine on an international menu composed of local produce while admiring
views of Albion Cove and the Pacific Ocean. Chef Stephen Smith offers fresh
coastal cuisine including shellfish, seafood chowder, prawns, sole, short ribs,
crab cakes, pork stew and more. The dessert menu is equally as appealing
with choices such as chocolate mousse, cheesecake, housemade sorbet and ice
cream. A pianist livens up the dining room on the weekends.
International. Dinner. Reservations recommended. Bar. $36-85

★★★CAFE BEAUJOLAIS
961 Ukiah St., Mendocino, 707-937-5614; www.cafebeaujolais.com

Surrounded by antique roses, edible flowers and unusual plants, this café,
housed in a Victorian farmhouse, serves cuisine made from locally grown
organic produce and freshly baked goods from its onsite bakery, The Brickery.
The main dining room features pale green walls, white linens and dark wood
floors for a calm, cozy atmosphere. The garden dining room on the enclosed
patio overlooks the green gardens. Entrées include roasted acorn squash with
wild and brown rice and pomegranate-zinfandel reduction; and pan-roasted
California sturgeon fillet with truffle emulsion sauce.
French, American. Lunch, dinner. Bar. $36-85

MENLO PARK
★★★★MADERA
Rosewood Sand Hill, 2825 Sand Hill Road, Menlo Park, 650-561-1540;
www.rosewoodhotels.com

With its massive, floor-to-ceiling windows, intriguing open kitchen and cozy
fireplaces, this restaurant inside the Rosewood Sand Hill resort is a beguiling
place to take a table and dig into locally sourced, seasonal California cuisine.
Chef Peter Rudolph grew up in the Bay Area and led the kitchen at San

WHICH RESTAURANTS HAVE THE BEST CONTEMPORARY AMERICAN FOOD?

Equus:
Take fresh local Sonoma County produce in Equus' seasonal fare, like sun-dried tomato and mushroom ravioli with artichokes, pancetta and tomato-basil sauce.

John Ash & Co.:
Oenophiles will want to eat here. Part of Vinters Inn, owned by winemakers Ferrari-Carano, it turns out delicious cuisine that pairs perfectly with wine.

Madera:
Madera's floor-to-ceiling windows and fireplaces make it an inviting place to dine, but dishes such as squab with pine nuts, carrots and kumquat confit make it a standout.

Francisco's Campton Place before coming to Madera, and brought with him a passion for the flavors and rich resources found in this region. At dinner, dishes might include pan-roasted squab with braised pine nuts, carrots and kumquat confit, or dayboat scallops with roasted chanterelle mushrooms, rapini and apple turnip purée. Sommelier Paul Mekis holds an advanced sommelier designation, and he puts his vast knowledge to good use in selecting a well-rounded wine list that puts a spotlight on star bottles from the region.
American. Breakfast, lunch, dinner. Bar. $36-85

SANTA ROSA
★★★EQUUS
Fountaingrove Inn, 101 Fountain Grove Parkway, Santa Rosa, 707-578-0149; www.fountaingroveinn.com
The California wine country menu of this contemporary restaurant inside the Fountaingrove Inn changes seasonally and relies on local Sonoma County produce. Entrées include sun-dried tomato and mushroom ravioli with artichokes, pancetta and tomato basil sauce; and seared sea scallops with curry sauce, coconut basmati rice and grilled pineapple relish. The restaurant also features an extensive wine list emphasizing West Coast wines.
American. Lunch, dinner. Reservations recommended. Bar. $16-35

★★★JOHN ASH & CO.
4330 Barnes Road, Santa Rosa, 707-527-7687; www.vintnersinn.com
Located next to the Vintners Inn, a country retreat operated by winemakers Ferrari-Carano, this sophisticated dining room serves simple dishes made with fresh, local ingredients from local farmers and producers, as well as the restaurant's own gardens. Entrées might include Moroccan spiced loin of California lamb with couscous or housemade chicken and sun-dried tomato sausage. The Front Room Bar and Lounge offers signature cocktails, wines and lighter fare.
American. Dinner. Reservations recommended. Outdoor seating. Bar. $36-85

★★★KENWOOD
9900 Highway 12, Kenwood, 707-833-6326; www.kenwoodrestaurant.com
This restaurant has many dining rooms to choose from with views of the Sugarloaf Mountains and the Kunde

Vineyards. Enjoy a simple California menu, including grilled chicken with wild rice, curry sauce and raisin chutney. For dessert, try the pineapple carpaccio with coconut ice cream or the dark chocolate truffle. Then retreat to the bar for a drink in front of the fire.

American. Lunch, dinner. Closed Monday-Tuesday. Reservations recommended. Outdoor seating. Bar. $16-35

RECOMMENDED

BODEGA BAY

THE BAY VIEW RESTAURANT AND LOUNGE

The Inn at Tides, 800 Coast Highway 1, Bodega Bay, 707-875-2751, 800-541-7788; www.innatthetides.com

Located at the Inn at the Tides, this upscale restaurant offers views of Bodega Bay and the harbor. The menu includes fresh, local seafood, meats and produce including dishes such as Sonoma duck breast with duck confit, beluga lentils and cherry-sage sauce; and pistachio-crusted rack of lamb with garlic-Yukon Gold mashed potatoes and a rosemary zinfandel glaze.

American. Dinner. Closed Monday-Tuesday. Bar. $16-35

GLEN ELLEN

THE FIG CAFÉ AND WINE BAR

13690 Arnold Drive, Glen Ellen, 707-938-2130; www.thefigcafe.com

Located in the center of Glen Ellen, this restaurant, which is housed in a craftsman cottage accented with flower-filled window boxes, serves fresh, seasonal French-influenced dishes in a casual setting. The menu features dishes such as stuffed brioche French toast, baby artichoke pizza and steamed mussels and fries.

French. Dinner, Saturday-Sunday brunch. Reservations recommended. Bar. $16-35

GLEN ELLEN INN

13670 Arnold Drive, Glen Ellen, 707-996-6409; www.glenelleninn.com

This chef-owned and operated restaurant is located in the village of Glen Ellen. The California menu features dishes such as ginger tempura calamari, braised lamb shank and a pulled Kahlua pork sandwich. The oyster grill and martini bar make this quaint restaurant a local favorite. The extensive wine list features more than 550 local wines.

American. Lunch (Friday-Tuesday), dinner. Outdoor seating. $16-35

SAFFRON RESTAURANT

13648 Arnold Drive, Glen Ellen, 707-938-4844

Owned by chef Christopher Dever, this intimate café features a daily changing menu of eclectic California cuisine. The restaurant's eleven tables are dressed with burgundy and white cloths and topped with sunflowers. A small, enclosed patio with heaters and a fountain provides additional space for alfresco dining.

American. Dinner. Closed Sunday-Monday. Reservations recommended. Outdoor seating. $16-35

SPA

★★★★SENSE, A ROSEWOOD SPA AT ROSEWOOD SAND HILL
2825 Sand Hill Road, Menlo Park, 650-561-1500; www.rosewoodhotels.com

This attractive spa is a sanctuary where natural wood and stone are used to create a calming environment that makes the most of the beautiful California setting. The 13 treatment rooms and locker areas are light-filled and luxe—the coed relaxation room is a unique, spacious and appealing space with doors that open onto a private open-air courtyard and fountain. Choose from a menu that carries out the California theme, including treatments such as the Forest Sanctuary, which begins with a eucalyptus exfoliation, then moves onto an herbal wrap and aromatherapy hot stone massage. Also offered are a range of facials, manicures and pedicures. The spa includes a movement studio, fitness center with cutting-edge equipment and a spa café with outdoor seating in a charming courtyard.

SAN FRANCISCO

With its Victorian architecture and open-minded nature, San Francisco has a look and feel that's different from any other city in the country, or even the world. Since its inception, thousands of people with pioneering spirits have packed up and moved west to this city on the bay, drawn by many things: beautiful landscapes, healthy living, cultural acceptance, an abundance of tech jobs—you name it. Tourists come in droves for many of the same reasons, and leave wowed by the vistas afforded by the city's many peaks, the incredible food, the laidback style and the surrounding vineyards, mountains, beaches and more.

There's no shortage of classic sights in this scenic city: From the Golden Gate Bridge to the Coit Tower and Lombard Street to cable cars, San Francisco is chock-a-block with distinctive elements wholly unique to the City by the Bay. But dig a little deeper, and you'll find the spots that locals love, from the Beat Museum (with its quirky rundown of the counter-cultural revolution) to the Cartoon Art Museum (no need for an introduction there) and from Chinatown's best dim sum spots to the colorful Chicano art murals in the Mission District.

Of course, California cuisine was born in the Bay Area. Helmed by chefs like Alice Waters, a culinary revolution took place there in the 1970s. The mantra: locally-grown, seasonal ingredients. These ideas are mainstream nowadays, but there is no better place to appreciate them than in the place where they first emerged. Seafood plucked from Pacific waters, produce grown in nearby valleys and rich, creamy just-made cheeses and butters are just a few of the treats you'll find on the menu in San Francisco. With a slew of talented chefs and an abundance of authentic ethnic eateries, the city is a serious destination for food.

When it comes to shopping, tie-dye hasn't completely died, and denim will always be worshipped. But the city has come a long way from its days as a low-key jeans-only type of town (though this is the home of Levi's and Gap, after all).

BEST ATTRACTIONS

WHAT ARE THE MUST-SEE SIGHTS ON A VISIT TO SAN FRANCISCO?

FERRY BUILDING MARKETPLACE

This former transportation hub is now a popular stop for foodies. The renovated landmark offers some of the Bay Area's best restaurants and specialty food shops.

GOLDEN GATE PARK

Larger than New York City's Central Park, this recreation area is packed with outdoor fun—from rollerblading to tennis courts and soccer fields to simply smelling the roses in the Shakespeare Garden—and is home to the California Academy of Sciences, de Young Museum and the Japanese Tea Garden.

UNION SQUARE

Built in 1847, a plethora of hotels, restaurants and shops surround this plaza today, making it one of the major tourist destinations in San Francisco.

Today, San Francisco boasts a unique style, a blend of fashion-forwardness and eco-consciousness that fits the city's character like a glove. Add a dash of DIY aesthetics, an affinity for vintage shops and a flair for international influences (Japanese and European among them), and you have a city of trendy, fashionable people who are comfortable in their own skin and who embrace mixing old and new.

Los Angeles has Hollywood and Seattle has coffee and grunge, but San Francisco is arguably the West Coast's cultural capital. Not only is it home to the legendary San Francisco Opera, which gives New York's Metropolitan Opera a run for its money, but it's also the stomping ground for the country's oldest ballet company, the San Francisco Ballet. If you're still looking for the city's flower power, a visit to Haight-Ashbury is in order. The neighborhood may be more yuppie than hippie these days, but the spirit of counter-cultural heroes like Grateful Dead and Janis Joplin still lives.

WHAT TO SEE

ALAMO SQUARE/PAINTED LADIES
712-720 Steiner St., San Francisco

Contrary to their name, the Painted Ladies aren't overly rouged harlots. Rather, they're narrow, Victorian-style buildings drenched in vibrantly colored paints. Approximately 48,000 homes were built in this style around the turn of the

HIGHLIGHT

WHAT ARE THE BEST THINGS TO SEE WHILE WALKING AROUND THE MARINA DISTRICT AND COW HOLLOW?

Two of San Francisco's toniest neighborhoods, the adjacent Marina District and Cow Hollow, both come from relatively humble beginnings. Originally tidal marshlands, the Marina District rose from the rubble of the 1906 earthquake, when the area was used as a dumping ground for debris. Cow Hollow takes its name from the dairy bovines that once grazed here. Today, these districts are home to yacht clubs, gorgeous Art Deco buildings and Victorian houses. Boutiques, restaurants and bars catering to a trendy clientele line the parallel Chestnut Street (Marina) and Union Street (Cow Hollow). Shop for vintage-inspired designer dresses at Ambiance or soft, fuzzy sweaters at **House of Cashmere** (*2764 Octavia St., 415-441-6925*), then grab delicious wood-fired pizza and other Italian treats at **A16** (*2355 Chestnut St. 415-771-2216*). Just be sure to call ahead, as the popular place is always booked. Afterward, relax with a bottle of burgundy at the stylish **Nectar Wine Lounge** (*3330 Steiner St., 415-345-1377; www.nectarwinelounge. com*). The neighborhood is also home to the historic 1960s club the Matrix, formerly owned by Jefferson Airplane's Marty Balin. Reopened as the **MatrixFillmore** (*3138 Fillmore St., 415-563-4180; www.matrixfillmore.com*) in 2001 by the city's own Mayor Gavin Newsom, the club no longer oozes a rock 'n' roll vibe, but the yuppie drinks are still tasty. Kick back on the plum velvet banquette with a peach tea mojito or white mocha martini and watch the weekend mating rituals begin. During the day, the Marina Green and Crissy Field provide the area's fit young residents with ample space for jogging, rollerblading, kite flying, Frisbee throwing or simply spreading out on a picnic blanket alongside the waterfront.

20th century, although many of the houses were covered in gray Army surplus stock during the two world wars. In the '60s and '70s, the colorist movement took hold, and many homeowners revived the bright lemon yellow, bubble-gum pink and periwinkle hues of the past. Elizabeth Pomada and Michael Larsen brought national attention to the houses with their 1978 book, *Painted Ladies: San Francisco's Resplendent Victorians*, and nowadays people flock to Alamo Square to snap shots of one particular row of sun-struck beauties. (Being featured on the catchy opening credits of the TV show *Full House* probably didn't hurt, either.)

ALCATRAZ ISLAND

The Embarcadero near Bay Street, Pier 33, San Francisco, 415-561-4900; www.nps.gov; for ferry tickets/reservations: 415-981-7625; www.alcatrazcruises.com

Escape to Alcatraz and explore the prison cells that once held some of America's most notorious criminals, including Al "Scarface" Capone, kidnapper George "Machine Gun" Kelly, Bonnie and Clyde's accomplice Floyd Hamilton and Robert "Birdman" Stroud. Surrounded by the Bay's treacherous waters, the reputedly "escape-proof" prison witnessed 14 breakout attempts. Although no successful prison breaks were ever confirmed, five escapees remain missing and are presumed drowned. Among Alcatraz's more interesting artifacts are the dummy heads created by three would-be escapees. Made from used toilet paper, cardboard, cement chips, and hair scraps from the barbershop floor, they're a testament to captive creativity. A penitentiary from 1934 to 1963, "The Rock" now provides sanctuary for thousands of seabirds. But the prison-turned-museum is a popular stop for people, too, so call a week ahead for reservations during the summer and holidays.

Admission: adults $26 day tours, $33 night tour; children 12-17 $26 day tours, $32 night tour; children 5-11 $16 day tours, $19.50 night tour; children under 5 free; seniors $24.50 day tours, $30.50 night tour. Hours vary.

AMERICAN CONSERVATORY THEATER
415 Geary St., San Francisco, 415-749-2228; www.act-sf.org

Home to the nationally acclaimed conservatory (alumni include Danny Glover, Annette Bening and Denzel Washington) and theater company of the same name, this gilded palace of Corinthian columns was built as part of the post-1906 earthquake reconstruction. Known for both its cutting-edge productions, such as David Mamet's controversial *Oleanna* and Tony Kushner's Pulitzer Prize-winning *Angels in America*, and its Victorian-era architecture, the ornate building ranks on the U.S. Department of the Interior's National Register of Historic Places. Not satisfied to rest on the laurels of its lush surroundings or on the annual success of classics like *A Christmas Carol*, the company has cultivated relationships with contemporary masters, among them Tom Stoppard and Mamet.

ANGEL ISLAND STATE PARK
The Embarcadero at Beach Street, Pier 39, San Francisco, 415-435-1915; www.angelisland.org; for ferry tickets/reservations: 415-705-8200; www.blueandgoldfleet.com

For beautiful vistas of San Francisco, the Marin Headlands and Mount Tamalpais, head to Angel Island, a small state park just off the coast of Tiburon. The 1.2-mile isle, which is filled with lush flora, also provides spectacular hiking and biking. The island has had many uses over the years—from a cattle ranch to an Army garrison to a controversial immigrant-processing station known as "The Ellis Island of the West"—before being converted into a national park in 1954. Now, the island offers volleyball and baseball, manicured picnic grounds, historical tours and a café serving barbecued oysters. Roller skates, scooters and Segways are forbidden. Ferries depart daily from San Francisco, Oakland and Tiburon.

Daily 8 a.m.-sunset.

AQUARIUM OF THE BAY
The Embarcadero and Beach Street, Pier 39, San Francisco, 415-623-5300; www.aquariumofthebay.com

Go on an underwater adventure without getting wet. The aquarium's three exhibits immerse you in the rich local marine life. A moving walkway glides through two 300-foot-long acrylic tunnels surrounded by more than 700,000 gallons of water and more than 20,000 aquatic animals, including swarming schools of anchovies, bright sea stars and angel sharks. If *Jaws* gave you nightmares, watch out—the aquarium is also home to 10-foot sevengill sharks, the largest in captivity. Get up close with the softer side of the Bay at the last exhibit, where you can pet live bat rays, leopard sharks, sea cucumbers (which are related to starfish and sea urchins, but are actually shaped like cucumbers) and other tide pool critters.

Admission: adults $15.95, seniors and children 3-11 $8. Summer, daily 9 a.m.-8 p.m.; Winter, Monday-Thursday 10 a.m.-6 p.m., Friday-Sunday 10 a.m.-7 p.m. Behind the Scenes Tour: adults $21.95, seniors and children 5-11 $14

ASIAN ART MUSEUM OF SAN FRANCISCO

200 Larkin St., San Francisco, 415-581-3500; www.asianart.org

Beginning as a wing in the de Young, this museum has since blossomed into the largest collection of Asian art in the U.S., housing nearly 17,000 pieces in the city's former Main Library (stunningly renovated by Gae Aulenti, designer of Paris' Musée d'Orsay). Trek through three floors of history and culture spanning 6,000 years and covering seven geographic regions. While the museum is rich in relics—it is home to the oldest known Chinese Buddha in the world—it also regularly exhibits contemporary artwork, including manga (the popular Japanese-style comics) and Japanese haute couture from the Kyoto Costume Institute. After taking in the visual feast, engage the rest of your senses in a Japanese tea ceremony class (purchase tickets online in advance) or drop in on one of the museum's revolving interactive programs, like a Chinese brush-painting demonstration.

Admission: adults $12, seniors $8, children 13-17 $7, children 12 and under free. Thursdays after 5 p.m. $5. Tuesday-Wednesday, Friday-Sunday 10 a.m.-5 p.m., Thursday 10 a.m.-9 p.m. Daily gallery and architectural tours free with admission. Free first Sunday of every month.

AUDIUM

1616 Bush St., San Francisco, 415-771-1616; www.audium.org

At its location since 1975, this unassuming San Francisco institution touts itself as the world's only "theatre of sound-sculptured space." After you take a seat, the lights dim. It gets darker and darker, until you can't see your own hand in front of your face. As light exits, sound takes center stage. Stan Shaff, Audium's composer and co-creator, works with a complicated system of 176 specially designed speakers. From behind the control panel, Shaff moves rivers, trains and chair-trembling hums around the theater to form an almost palpable tension. The surprisingly disorienting experience has attracted a roster of creative thinkers, including architects, filmmakers, multi-media artists and scientists.

Admission: $15. Friday, Saturday 8:30 p.m. (arrive to the theater by 8:15 p.m.). No children under 12.

BAKER BEACH

Lincoln Boulevard and Bowley Street, San Francisco, 415-561-4300; www.nps.gov

San Francisco isn't known for its beaches, mostly because it's just too cold or cloudy to use them most of the year. There are, however, a handful of swelter-ing, clear-as-crystal days in the summer that demand that you grab your towel and sunblock and head to Baker Beach. During these times, the mile stretch of golden sand becomes a microcosm of San Francisco, featuring a rollicking mix of college students, businessmen playing hooky, parents, dog walkers and, down at the northern-most end by the Golden Gate Bridge, nudists (who flock to the beach no matter what the conditions are). It's an eclectic group, which might explain why the original Burning Man Festival (the annual art event dedicated to radical self-expression now held in Nevada's Black Rock Desert) was launched here back in 1986.

BARBARY COAST TRAIL
All over the city, San Francisco, 415-454-2355; www.barbarycoasttrail.org
From the birthplace of the Gold Rush to the beginning of the Beats, this fascinating walking tour takes you through San Francisco's storied past. Wild and rowdy tales of shanghaied sailors, streetwalkers and Pony Express riders accompany your every step as you wind your way through 3.8 miles of the city's rich history. Less scandalous highlights include the first Asian temple in the U.S., as well as the oldest Catholic cathedral west of the Rockies. Like bronze bread crumbs, 170 medallions and arrows embedded in the sidewalk mark the trail's path. Download one of the three themed audio tours from the website, purchase the printed guide online or at several local bookstores (including the Union Square Borders and Stacey's Bookstore on Market Street) and set out on your own, or arrange for a guided tour with author and trail creator Daniel Bacon. For a varied and fascinating look at San Francisco's history, fuel up with an espresso at North Beach's beatnik hot spot Vesuvio Café and then follow along to the beat of the "Poets, Paesanos and Windjammers" audio tour.
Guided tours are available by appointment only: $22 per person with a $352 group minimum.

BEACH BLANKET BABYLON
Club Fugazi, 678 Green St., San Francisco, 415-421-4222;
www.beachblanketbabylon.com
Since opening in 1974, Beach Blanket Babylon has become a Bay Area institution, selling out almost every performance. While the wacky musical revue uses the same story structure as it did during the Ford administration (Snow White tries to find Prince Charming outside the Bay Area but realizes there's no place like home), its producers update it constantly, offering witty digs at whoever's in the headlines, be it the Obamas, the McCains, tabloid regular Amy Winehouse, Arnold Schwarzenegger or Oprah. Campy as a Liza Minnelli marathon, the show features elaborate musical numbers, spot-on satire and really big hats. You never know who'll be sitting next to you, as some of the comedic targets—Nancy Pelosi, for instance—occasionally pop by to watch their likenesses cavort onstage.
Hours and prices vary; check website for details.

THE BEAT MUSEUM
540 Broadway, San Francisco, 800-537-6822; www.thebeatmuseum.org
Open since 2006, this small space tells the tales behind the lives of Jack Kerouac, Allen Ginsberg, Neal Cassady and other bohemian icons of the '50s and '60s movement. Just around the corner from Lawrence Ferlinghetti's City Lights Bookstore and Jack Kerouac Alley, the museum features everything from commemorative bobblehead dolls to yo-yos, personal correspondence and long out-of-print books, providing illustration of how the Beats changed the way people think about poetry and fiction.
Daily 10 a.m.-7 p.m.

HIGHLIGHT

WHAT ARE THE BEST PLACES IN SAN FRANCISCO FOR FAMILY FUN?

CALIFORNIA ACADEMY OF SCIENCES

The California Academy of Sciences brims with life—wander through the rainforest dome, take a trip below the flooded forest, embark on a virtual space odyssey, see rare animals and so much more.

THE EXPLORATORIUM

More than 400 works illuminating the mysteries of visual perception, sound and touch, including acoustic parabolic dishes that allow you to hear whispering from across a noisy room, make this one of the most entertaining science museums in the country.

FISHERMAN'S WHARF

Fisherman's Wharf is always mobbed, but you're bound to have at least a couple of hours of fun playing the antique arcade games and seeing the 900 barking and brawling sea lions that have set up camp on Pier 39's floating docks.

BISCUITS & BLUES
401 Mason St., San Francisco, 415-292-2583; www.biscuitsandblues.com

Shake off the chilly fog with some red-hot blues at this down-home basement club, where the cocktail tables practically hug the stage. Local favorites such as Lavay Smith & Her Red Hot Skillet Lickers and national touring artists swing through this cozy, all-ages joint Tuesday through Saturday and every other Sunday. Noted jazz guitarist Lloyd Gregory occasionally performs with standout guest singers. Known almost as much for its food as its excellent sound system, the venue churns out flaky biscuits and signature Southern fried chicken. Just try to resist the chocolate pecan pie flavored with bourbon. Specialty cocktails are poured at the silver Formica bar.

Restaurant: Tuesday-Thursday 6-11 p.m., Friday-Saturday 3:30-11 p.m., Sunday-Monday hours vary. Music: Tuesday-Thursday 8-11:30 p.m., Friday-Saturday 3:30-11:30 p.m., Sunday-Monday hours vary depending on special performances.

CABLE CAR MUSEUM
1201 Mason St., San Francisco, 415-474-1887; www.cablecarmuseum.org

Housed in the historic Washington/Mason cable car barn and powerhouse, San Francisco's oldest and hardest-working icon is celebrated in this informative museum. After witnessing the brutal death of horses that slipped on a steep cobblestone street while struggling to pull a streetcar, Andrew Smith Hallidie was inspired to invent an alternative mode of transportation. A godsend to humans and horses alike, the first cable car was successfully tested in 1873. It quickly caught on and an extensive network of 53 miles of track eventually crisscrossed the city. More than just a monument to a bygone era, the museum overlooks the engines and whirring wheels that power and pull the Powell-Mason, Powell-Hyde and California Street lines. Downstairs, you can view the sheaves and cable lines entering the building through their underground channel.

April-September, daily 10 a.m.-6 p.m.; October-March, daily 10 a.m.-5 p.m.

CALIFORNIA ACADEMY OF SCIENCES

55 Music Concourse Drive, Golden Gate Park, San Francisco,
415-379-8000; www.calacademy.org

From the rolling green hills of its "living roof" to its 25-foot-deep coral reef aquarium, the California Academy of Sciences' new home (opened in September 2008) brims with life. Wander through the rainforest dome as free-flying birds and butterflies swoop and flutter around you. Take a trip below the flooded forest and hang out with the anacondas and piranhas while gazing up through a 25-foot-long acrylic tunnel. Or ditch the earthly environs altogether and embark on a virtual space odyssey with real-time NASA feeds of shuttle launches and missions in the planetarium. Old favorites have also returned, including a rare albino alligator (there are about 40 worldwide; their lack of camouflage makes it nearly impossible for them to survive outside of captivity) and the Tusher African Center's ridiculously cute colony of South African penguins (only 150,000 exist in the wild). Penguins may look like tuxedoed maître d's, but they're not particularly polite when it comes to their food. Stop by during one of their twice-daily feeding frenzies to catch them at their feistiest.

Admission: adults $24.95, seniors and children 12-17 $19.95, children 4-11 $14.95, children under 4 free. Monday-Saturday 9:30 a.m.-5 p.m., Sunday 11 a.m.-5 p.m. Free every third Wednesday of the month.

CARTOON ART MUSEUM

655 Mission St., San Francisco, 415-227-8666; www.cartoonart.org

This museum takes its funny pages very seriously. Initially a traveling exhibit organized by a group of collectors, the museum settled into its first home in 1987 thanks to a generous endowment from *Peanuts* creator Charles M. Schulz. The museum gives the art form an invigorating dose of cultural perspective and context: Past exhibits have examined the role of women and African-Americans in comics and explored the power of political cartoons. The Cartoonist-in-Residence program, which invites you to watch over an artist's shoulder as he or she draws in public for two hours, brings the two-dimensional panels to life. Enthusiasts will go on a shopping binge in the museum store, which features collectibles and hard-to-find comics by Bill Griffith, Adrian Tomine and Aleksandar Zograf, among others.

Admission: adults $7, seniors and students $5, children 6-12 $3, children 5 and under free. Tuesday-Sunday 11 a.m.-5 p.m. First Tuesday of every month is "Pay What You Wish" Day.

CASTRO THEATRE

429 Castro St., San Francisco, 415-621-6120; www.thecastrotheatre.com

Built in 1922, this movie palace is one of the few of its size, age and grandeur left. Holding more than 1,400 attendees, the room is truly magnificent—from its Art

Deco chandelier to its iconic vertical sign to its Spanish-influenced façade, not to mention the mighty Wurlitzer organ, which is still played before select shows. Since 1976, the theater has shown mainly repertory films, offering weeklong tributes to famed directors like Antonioni, as well as hosting the LGBT-focused Frameline, hard-boiled Noir City and international Berlin & Beyond film festivals. The Castro shows films the way they were meant to be seen.

CHINATOWN
Grant Avenue and Stockton Street, San Francisco; www.sanfranciscochinatown.com

Chinatown buzzes with quaint trinket shops, steaming dim sum parlors and green grocers overflowing with tropical produce, but its history is rather scandalous. Back in 1906, when much of the community was destroyed in the legendary earthquake and fire, city officials tried to move the entire north-eastern neighborhood south to Hunters Point. When Chinese officials and American merchants balked, they came upon a compromise, rebuilding the area as a tourist destination, complete with vague notions of what China is "really" like. Today, most of the actual Chinese community lives in the Richmond or Sunset neighborhoods, far removed from the toyshops and angled rooftops of Chinatown. Despite its manufactured past, there's no denying the area's vibrant mercantile present: Exotic delicacies such as armadillos and pigs' noses press up against store windows while fish wriggle in ice buckets on the sidewalk. Fill up on dim sum at the three-storied **Gold Mountain Restaurant** *(644 Broadway, 415-296-7733)* or the **Hang Ah Tea Room** *(1 Pagoda Place, 415-982-5686)*, San Francisco's oldest dim sum establishment. Then stop by the **Golden Gate Cookie Factory** *(56 Ross Alley, 415-781-3956)* for a tasty peek into your future and a look at how fortune cookies are made.

COBB'S COMEDY CLUB
915 Columbus Ave., San Francisco, 415-928-4320; www.cobbscomedy.com

Since 1982, Cobb's has consistently been one of the best places in San Francisco to get your laughs in. Familiar funny faces from *Saturday Night Live* (Tracy Morgan, Kevin Nealon), *The Daily Show* (Rob Riggle, John Oliver) and Comedy Central specials (Patton Oswalt) headline here. The 400-seat venue is first-come, first-served, so get there early if you want a choice between a front-and-center seat and a spot safely out of the comics' line of fire. Skip the club's overpriced and mediocre dinner menu and eat out at one of the many fantastic North Beach options beforehand. Ordering food doesn't count toward the seemingly ubiquitous comedy club two-drink minimum anyway. While the crowd varies, you can count on well-dressed dates at tables for two and groups of college-aged kids sporting baseball caps.
Thursday-Sunday 8 p.m., Friday-Saturday 8 p.m. and 10:15 p.m. 18 and older; two-drink minimum.

COIT TOWER
1 Telegraph Hill Blvd., San Francisco, 415-362-0808

No longer one of the tallest buildings in San Francisco, Coit Tower's Telegraph Hill location still offers spectacular 360-degree panoramas of downtown and the Bay from its observation deck. Rescued as a child from a fire, wealthy eccentric Lillie Hitchcock Coit put a third of her fortune toward the construction of the

210-foot tower—a monument to honor the city she loved and its volunteer firemen. However, contrary to popular belief, the fluted column is not meant to resemble a fire hose nozzle. You can check out the lobby's Diego Rivera-inspired WPA murals for free, but the elevator ride to the top costs a few bucks. Avoid the traffic jam on Telegraph Hill Boulevard (which leads to the parking lot) and take the steep Filbert Steps to the top instead; the cute garden cottages and intermittent views make the climb more than worthwhile (the tower functions as a lookout today).

Admission: adults $4.50, seniors $3.50, children 6-12 $2, children under 6 free. Daily 10 a.m.-5 p.m.

CURRAN THEATRE
445 Geary St., San Francisco, 415-551-2000; www.shnsf.com

Replete with crystal chandeliers, buttery gold bas-relief ceilings and box seating, the Curran Theatre has been cultivating Broadway glamour in San Francisco since its 1922 premiere. It even doubled for a New York stage in the classic 1950 Bette Davis film *All About Eve*. Along with the Golden Gate Theatre and the Orpheum Theatre, the Curran is owned by Tony Award-winning producer Carole Shorenstein Hays and her partner, Robert Nederlander, part of the Nederlander-family theater legacy. The theater-loving pair began buying and restoring the trio of crumbling playhouses more than 30 years ago with the purchase of the Curran. Under their umbrella organization SHN (Shorenstein Hays Nederlander), the two continue to bring East Coast spectacles (*Jersey Boys, Billy Elliot*) and modern drama (*August: Osage County, Next to Normal*) to the West Coast through their "Best of Broadway" series.

DE YOUNG MUSEUM
50 Hagiwara Tea Garden Drive, Golden Gate Park, San Francisco, 415-750-3600; www.famsf.org

Extending above the tree line like a modern-day Mayan temple, the new de Young is a striking structure. Designed with the natural world in mind, the building's perforated copper casing replicates the dappled sunlight shining through the surrounding park's trees. Even the walkway includes a clever allusion to the environment with British artist Andy Goldsworthy's cracked-sidewalk sculpture *Drawn Stone*. Inside, the museum displays a variety of special exhibitions—you might catch an Yves Saint Laurent fashion retrospective or see the artifacts of King Tut—and possesses an eclectic permanent collection, which includes American art spanning the 17th and 20th centuries and ancient murals from Teotihuacán. An observation deck provides a panoramic view of the city. But for a more down-to-earth vista, the museum's bustling café spills out into the Barbro Osher Sculpture Garden, which features a giant blue safety pin by Claes Oldenburg and Coosje van Bruggen. The museum isn't just a daytime destination, either. The party atmosphere of its Friday-night program-ming, which often includes live music and a cocktail bar, has made it a hot evening stop as well.

Admission: adults $10, seniors $7, children 13-17 and college students $6, children 12 and under free. $10 surcharge for special exhibitions. Tuesday-Sunday 9:30 a.m.-5:15 p.m., Friday 9:30 a.m.-8:45 p.m. Free docent tours daily; check museum schedule. Free first Tuesday of every month.

THE EXPLORATORIUM

3601 Lyon St., San Francisco, 415-561-0360; www.exploratorium.edu

Kids can channel their inner mad scientists at the Exploratorium, one of the most entertaining science museums in the country. Children come to use the acoustic parabolic dishes, which allow them to hear mom and dad whispering from across the noisy room. But the fun exhibit has a purpose other than spying on your parents: It's one of the more than 400 works that illuminate the mysteries of visual perception, sound and touch. Housed in the Palace of Fine Arts, the interactive museum was built in 1969 by Manhattan Project physicist Frank Oppenheimer. Be sure to try your own experiments with the Wave Organ, which is built from pipes and concrete and juts into the nearby ocean, and the Tactile Dome, a pitch-black maze of chutes and ladders and all sorts of touchy-feely textures beloved by children and teenagers alike.

Admission: adults $15, children 13-17 $12, children 4-12 $10, children 3 and under free. Tuesday-Sunday 10 a.m.-5 p.m. Tactile Dome: $20; children under 7 not allowed; reservations recommended.

FERRY BUILDING MARKETPLACE

1 Ferry Building, San Francisco, North Beach, 415-693-0996; www.ferrybuildingmarketplace.com

Built in 1898, the Ferry Building was once a lively transportation hub, welcoming train travelers from the East and ferryboat passengers from across the Bay. Now a popular stop for foodies, the renovated landmark offers some of the Bay Area's best restaurants and specialty food shops. Ferry Plaza Wine Merchant boasts a unique selection of wines from smaller producers and a wine bar where customers can sit and sip the merchandise. The popular Vietnamese restaurant Slanted Door features a wall of windows overlooking the Bay. Winemaker Joel Gott's place, Gott's Roadside, has delicious burgers, fries and half-bottles of wine, while Marketbar is a great spot for sharing seasonal Mediterranean plates. It's also fun to wander through the building's three-story-high, sunlit hall and browse the shops. Pick up a coffee at Blue Bottle Coffee, some cheese at Cowgirl Creamery and scoops of gelato at Ciao Bella. On Saturday, Tuesday and Thursday mornings, head toward the iconic 240-foot-tall clock tower for the Ferry Plaza Farmers Market and pick up a farm-fresh breakfast of locally grown organic produce and artisanal breads, cheeses and preserves. Saturday's market regularly draws 10,000 to 15,000 happily munching shoppers, making it a great place to people-watch while enjoying your meal at one of the outdoor tables.

Monday-Friday 10 a.m.-6 p.m., Saturday 9 a.m.-6 p.m., Sunday 11 a.m.-5 p.m. Ferry Plaza Farmers Market: Tuesday, Thursday, Saturday 10 a.m.–2 p.m. San Francisco City Guides walking tours: Saturday, Thursday and Tuesday at noon.

THE FILLMORE

1805 Geary Blvd., San Francisco, 415-346-6000; www.livenation.com

Rock history was made here. At the height of the '60s counter-culture revolution, rock promoter Bill Graham lit the stage with electric performances by the likes of Janis Joplin, the Grateful Dead and Jimi Hendrix—all of it catalogued in the famed psychedelic concert posters that now adorn the venue's walls. A holdover from its hippie heritage, a bucket of free apples still welcomes you at

HIGHLIGHT

WHAT ARE THE CITY'S TOP MUSEUMS?

CARTOON ART MUSEUM

If you're a fan of comics, you'll love this museum. Special exhibits have explored the power of political cartoons, and the shop includes collectibles.

DE YOUNG MUSEUM

The museum displays a variety of special exhibitions—from an Yves Saint Laurent fashion retrospective to the artifacts of King Tut—and possesses an eclectic permanent collection, which includes American art spanning the 17th and 20th centuries and ancient murals from Teotihuacán. What's more, an observation deck provides a panoramic view of the city.

SAN FRANCISCO MUSEUM OF MODERN ART:

The museum's world-class collection of more than 25,000 works of modern and contemporary art ranges from Henri Matisse's 1905 masterpiece *Femme au chapeau* (Woman with a Hat) to Jeremy Blake's 21st-century digital animation. The museum boasts a massive photography collection and frequently hosts blockbuster touring exhibitions as well.

the top of the stairs. Inside, the one-time dance hall, with its glittering chandeliers and wooden floor, now hosts a mix of musical talent, from rock to hip hop to the occasional country crooner. For a clear view of the stage, arrive early for a seat at one of the balcony tables.

Box office: Sunday 10 a.m.-4 p.m. and 30 minutes before the doors open until 10 p.m. on show nights, excluding major holiday weekends and special event nights.

FISHERMAN'S WHARF

Taylor Street and the Embarcadero, San Francisco, 415-674-7503; www.fishermanswharf.org

While a few fishing boats still set sail from here, much of the wharf's maritime past has been overwhelmed by its present-day resemblance to a shopping mall. If you're searching for that perfect sweatshirt, keychain or shot glass with San Francisco boldly printed on it, you'll find plenty of choices in the kitschy shops that stretch from Ghirardelli Square to Pier 39. Locals claim to avoid this place like the plague (slow-moving vacationers being the plague), but only a true curmudgeon could resist smiling at the carnival-like spectacle. The trick is to get out before you get duped into a shell game (beware—it's a scam) and the cheesiness loses its flavor. While you're here, drop a few coins at Musée

Mécanique, home to the mechanical (some say maniacal) Laffing Sal and a collection of other mechanized contraptions, antique arcade games and player pianos. It won't cost you a dime to see the real stars of the wharf: Some 900 barking and brawling sea lions have set up camp on Pier 39's floating docks, and it's the best show around. The food isn't all bad, either. Get a taste of Dungeness crab from one of the seafood street vendors. Or grab some steaming clam chowder in a bread bowl from **Boudin Bakery** *(Pier 39, 415-421-0185; www. boudinbakery.com)*; it has been pulling sourdough bread out of its ovens in San Francisco since 1849.

FORT POINT

End of Marine Drive on the Presidio, Presidio/Golden Gate National Recreation Area, San Francisco, 415-556-1693; www.nps.gov

Located under the narrows of the Golden Gate, the fort affords some of the most awe-inspiring views of the bridge's massive orange-vermillion beams and the bay below. Built between 1853 and 1861, the three-tiered brick fortress was armed with 102 cannons at its greatest strength, but never fired a single shot in battle. However, it was almost attacked by a Confederate raider, the CSS *Shenandoah*; the ship was sailing toward the harbor when it learned that the war had ended. This National Historic Site's exhibits focus on Civil War-era history, including the role of African-American soldiers and women in the military. A cannon-loading demonstration will show you how to fire one off like a Civil War artilleryman—you never know when that skill will come in handy.

Thursday-Monday 10 a.m.-5 p.m. Pier crabbing demonstration: March-October, Saturday 10 a.m.-noon. Candlelight tour: November-February, Saturday evenings. Call for reservations.

GHIRARDELLI SQUARE

900 North Point St., San Francisco, 415-775-5500; www.ghirardellisq.com

Ghirardelli Square has been a major tourist attraction since 1964, when local businessman William Roth bought the old chocolate factory and transformed it into shops and offices. Added to the National Register of Historic Places in 1982, the square has recently undergone another redesign, with the upper offices being converted into a high-end residence club run by the Fairmont hotel chain. Ghirardelli Square still remains true to its sweet-tooth roots, though. Hit the original Ghirardelli Ice Cream and Chocolate Shop for a traditional hot fudge sundae (you'll need a partner and two spoons to finish one), and a look at manufacturing equipment from the 1852 factory. Or follow the delicious smell over to Kara's Cupcakes for a trendier treat. Batches are baked from scratch all day long, so you have a chance of getting a warm one straight from the oven. Try the melt-in-your-mouth chocolate cupcake with peanut butter and milk chocolate ganache frosting—all made from locally sourced ingredients.

GOLDEN GATE BRIDGE

Lincoln Boulevard and Highway 101, San Francisco, 415-455-2000; www.goldengatebridge.org

Emblazoned on sweatshirts and tchotchkes, the bridge is San Francisco's defining landmark. Built between January 1933 and May 1937, its two main towers reach 746 feet above the water and span 4,200 feet between them. Upon completion, it was the longest suspension bridge in the world. But it is more than a testament to innovative engineering. Its elegant Art Deco design and distinctive color (officially dubbed international orange; the reddish-orange shade makes it visible to passing ships) give rise to one of the world's most beautiful bridges. Its nearly two-mile stretch of sidewalks offers pedestrians and cyclists breathtaking, albeit windy, views of the ocean opening up on one side and the city skyline glittering on the other. The stirring vistas and looming towers make crossing the bridge an exhilarating experience.

Admission: free to pedestrians and cyclists, $6 southbound by car. Open to pedestrians April-October 5 a.m.-9 p.m.; November-March 5 a.m.-6 p.m. Cyclists have toll-free access to the bridge's sidewalks 24 hours a day.

GOLDEN GATE PARK

Fulton at 36th Avenue and Lincoln at 41st Avenue, San Francisco,
415-831-2700; www.parks.sfgov.org

Larger than New York City's Central Park, this 1,017-acre recreation area is packed with more outdoor fun than you can throw a Frisbee at—from roller-blading along John F. Kennedy Drive on Sunday to sharpening your marks-manship skills at the archery range to simply pondering whether a rose by any other name would smell as sweet in the Shakespeare Garden. There are almost too many ways to enjoy a day at this park. Among the seemingly endless possibilities are 21 tennis courts, four soccer fields, three lawn-bowling greens and swing dancing lessons in the street. Built atop ocean dunes in the 1870s, this verdant rectangle teems with plant and animal life, too, including duck-filled lakes, some of the best fly-casting pools in the country and even a bison paddock. The gorgeous domed Conservatory of Flowers (one of the oldest wood-and-glass-pane greenhouses in the world) contains more than 10,000 plants from around the globe. Home of the California Academy of Sciences and the de Young Museum, the park also offers plenty of indoor entertainment. If all this activity leaves you breathless, sit for a spell and sip some tea in the lovely Japanese Tea Garden.

GOLDEN GATE THEATRE

1 Taylor St., San Francisco, 415-551-2000; www.shnsf.com

From its 1920s vaudeville heyday to the 1960s Cinerama screenings to its decline and closure in the 1970s, this theater has seen more than its share of drama. Buried under decades of alterations, it returned to its Art Deco decadence in 1979. Over the years, the 2,426-seat theater has reverberated with the sounds of Louis Armstrong, Frank Sinatra, Bette Midler and Liza Minnelli. Still making the most of its acoustics, the theater showcases mega-hit musicals such as *Hairspray, Mamma Mia!, Chicago,* and *Rent.*

GREAT AMERICAN MUSIC HALL

859 O'Farrell St., San Francisco, 415-885-0750; www.musichallsf.com

Opened in 1907, this former bordello has left its seamy past behind and is now one of the most civilized, but still intimate, live-music venues around. This is not to say that San Francisco's oldest nightclub has lost its sense of fun—it regularly books the best in rock, jazz and world beats. But it's hard not to feel a little reverent when surrounded by the ornate balconies, marble columns, frescoed ceiling and gleaming oak dance floor. Tasty bar bites, including burgers and nachos, are available. For an additional $25, you can chow down on a surprisingly sophisticated meal (such as grilled Niman Ranch pork served

HIGHLIGHT

WHAT IS THERE TO SEE IN HAIGHT-ASBURY?

During 1967's Summer of Love, flower children, free-love followers and people looking to score psychedelic drugs headed straight for Haight-Ashbury. Nowadays, the only thing you can score at that historic corner is an ice cream cone from the Ben & Jerry's shop. But the hippie-turned-yuppie haven hasn't lost touch with all of its nonconformist roots. There are still places in Haight-Ashbury with that old-time countercultural character.

The neighborhood used to be a home for music legends. Snap a picture in front of rocker **Janis Joplin's apartment** (*122 Lyon St.*), which she rented near the famed Haight-Ashbury intersection. On the other end of the housing spectrum, the Colonial Revival-style **Jefferson Airplane Mansion** (*2400 Fulton St.*), toward the northeastern tip of Golden Gate Park, is a great photo op. Haight-Ashbury's best-known residents may be the Grateful Dead. See the **Grateful Dead House** (*710 Ashbury St.*), where the tie-dye-loving band lived from 1966 to 1968 and where most of the members were busted in a 1967 police drug raid. Although the bands may be long gone, you can find traces of the area's musical past. Just head down Haight Street to find the best record store in the city, Amoeba Records, where you can find all the classics on vinyl.

True to their free-love spirit, the '60s psychedelic bands played plenty of public shows in Golden Gate Park, including the Gathering of the Tribes, a momentous Human Be-In in which rock bands and beatnik poets such as Allen Ginsberg rallied to legalize LSD on January 14, 1967. During the gathering, LSD proponent and former Harvard professor Timothy Leary famously told the flowers-in-their-long-hair masses to "Tune in, turn on, drop out." Make your way to the Polo Fields to see where Jefferson Airplane, the Grateful Dead and Quicksilver Messenger Service all performed during the show. Or you can see modern-day hippies right near the park's Haight Street entrance on the aptly named Hippie Hill—instead of fighting for flower power, these folks strum guitars or thump around in drum circles.

Now a popular place for jogging and pick-up basketball games, the shady Panhandle leading up to the park's entrance was once a frequent spot for impromptu concerts. On October 6, 1966, the Grateful Dead and Big Brother and the Holding Company protested the illegalization of LSD with a free concert here.

The hippie movement wasn't only about rock 'n' roll, bell bottoms and free love; followers wanted to change the country and make it less about commercialism and more about spirituality and being environmentally conscious. Head to **Bound Together Books** (*1369 Haight St., 415-431-8355; www.boundtogetherbooks.wordpress.com*) to get a taste of the subversive ideology of the time. Though the shop opened its doors in 1976, its radical vibe is reminiscent of the '60s. The self-described anarchist collective bookstore sells tomes you won't find in traditional bookshops, including political literature, comics, magazines and DVDs. After looking through the stacks, take a look at the newly restored mural on the side of the shop, which features famous anarchists such as Emma Goldman and Sacco and Vanzetti. It's one of the few remaining spots with that Summer of Love flavor. Ben & Jerry's, while it does offer the tasty Cherry Garcia ice cream, doesn't count.

with sweet potato mash and poblano cream sauce with a sour cherry compote) while rocking out in style at a reserved table. All shows are open to those ages 6 and older, so feel free to bring the whole family.
Check website for upcoming musical acts, show times and ticket prices.

HAIGHT-ASHBURY
Haight and Ashbury streets, San Francisco

Thanks to 1967's "Summer of Love" (and the ensuing inflammatory media coverage), the Haight-Ashbury neighborhood has become synonymous with the hippie ideal. The concepts of peace, love and psychedelic drugs remain stuck to the region, but for the most part, these days the houses are full of yuppies instead of musicians. In fact, the Haight has become more of a shopping mecca than a counter-cultural breeding ground—albeit one that sells everything from rock posters to used records. Get lost in the seemingly endless rows of CDs and vinyl at **Amoeba Records** or search for hipster castaways and vintage treasures at **Wasteland** *(1660 Haight St., 415-863-3150; www.wastelandclothing.com)*, a popular second-hand clothing store.

JAPANESE TEA GARDEN
Hagiwara Tea Garden Drive, Golden Gate Park, San Francisco, 415-668-0909; www.japaneseteagardensf.com

The Japanese Tea Garden's artful landscaping makes it one of the most popular tourist attractions in Golden Gate Park. That popularity has brought large crowds and loud grumblings about ticket prices, but if you time things right, you'll get a nice meditative experience among the sculpted hedges and winding paths. Originally built in 1894 for the California Midwinter International Exposition, the five-acre garden now features an abundance of intriguing sights, from a giant bronze Buddha to a drum bridge over a koi pond to a Mt. Fuji Hedge honoring Makoto Hagiwara, the first caretaker of the garden and the creator of the fortune cookie. Make sure to save enough time to sample from the Asian-focused tea menu and savor your last drops of relaxation.
Admission: adults $7, seniors and children 12-17 $5, children 5-11 $2, children under 5 free. March-October, daily 9 a.m.-6 p.m.; November-February, daily 9 a.m.-4:45 p.m.

JAPANTOWN
1625 Post St., San Francisco; www.sfjapantown.org

Japantown (or, as it's known to locals, "Nihonmachi") grew out of the Earthquake of 1906, after which Japanese people settled in the Western Addition neighborhood, opening Nipponese restaurants and stores. The area didn't come into its own as a tourist destination until 1968, when several international conglomerates erected Japan Center, three malls on five acres devoted to Japanese eateries, bookstores, grocery stores, hotels, shops and even a spa. One of only three remaining Japantowns in the continental U.S., Nihonmachi hosts both the spring **Cherry Blossom Festival,** a street fair featuring a parade, traditional cuisine, crafts and taiko drummers, and the boundary-pushing **San Francisco International Asian American Film Festival,** offering a place where tradition meets technology and progress coexists with the past. Even if you can't read katakana, you'll still enjoy flipping through the manga illustrations at the **Kinokuniya Bookshop** *(1581 Webster St., 415-567-7625)*. After browsing through the kimono shops and anime-filled DVD stores, treat yourself to a steaming bowl of udon or soba noodles at **Mifune Don** *(415-346-1993)*— forget chicken noodle soup, this restaurant's hearty broth is the real comfort food. For even deeper relaxation, take a dip in **Kabuki Springs and Spa**'s hot pool and follow it with a shiatsu massage. Of course, no trip to Japantown would be complete without a humiliating round of karaoke. Grab the mike at **Festa Karaoke Lounge** *(1825 A Post St., 415-567-5866; www.festalounge.com)* and belt one out to the back row.

LOMBARD STREET
Between Hyde and Leavenworth streets, San Francisco

Lombard is known as "The Crookedest Street in the World." This designation doesn't stem from any illegal deeds or wrongful actions committed there; rather, the title comes from one block of the throughway between Hyde and Leavenworth streets, in which the avenue takes eight sharp turns. (The switchbacks were added in 1922, when they were deemed necessary for people to navigate the sharp decline.) Nowadays, tourists go out of their way to traverse the strip, which features vibrant flowers and a speed limit of 5 miles per hour. Shutterbugs can't resist the postcard-perfect red cobblestone and dense green shrubbery, making it one of the world's most photographed streets.

MAGIC THEATRE
Fort Mason Center, San Francisco, 415-441-8822; www.magictheatre.org

Named after a scene in Hermann Hesse's novel *Steppenwolf,* in which the main character receives an invitation to an "Anarchist Evening at the Magic Theatre/ For Madmen Only/Price of Admission Your Mind," this theater has been engaging audiences' minds for more than 40 years, and it shows no signs of slowing down in middle age. The theater prides itself on nurturing emerging voices and its exclusive dedication to developing new work. This commitment to untested projects has paid off. More than 200 plays have debuted here— including *Dr. Faustus* by David Mamet and Pulitzer Prize winner *Buried Child* by Sam Shepard (playwright in residence 1975-1983).

MISSION DISTRICT
Between U.S. Route 101, Church Street, Cesar Chavez Street and Duboce Avenue, San Francisco; www.sfmission.com

The Mission District is one of the most diverse in San Francisco. Nowhere else can you see avant-garde playwrights quaffing microbrews next to sorority sisters, watch middle-class families dodge Frisbees thrown by dot-com millionaires or witness giddy newcomers ordering lattes from older folks who have lived in the Mission for decades. Once firmly Irish but now half Latino, the neighborhood draws folks from all sections of town who come for the fantastic restaurants, upscale bars, inexpensive taquerías, eclectic film houses and live music venues. All this diversity keeps the Mission interesting, especially when the weather is nice and the sidewalks, cafés and parks fill with people.

MISSION DISTRICT MURALS
Precita Eyes, 2981 24th St., San Francisco, 415-285-2287; www.precitaeyes.org

San Francisco is a city of local color—both literally and figuratively. There are about 1,500 murals painted on various walls and buildings throughout the city, each telling different tales of fallen comrades, mythological heroes and abstract thoughts. The Mission District houses a large concentration of the city's murals, thanks in part to groups like the now-defunct Mujeres Muralistas, the Chicano art mural movement of the '70s, and the current **Precita Eyes Mural Arts Center**. The organization also hosts classes on mural painting, and offers walking and biking tours of the 80-plus pieces near its storefront. The Mission murals prove that art can be both evocative and instructive, and they offer a nice alternative to a museum on a beautiful day.

Admission for tours: adults $12, seniors and students $8, children 13-17 $5, children under 12 $2. Saturday-Sunday 11 a.m. and 1:30 p.m.

MISSION DOLORES

3321 16th St., San Francisco, 415-621-8203; www.missiondolores.org

Constructed by Spanish settlers in 1776, Mission Dolores is the oldest remaining structure in San Francisco. Not surprisingly, the original log-and-thatch building has undergone many renovations over the years, most notably during the California Gold Rush, when parts of it were leased or sold as saloons and gambling facilities, and after the 1906 earthquake, during which much of the surrounding areas were scorched. Around 1913, the larger, grander Mission Dolores Basilica was erected next door. Since then, patrons and tourists have flocked to witness the chapel's sleek adobe elegance, with its mesmerizing painted ceiling beams (the design was inspired by the Ohlone tribe's face paint) and the elaborate golden altars brought from Mexico around the turn of the 19th century. The Basilica's ornate Catholic grandeur is spectacular, resplendent with intricate tile work, stunning stained-glass windows and a wide domed ceiling. If the sheer beauty isn't enough for you, maybe the opportunity to see one of Alfred Hitchcock's locations from the classic film *Vertigo* will convince you.

Suggested donation: adults $5, seniors and students $3. May-October, daily 9 a.m.-4:30 p.m.; November-April, daily 9 a.m.-4 p.m.

MUSEUM OF CRAFT AND FOLK ART

51 Yerba Buena Lane, San Francisco, 415-227-4888; www.mocfa.org

From exhibits featuring the work of four generations of African-American quilt makers to the intricate needlework of contemporary tattoo artists, this museum has woven together traditional and contemporary crafts and folk art from around the world for more than 25 years. Given its focus, the place begs involvement. Explore your creative side in one of its hands-on workshops. If you have kids, keep an eye out for the family activity days led by the museum's school program staff. After being inspired by all the fine craftsmanship, you can pick up a handcrafted item, like a blown-glass vase shaped like a splashing droplet or a whimsical ceramic tea set perfect for a Mad Hatter's party; the museum's gift shop represents more than 50 established and emerging artists.

Admission: adults $5, seniors $4, children under 18 free. Monday-Friday 11 a.m.-6 p.m., Saturday-Sunday 11 a.m.-5 p.m. Free Tuesday.

NORTH BEACH

Between Columbus Avenue and Telegraph Hill, Broadway and Bay Street, San Francisco; www.sfnorthbeach.org

In these days of globalization, big-box stores and the homogenization of culture, North Beach stands out as a welcome exception. Situated in the northeast section of the city, the traditionally Italian neighborhood prides itself on being old-fashioned, having instituted legislation to keep out chain stores and skyscrapers. Still, old-fashioned doesn't mean dowdy, as its small restaurants, intimate cafés and unique shops share blocks with rowdy bars and lascivious gentlemen's clubs. Food is the main attraction. Tourists can't seem to get enough of the garlic-heavy menu and funky décor at **The Stinking Rose** (*325 Columbus Ave., 415-781-7673; www.thestinkingrose.com),* but tiny **L'Osteria del Forno** (*519 Columbus Ave., 415-982-1124; www.losteriadelforno. com)* is the local favorite for authentic Italian dining. From its single oven, this sliver of an eatery consistently turns out some of the tastiest pizza slices and focaccia sandwiches in town. Fans of *On the Road* may also want to check out such Beatnik landmarks as Kerouac Alley, Vesuvio Café, the Beat Museum and City Lights Bookstore.

ODC/DANCE
315 Shotwell St., San Francisco, 415-863-6606; www.odcdance.org

Proving that New York doesn't have a lockdown on modern dance, ODC/ Dance has been choreographing gorgeous, witty, gravity-defying productions on the West Coast since 1976. Choreographers Brenda Way, KT Nelson and Kimi Okada have received numerous accolades among them, including four Isadora Duncan Dance Awards and a Guggenheim Fellowship. Hailed for its exhilarating mix of progressive physicality and ballet precision, the company has a collaborative spirit that's led to work with writers (Leslie Scalapino, Rinde Eckert), actors (Robin Williams) and visual artists (Wayne Thiebaud, Eleanor Coppola) as well. Get a behind-the-scenes look at how the dancers' athletic flights of fancy come together at one of their "unplugged" performances, which feature works-in-progress followed by conversations with the artists. Despite its avant-garde reputation, the company delves into whimsy and warmth in its annual November-December production of *The Velveteen Rabbit* at the Yerba Buena Center for the Arts. The facility recently underwent a two-year, $9 million renovation and expansion.

ORPHEUM THEATRE
1192 Market St., San Francisco, 415-551-2000; www.shnsf.com

Walking through the engraved wooden doors of the Orpheum Theatre is like stepping back in time. The theater, which has been around since 1926, was spared the wrecking ball by Carole Shorenstein Hays and Robert Nederlander's theater triumvirate and has since undergone a $20 million restoration. Styled after a 12th-century Spanish palace, the wall carvings are so detailed that you can almost hear the sculptural lions roaring with the crowd. Similar to the Golden Gate Theatre, the Orpheum has witnessed audiences' changing tastes—from vaudeville to 3-D movies. The 2,200-seat venue now brings down the house with top touring productions of Broadway shows like *The Phantom of the Opera* and *Wicked*.

PALACE OF FINE ARTS
3301 Lyon St., San Francisco, 415-567-6642; www.palaceoffinearts.org

The Palace of Fine Arts is one of the most popular spots for snapping wedding photos in San Francisco. Where else can you pose before a Roman-style rotunda with giant columns, a lagoon full of ducks and geese and a bevy of lush Monterey cypresses? The palace was originally constructed as part of the 1915 Panama-Pacific International Exposition, which celebrated the completion of the Panama Canal and San Francisco's resurrection following the 1906 earthquake. Built to look like a ruin, the palace's eight domed structures eventually fell into actual disrepair, until they were bulldozed in the mid-'60s. One dome and the rotunda were immediately reconstructed—right down to the famed weeping women who adorn the top of the colonnades—and the Exploratorium science museum and a 1,000-seat theater were built next door. Today, along with the bride and groom, you'll find everyone from locals and tourists to film crews (the site has been used for scenes in *The Rock*, *Time After Time* and *Vertigo*) utilizing the romantic setting.

PATRICIA'S GREEN
Octavia Boulevard, between Hayes and Fell streets, San Francisco

Formerly known as Hayes Green, locals consider this patch of green an extension of where they live (and if they had their way, no one would know about it). Named after the activist who persuaded the city to take the freeway down, people from the neighborhood come here to picnic, read under a palm tree, sip coffee and send emails or simply people watch from one of the stone benches. Kids also love the play area. Temporary public artworks are sometimes on display. After wandering the shops of Hayes Valley, grab the perfect cup of coffee at Blue Bottle Coffee (*66 Mint St., 415-351-9276; www.bluebottlecoffee. net*) and relax in this lovely park.

PRESIDIO GOLF COURSE & CLUBHOUSE
Arguello Boulevard and Finley Road, San Francisco, 415-561-4661;
www.presidiogolf.com

Back in the day, only military leaders like Teddy Roosevelt and Dwight Eisenhower could marvel at the greens of the Presidio Golf Course. But in 1995, when the Army facilities were converted to a national park, these illustrious fairways became open to the public. Now, you too can play with military precision, winding your way through eucalyptus tree groves and nefarious sand traps, all the while soaking in the breathtaking Bay scenery. Conveniently located 10 minutes from downtown San Francisco, the course is overseen by Arnold Palmer Golf Management, which knows a thing or two about winning tough battles.

Admission: Monday-Thursday: non-resident $49-$125, resident $25-$79, children $20; Friday: non-resident $49-$145, resident $35-$85, children $20; Saturday-Sunday: non-resident $49-$145, resident $35-$99, children $15. Daily, dawn-dusk.

PUNCH LINE COMEDY CLUB
444 Battery St., San Francisco, 415-397-4337;
www.punchlinecomedyclub.com

Although the city's oldest comedy club regularly hosts big-name comedians, it's perhaps better known as a place to catch stars on the rise. Ellen DeGeneres, Rosie O'Donnell, Chris Rock, Dave Chappelle, Margaret Cho, Jay Leno and Whoopi Goldberg all sharpened their wits under the Punch Line's limelight before becoming household names. Touring comics headline Tuesday through Saturday nights, but Sunday is reserved for nurturing nascent local talent. Yuck

HIGHLIGHT

WHAT'S THE BEST WAY TO SEE SAN FRANCISCO IN ONE DAY?

To really get a feel for San Francisco, start out with its most iconic structure: the Golden Gate Bridge. Take a refreshingly crisp stroll along the massive reddish-orange bridge for a spectacular view of the city, the ocean and the rolling green hills of Marin County on the other side of the bay. Keep walking and head over to the Palace of Fine Arts for a breather under the Roman-style rotunda and to snap a photo or two of the gorgeous grounds.

When you start getting restless, let out your inner child inside the Exploratorium science museum next door. There you can check out hundreds of science, art and human-perception exhibits, such as Mind, a collection of 40 interactive displays that show how your mind works. One of our favorites is See Yourself Sweat, which magnifies a patch of your skin as you think about ideas or images. Your thoughts trigger immediate sweating, which shows a physiological reaction to a cognitive event. If science makes you snore, check out the art galleries and museums over at Fort Mason. There you can peruse places like SFMOMA Artists Gallery, which features contemporary art from Northern California artists.

If you're looking for the true tourist experience, hit the shops and sights of Fisherman's Wharf, which stretches from Ghirardelli Square to jam-packed Pier 39. Fisherman's Wharf is touristy, but you'll join the crowds at Pier 39 and melt when you see the 900 or so barking sea lions hanging around the floating docks. Have some clam chowder in a sourdough bread bowl at **Cioppino's on the Wharf (400 Jefferson St., Fisherman's Wharf, 415-775-9311; www.cioppinosonthewharf.com)**. Here, you can sit outdoors and take in the wharf views.

Make a reservation for the scenic ferry ride out to Alcatraz, where you'll get a fascinating look inside the notorious escape-proof island penitentiary, whose cells housed big-time criminals such as Al Capone. End your day at the nationally acclaimed Vietnamese restaurant The Slanted Door. You'll devour the deliciously tender "shaking" beef and greaseless fried imperial rolls. Even better than the fresh eats is the waterfront restaurant's amazing view of the bay.

WHAT'S THE BEST WAY TO SEE SAN FRANCISCO IN THREE DAYS?

For your second day, fortify yourself with some fresh organic eats at the Ferry Plaza Farmers Market. Make like a local and pick up some artisanal bread and cheese and then grab a bench along the waterfront for a lovely view while you eat your breakfast.

Afterward, get a double dose of culture at the San Francisco Museum of Modern Art and its neighbor Yerba Buena Center for the Arts across the street. SFMOMA offers a great collection of modern work from artists such as Henri

WHAT'S THE BEST WAY TO SEE SAN FRANCISCO IN THREE DAYS? *(continued)*

Matisse. Don't miss the massive photography collection, which showcases snapshots from famous shutterbugs such as Ansel Adams and Dorothea Lange. YBCA is a more daring museum: It doesn't have a permanent collection. Instead it rotates an ever-changing menu of exhibits that mix pop culture and fine art, such as a recent retrospective of illustrator R. Crumb's work.

When you've gotten your fill of museums, it's time to shop. Forge ahead into downtown's crowded shopping mecca, Union Square. You'll need your credit cards to hit high-end boutiques such as Gucci, Chanel, Prada and the country's only Goyard store. After your shopping spree, make plans to see a play at the American Conservatory Theater. At the Victorian-era theater, which is listed on the National Register of Historic Places, you'll see cutting-edge drama like David Mamet's much talked-about *Oleanna* (which appeared here in 1994). For lighter fare, go to the Curran Theatre in the nearby theater district. The Curran offers foot-tapping fun productions such as *Jersey Boys*.

When the show is over, hop on a cable car and ride up toward North Beach for an authentic Italian dinner. Those in the know head to L'Osteria del Forno for great pizza. Finish absorbing the day over a cocktail at the venerable **Tosca Café (242 Columbus Ave., North Beach, 415-986-9651)** or at the Clift Hotel's glamorous Redwood Room.

Spend your last day in Golden Gate Park walking, biking, rollerblading, fly fishing, row boating, visiting the bison or simply stopping to smell the roses—or one of the other 1,700 plant species—at the domed Conservatory of Flowers. When you've had enough of the great outdoors, head inside the de Young Museum for its eclectic collection, which includes American art spanning the 17th and 20th centuries and ancient murals from Teotihuacán. Don't forget to stop by the museum's observation tower to see a beautiful panorama of the city.

Walk over to the California Academy of Sciences to check out its exotic animal exhibits. Don't miss the rare albino alligator and the cute South African penguins. Before you leave the park, relax and sip some tea and nosh on snacks under the cherry trees in the Japanese Tea Garden.

Say goodbye to the park and make your way to the Haight-Ashbury neighborhood—no trip to San Francisco would be complete without a visit here. You can browse shops such as CD and vinyl haven Amoeba Records or vintage treasure trove **Wasteland (1660 Haight St., Western Addition, 415-863-3150)** for a sense of San Francisco's hippie history. End your last day by rocking out at The Fillmore, whose stage has been worked over by music greats like Janis Joplin and Jimi Hendrix. If you're not a rocker, get a side of jazz with your sushi at Yoshi's, which hosts two shows nightly. It's a mellow way to draw your vacation to a close.

it up as these newcomers shine or totally bomb. But be kind—thanks to the low stage and close seating, comics often engage, or rather pick on, the audience here. *Sunday-Thursday 8 p.m., Friday-Saturday 8 p.m. and 10 p.m. 18 and older; two-drink minimum.*

SAN FRANCISCO 49ERS

Candlestick Park, 490 Jamestown Ave., San Francisco, 418-464-9377; www.sf49ers.com

The 49ers' record five Super Bowl wins makes them one of the most successful franchises in NFL history. However, their last title came in 1994, and recent years have been mediocre at best. While the faithful still turn out in red and gold to support or chastise the team, most of the drama has been happening off field. Following the city's inability to come up with a feasible plan to replace the worn-down Candlestick Park, a new stadium is being built in Santa Clara. Expected to be complete by the 2014 season, the stadium will feature pedestrian plazas, an open design, a 49s Hall of Fame, a team store and commercial community space.

SAN FRANCISCO BALLET

War Memorial Opera House, 301 Van Ness Ave., San Francisco, 415-865-2000; www.sfballet.org

Founded in 1933, this is the country's oldest professional ballet company and one of its largest. Under the direction of Helgi Tomasson (a longtime lead dancer for legendary choreographer George Balanchine) for 25-plus years, the San Francisco Ballet has risen from a regional troupe to one of the world's premier companies. While firmly grounded in the classical ballet tradition, the company is known for pioneering newly commissioned works and innovative spins on classics. Its annual *Nutcracker* production in December is nothing shy of magical. You'll leave dancing like a sugarplum fairy, or rather wishing you could. The regular repertory season runs from the end of January through May in the War Memorial Opera House.

SAN FRANCISCO GIANTS

AT&T Park, 24 Willie Mays Plaza, San Francisco, 415-972-2000; www.sanfranciscogiants.com

Following the loss of Barry Bonds, there's been a marked lack of excitement surrounding the Giants, except when pitcher Tim Lincecum—of the 99-mile-per-hour fastball and unorthodox delivery—is playing. Nowadays, the biggest attraction may be the park itself, which has gone through several name changes, but is currently known as AT&T Park. Even if you don't paddle a kayak into McCovey Cove to catch homers, you're sure to enjoy the stadium's stunning views, idiosyncratic layout, intense garlic fries and gorgeous brick wall (complete with viewing areas for fans who can't afford a ticket). One or two more brawny hitters, and the Giants will chase the ring again.

SAN FRANCISCO MUSEUM OF MODERN ART

151 Third St., San Francisco, 415-357-4000; www.sfmoma.org

Designed by noted Swiss architect Mario Botta, SFMOMA's burnt-sienna brick exterior and iconic black-and-white central cylinder stand in stark contrast to the surrounding glass and steel towers. The art housed inside isn't shabby, either. The museum's world-class collection of more than 25,000 works of modern and contemporary art ranges from Henri Matisse's 1905 masterpiece *Femme au chapeau* (Woman with a Hat) to Jeremy Blake's 21st-century digital animation. Along with its impressive catalogue of painting, sculpture, architecture, and design and media art, the museum boasts a massive photography collection, including work by Ansel Adams, Ilse Bing, Alfred Stieglitz and Dorothea Lange. As one of the country's largest modern art museums, SFMOMA frequently hosts blockbuster touring exhibitions as well. Past exhibits have featured Olafur Eliasson, Matthew Barney, Diane Arbus and Gerhard Richter. Refuel after taking in the works in the museum by heading to the café and ordering up one of the Italian-inspired panini or pastas.

Admission: adults $15, seniors and students $9, children under 12 free; Thursday 6-9 p.m. half-price. Monday-Tuesday, Friday-Sunday 11 a.m.-5:45 p.m., Thursday 11 a.m.-8:45 p.m. Spotlight tours: Friday-Sunday noon-12:30 p.m.; meet in the Haas Atrium. Daily tours: 11:30 a.m., 12:30 p.m., 1:30 p.m. and 2:30 p.m.; Thursday 7:15 p.m.; meet in the Haas Atrium. Free first Tuesday of every month.

SAN FRANCISCO OPERA

War Memorial Opera House, 301 Van Ness Ave., San Francisco, 415-864-3330; www.sfopera.com

The Beaux Arts architecture of the War Memorial Opera House belies the innovative spirit of the San Francisco Opera. Second only to New York's Metropolitan Opera in North America, this internationally recognized company is known for its inventive takes on classics (Puccini's *La Bohème* and Verdi's *La Traviata*) as well as for championing new work (*Doctor Atomic* by John Adams and *The Bonesetter's Daughter*, adapted from Bay Area author Amy Tan's best-selling novel). Thanks to its commitment to pulling the art form into the 21st century, there's no need to bring your opera glasses here. Its high-definition video projections allow even the folks in the balcony seats to see the divas sweat.

SAN FRANCISCO SYMPHONY

Louise M. Davies Symphony Hall, 201 Van Ness Ave., San Francisco, 415-864-6000; www.sfsymphony.org

Under the direction of Classical Music Hall of Famer Michael Tilson Thomas, the symphony has been honored for its pioneering programming and its celebration of American composers. The 100-year-old orchestra's tradition of excellence has attracted a who's-who list of conductors and composers, including Leopold Stokowski, Leonard Bernstein, Igor Stravinsky, Sergei Prokofiev, Maurice Ravel, Aaron Copland and John Adams. The symphony also boasts its own chorus, whose vocal prowess has been featured on the soundtracks for *Amadeus*, *The Unbearable Lightness of Being* and *Godfather III*. Hear the 11-time Grammy Award-winning symphony live in the sparkling Louise M. Davies Symphony Hall, home to the Ruffatti organ, the largest concert-hall organ in North America.

SAN FRANCISCO ZOO

Sloat Boulevard at Great Highway, San Francisco, 415-753-7080; www.sfzoo.org

While the San Francisco Zoo doesn't have the most stellar reputation (critics have complained of shabby surroundings and the precarious health of some of the animals), it is still home to exotic and rescued animals from all over the world, and it welcomes nearly a million visitors a year to its 100-acre ocean-side spread. Followers of Animal Planet's hit "drama" *Meerkat Manor* will adore the zoo's outdoor meerkat exhibit. With only a low glass barrier separating human from meerkat, even the littlest fans can get an intimate look at the tight-knit family in its simulated savanna abode, replete with red soil and termite mounds. Nearly 700 mammals, birds, reptiles and insects call the zoo home. So even if meerkats aren't your thing, a critter more to your liking is bound to be pouncing, slithering or swinging around one of the enclosures. Kids flock to the historic "Little Puffer" miniature steam-train ride (built in 1904)—which chugs past the bear grottos and offers views of Eagle Island and the Latin American exhibit "Puente Al Sur"—and the hand-carved wooden Dentzel Carousel (built in 1921). For those wanting to chow down with the animals, the zoo's Twitter account will keep you updated on exactly when feeding times begin with text message alerts to your cell phone or online.

Admission: non-resident adults $15, seniors $12, children 4-14 $9, children under 4 free; resident adults $12, seniors $7.50, children 4-14 $5.50, children under 4 free. Free first Wednesday of every month for residents. March 13-November 5, daily 10 a.m.-5 p.m.; November 6-March 12, daily 10 a.m.-4 p.m.

SURFING

Known for big waves and big sharks, Northern California surfing isn't for amateurs. If the threat of sharks isn't enough to give you goose bumps, there's always the icy-cold water to chill you to the bone. But for those ready to zip into a wetsuit and brave the fierce rip currents, the winter wave payoff can be big. Most surfing in San Francisco happens at **Ocean Beach** between Kelly's Cove (north end, by the Cliff House) and Sloat Boulevard at the south end (in the Sunset District, near Richmond). It picks up mighty swells and has plenty of space for a city's worth of surfers to spread out. When the waves are big, paddling out can be a rougher workout than you expect. Experienced surfers also hit San Francisco's north side at **Dead Man's Break** (around the corner from China Beach) and **Fort Point** under the Golden Gate Bridge (off the Presidio) to hang 10.

TEATRO ZINZANNI
The Embarcadero, Pier 29, San Francisco, 415-438-2668; www.zinzanni.org

Imagine eating an extravagant meal right in the middle of a Cirque du Soleil performance, and you get a sense of the chaotic opulence that is Teatro ZinZanni. Staged along the Embarcadero in a giant, mirrored circus tent, the extravaganza offers a three-hour, five-course meal unlike any other. While the food is decent, it's not the main draw. Instead, folks go for the over-the-top entertainment, which can include acrobats, aerialists, comedians, opera singers, contortionists, tap dancers, magicians and jugglers.

Admission: Wednesday-Thursday, Sunday $117; Friday $136; Saturday $145. Wednesday-Saturday 6:55 p.m., Sunday 5:55 p.m. Cocktail lobby doors open 55 minutes before shows start.

UNION SQUARE
Geary and Powell streets, San Francisco; www.unionsquareshop.com

Union Square is one of the major tourist destinations in San Francisco, mainly because of the shopping opportunities, but also because of the plethora of hotels, theaters and bars in the area. The plaza itself, which was built in 1847 and named for the Union Army rallies that took place here, has been renovated many times, including when the world's first underground parking garage was added. But the real attractions are of course the upscale boutiques, among them Louis Vuitton, Gucci, Chanel, Prada and Marc Jacobs.

WASHINGTON SQUARE
Columbus and Union streets, San Francisco

Situated near many different neighborhoods, Washington Square epitomizes the variety of San Francisco life. Elderly folks amble down from Chinatown for their morning tai chi exercises. American and European tourists sprawl on the grass, exhausted from gorging at nearby restaurants and shops. Craggy Italian gentlemen pause from bocce games and to reminisce about Joe DiMaggio (who was first married at Saints Peter and Paul Roman Catholic Church, which sits along the north side of the square). Local barhoppers stretch out in the sun, recovering from the debauchery of the night before. In this small, tree-lined square, people-watching is both vibrant and relaxed, much like North Beach itself.

WHALE WATCHING
The Oceanic Society, San Francisco Marina Yacht Harbor, San Francisco,
415-474-3385, 800-326-7491; www.oceanic-society.org

Whale watching is an imprecise science. Sometimes you get lucky; other times you don't. However, with several migration patterns taking whales right past the San Francisco coastline, you have a decent chance of seeing some kind of oceanic life when you go out on the Bay. Blue whales—the largest animals in the world—tend to migrate from June through November, as do the ever-graceful humpbacks. If you visit between December and May, you're more likely to see gray whales, which travel from their Arctic feeding grounds to Baja to breed and give birth. Even if you don't see a whale during your trip, you're likely to spy puffins, various seals and sea lions—cute alternatives if you can't catch a humpback.

Admission: $120. Saturday-Sunday 8 a.m.-4 p.m.

WILD PARROTS OF TELEGRAPH HILL
Besides Coit Tower resting at its top, Telegraph Hill is perhaps best known for the flock of feral parrots, primarily cherry-headed conures that regularly swoop through and hang out in the branches of the neighborhood's lush gardens. The birds were the focus of self-appointed guardian Mark Bittner's bestselling book *The Wild Parrots of Telegraph Hill* and the subsequent documentary film of the same title. Despite their colloquial name, the parrots roost in the grassy area across from the Ferry Building, and their bright red and green plumage can be spotted from as far as Washington Square Park and Fort Mason. Once common practice, hand-feeding the parrots is now a misdemeanor. If you're caught food-handed, you could get slapped with a $100 fine.

WINDSURFING
On any given day, brightly colored sails dot the Bay's beautiful blue waters. But don't be fooled by the pretty picture. These choppy waves aren't for beginners. Powerful tides and currents can suck novice windsurfers out to sea. Then there are the strong and variable winds to contend with and the dense fog that can

reduce your vision to zero. Not to mention the hypothermia-inducing water temperatures. That said, **Crissy Field** *(Marine Drive, Presidio; www.parksconservancy.org)* is the most popular spot for those who know what they're doing and others who like to watch from the safety of the shoreline. Windy weekends draw hundreds of windsurfers into the water. Conditions are best from mid-March through September here. Beginners may want to head for tamer waters across the Bay at the Berkeley Marina or Alameda's Crown Beach.

YERBA BUENA CENTER FOR THE ARTS
701 Mission St., San Francisco, 415-978-2787; www.ybca.org

Situated alongside the picnic-ready Yerba Buena Gardens, the YBCA's two galleries form the cultural cornerstone of the surrounding entertainment complex. Unlike SFMOMA across the street, the YBCA doesn't have a permanent collection. The center focuses on work that explores the intersection of pop culture and fine art, such as its retrospective of underground comic artist R. Crumb and the popular *Beautiful Losers* exhibit, which included painting, sculpture and photography along with graffiti and clothing design born out of punk and hip-hop subcultures (and now a documentary with the same name). The center has been pushing the boundaries of art and performance ever since opening its doors in 1993. As part of its commitment to community and cutting-edge work, the center holds a triennial exhibit of emerging Bay Area artists.

Admission: when all galleries are open, adults $7, seniors, students and teachers $5; when galleries are partially open, $5 adults, seniors, students and teachers $3. Free first Tuesday of every month. Thursday-Friday 2-8 p.m., Saturday noon-8 p.m., Sunday noon-6 p.m. First Tuesday of every month noon-8 p.m.

YOSHI'S SAN FRANCISCO AT FILLMORE HERITAGE CENTER
1330 Fillmore St., San Francisco, 415-655-5600; www.yoshis.com

Jazz and sushi may seem like an unusual pairing, but at Yoshi's they go together like white on rice or Miles Davis on trumpet. Founder and namesake Yoshie Akiba has been serving Japanese cuisine and world-class jazz to the other side of the Bay since 1977, at his Oakland location *(510 Embarcadero West, 510-238-9200)*. Thirty years later, the chic second club opened its doors in San Francisco's historic Fillmore district. The club hosts two shows a night. If you're dining before the second show, present your ticket to your server, and he'll save you one of the 417 seats in the jazz house—and there isn't a bad seat among them. The crowd itself is an entertaining mix of head-bopping enthusiasts in jeans and T-shirts, cocktail-sipping women in stilettos and dapper fellows in fedoras.

ZEUM
221 Fourth St., San Francisco, 415-820-3320; www.zeum.org

If you take your kid to Zeum, you may realize there isn't a place this cool for adults. Open since 1998 inside the Yerba Buena Garden complex, Zeum has several exhibits where children learn how to make animated cartoons, film music videos, craft musical soundtracks and produce their own movie, talk show or television broadcast. Zeum offers workshops with visiting artists who teach wacky things like how to make blinking electronic insects. Kids can also learn about and ride the historic 1906 Charles Looff Carousel.

Admission: adults $10, children 3-18, seniors $8, children under 3 free. School year, Wednesday-Friday 1-5 p.m., Saturday-Sunday 11 a.m.-5 p.m.; summer, Tuesday-Sunday 11 a.m.-5 p.m. Zeum Carousel: daily 11 a.m.-5 p.m.

WHERE TO STAY

★★★ARGONAUT HOTEL
495 Jefferson St., San Francisco, 415-563-0800; www.argonauthotel.com

Everything's in ship-shape at the Wharf's newest boutique hotel. Housed in what was once a warehouse of the largest fruit and vegetable cannery in the world, this nautical-themed hotel features plank floors in the lobby, crisp navy and yellow fabrics and white-washed furnishings, as well as amazing panoramas of the waterfront and Alcatraz. Next door, the Blue Mermaid Chowder House & Bar delivers seafood to landlubbers; the bronze mermaid sculptures may be a little on the silly side, but Fisherman's Wharf wouldn't be fun without that sort of thing.

252 rooms. Business center. Fitness center. Pets accepted. $251-350

★★★CAMPTON PLACE HOTEL
340 Stockton St., San Francisco, 415-781-5555; www.tajhotels.com

Campton Place is a haven of serenity right on San Francisco's frenetic Union Square. The hotel is steps from Nob Hill's shops and restaurants, which makes the sophisticated vibe and thoughtful service all the more welcome. The rooms and suites have a modern, fresh look, with pear-wood paneling, unique photography and cushy but minimal furnishings. Most rooms have window seats with a view of the city—perfect for daydreaming or curling up with a book—and the hotel's rooftop fitness center boasts terrific skyline vistas. The onsite dining room, Campton Place Restaurant, serves great contemporary American fare.

110 rooms. Restaurant, bar. Fitness center. Pets accepted. $351 and up

★★★CLIFT
495 Geary St., San Francisco, 415-775-4700; www.clifthotel.com

You don't have to be a fashionista to stay here, but it doesn't hurt. Philippe Starck's brilliantly eclectic design vision for this boutique hotel balances a Dalí-inspired lobby with an incredible collection of furniture, and bright guest rooms tricked out with floor-to-ceiling mirrors and ivory-and-lavender color schemes. Located just two blocks off Union Square, it's near all the area's tourist draws without being dominated by the noise and crowds. A young clientele dines on farm to table organic cuisine in the dark and sexy Velvet Room, but for a little history, grab a cocktail at the Redwood Room, a landmark lounge that has been restored to its Art Deco glory.

372 rooms. Restaurant, bar. Business center. Fitness center. $251-350

★★★THE FAIRMONT SAN FRANCISCO
950 Mason St., San Francisco, 415-772-5000; www.fairmont.com

Sitting at the peak of Nob Hill, this historic hotel aims to dazzle from the moment you step into its palatial lobby. Its Old World ambience extends to the rooms, where marble baths and chaise lounges invite lingering. Things are livelier at the Tonga Room, a tiki restaurant with decorative indoor rain

WHAT ARE THE MOST LUXURIOUS HOTELS IN SAN FRANCISCO?

Four Seasons Hotel San Francisco
Polished service, sophisticated, elegant rooms and some of the city's best views make this modern tower a top choice.

The Ritz-Carlton, San Francisco
The amenities at this Nob Hill hotel match the grandeur of its circa 1909 building, from the Five Star dining at the Dining Room to the classically decorated rooms.

The St. Regis San Francisco
Staying here is like staying in a design showcase—rooms are loaded with tech toys like flat-screen TVs, Mid-century modern furniture, and uber-comfortable beds draped in Pratesi linens.

showers. The Laurel Court offers a more refined atmosphere to take in fresh seafood dishes. Higher tower rooms have good views, but the view in the lobby isn't too shabby, either—it recently went through a restoration that makes it one of the city's most opulent.

591 rooms. Restaurant, bar. Business center. Fitness center. Spa. Pets accepted. $251-350

★★★★★FOUR SEASONS HOTEL SAN FRANCISCO
757 Market St., San Francisco, 415-633-3000; www.fourseasons.com

San Francisco does not experience four distinct seasons—it's mild no matter when you visit. Likewise, the Four Seasons provides posh lodgings all year long. The glassy exterior of the tower looks sleek and modern, but the décor inside provides a soothing oasis. Rooms have a comfortable, sophisticated design that includes black lacquered coffee tables, granite-topped end tables, fabric wall coverings and headboards, plush carpeting and a chic color scheme of rich mocha and soft teal with pewter, silver and gold accents. (Request a corner room to see more of the city through floor-to-ceiling windows.) The restaurant, Seasons, focuses on surf-and-turf classics with a wine list that draws liberally from vineyards in nearby Sonoma and Napa counties. To burn off those calories, head to the 127,000-square-foot Sports Club/LA that overlooks Market Street. Before setting off to visit the nearby San Francisco Museum of Modern Art, art aficionados should download the podcast guide to the hotel's impressive collection, which includes works by Matisse and Klee.

277 rooms. Restaurant, bar. Business center. Fitness center. Pool. Spa. Pets accepted. $351 and up

★★★GRAND HYATT SAN FRANCISCO
345 Stockton St., San Francisco, 415-398-1234; www.grandsanfrancisco.hyatt.com

Popular with tourists and business travelers alike, this 36-story hotel boasts a fantastic Union Square location and floor-to-ceiling windows. Grandviews, a restaurant on the top floor, supplies sweeping vistas of Alcatraz and the Golden Gate Bridge, along with its French-accented American cuisine. A large 24-hour fitness center provides workout options, while the rooms themselves are spacious, if a bit impersonal. Our advice: Request a room away from Stockton Street, as the doormen's cab whistles blare on late into the night.

685 rooms. Restaurant, bar. Business center. Fitness center. Pets accepted. $151-250

★★★HOTEL ADAGIO
550 Geary St., San Francisco, 415-775-5000; www.thehoteladagio.com

After a 2003 facelift, the Adagio has become a stylish option for travelers seeking a bit of contemporary design. The hotel's style mixes a dash of Spanish Colonial (Moorish archways) with clean, contemporary touches (sleek couches and whimsical light fixtures). The onsite restaurant, Bar Adagio, draws a hip crowd seeking Mediterranean small plates. You'll appreciate the close-to-it-all location and soothing earth tones of the modern rooms, which feature plush beds and Egyptian linens. If you need to travel a little farther than nearby Union Square, the hotel offers complimentary car service each morning for business travelers.

171 rooms. Restaurant, bar. Business center. Fitness center. $151-250

★★★HOTEL DRISCO
2901 Pacific Ave., San Francisco, 415-346-2880; www.jdvhotels.com

Live like a local for the night at this century-old hotel. Tucked among multi-million-dollar homes in the posh Pacific Heights neighborhood, this hostelry provides a glimpse into a lively residential area. Mahogany wood encases the front desk area, while traditionally decorated guest rooms feature overstuffed sofas, marble sinks in the bathrooms, crown molding and a creamy color palette. Amenities are top-notch: A lounge with tea and coffee, a bath-goods bar in your room and evening wine service make this a very gracious stay.

48 rooms. Complimentary breakfast. Business center. Fitness center. $251-350

★★★HOTEL GRIFFON
155 Steuart St., San Francisco, 415-495-2100; www.hotelgriffon.com

For a city surrounded on three sides by water, surprisingly few hotels provide the chance to stay near the waterfront. Not so at Hotel Griffon, located a stone's throw from the Bay Bridge. Decked out with exposed brick walls, berber carpeting and quilted duvets, the recently remodeled rooms are comfortable and inviting The new onsite restaurant, Perry's on Embarcadero, is a rendition of a Union Square original that has been there for 40 years. Some of the best dining in town can also be found right outside the hotel. Complimentary car service is provided to the financial district for those visiting San Francisco on business weekdays from 7 to 11 a.m.

62 rooms. Business center. $251-350

★★★HOTEL MONACO
501 Geary St., San Francisco, 415-292-0100; www.monaco-sf.com

This Theater District boutique hotel from Kimpton is all about whimsy, from the lobby tarot card readings to the rent-a-goldfish service. There's even a Grace Slick suite filled with Jefferson Airplane memorabilia and Slick's own original paintings. Just because the hotel offers off-beat perks doesn't mean it skimps on amenities. A roomy spa offers massages and pedicures, while the Grand Café brasserie turns out regional French cuisine in a former ballroom. Frette sheets, canopy beds and fleur-de-lis textiles give a nod to the South-of-France inspiration, drawing guests who crave a little fun with their experience.

201 rooms. Business center. Fitness center. Spa. Pets accepted. $251-350

★★★HOTEL NIKKO

222 Mason St., San Francisco, 415-394-1111; www.hotelnikkosf.com

Say "konnichiwa" (that's hello and good afternoon in Japanese) to the San Francisco outpost of this Asian hotel chain, which has a Japanese feel without being too literal about it. The décor is traditional—lots of beige-on-beige warm tones and a few bold splashes of red—and the views of Union Square are lovely. Although the hotel caters to conventioneers and business travelers, the amenities are better than what many hotels in its class have to offer: ANZU, an Asian fusion restaurant, attracts locals for its sushi and Sunday brunch, and the sky-lit indoor pool will please fitness fans. A small spa includes shiatsu massage and steam rooms.

532 rooms. Restaurant, bar. Business center. Fitness center. Pool. Spa. Pets accepted. $251-350

★★★HOTEL PALOMAR

12 Fourth St., San Francisco, 415-348-1111; www.hotelpalomar-sf.com

Easily identifiable by its mint-green tiled exterior, the Palomar aims to draw an artsy crowd with its Escher-esque patterned floors and plenty of art placed throughout the hotel. There's nothing surreal about the attention to detail; staffers are known to leave notes offering their assistance and the bathrooms are generously stocked with Aveda products. Alligator-print carpeting and persimmon wood furniture give a decidedly international flair. The Fifth Floor restaurant is heralded for its take on southern French cooking. All in all, it's a great place to get in touch with your inner artiste.

195 rooms. Restaurant, bar. Business center. Fitness center. Pets accepted. $151-250

★★★HOTEL REX

562 Sutter St., San Francisco, 415-433-4434; www.thehotelrex.com

A bibliophile's dream, this boutique hotel has the rich ambience of a literary salon. Walls of books, leather chairs and original portraits make you feel like you're part of the intelligentsia, while the cozy but bright rooms feature cheerful yellow walls balanced by dark wood furniture. Downstairs, Café Andrée serves breakfast, lunch and dinner, and offers ethnic dishes and homemade pasta in a dining room that looks more like a library than a hotel eatery.

94 rooms. Restaurant, bar. Business center. Pets accepted. $151-250

★★★HOTEL VITALE

8 Mission St., San Francisco, 415-278-3700; www.hotelvitale.com

Opened in 2005, this minimalist hotel has an unbeatable location across from the Ferry Building. Its rooms are modern but warm, with soothing powder-blue accents and Fresh toiletries to add to the comfort. A series of patios makes it easy to soak up views of the Bay, while a spa and yoga studio (with complimentary classes) provide opportunities to chill out. Although the hotel doesn't have a pool, the staff does hand out passes to the YMCA lap pool. The off-lobby restaurant, Americano, draws a crowd of professional singles, giving the Vitale the feel of a cool local hangout rather than an isolated hotel.

200 rooms. Restaurant, bar. Business center. Fitness center. Spa. Pets accepted. $351 and up

★★★THE HUNTINGTON HOTEL

1075 California St., San Francisco, 415-474-5400; www.huntingtonhotel.com

Even on a foggy night, this historic hotel's rooftop sign lights up the top of Nob Hill. Built in 1922, it retains its old-fashioned character through rich velvets, silks and damasks in the lobby and guest rooms. The hotel was originally crafted as an apartment building, so you'll appreciate the larger-than-average layouts—as well as homey touches like complimentary tea or sherry service upon your arrival. There's plenty to do to relax in style: The Nob Hill Spa is larger and more luxurious than the average hotel spa, and the Big 4 restaurant serves American cuisine in a classic wood-paneled room. Guests have included the likes of Pablo Picasso and Lauren Bacall, so you know this stately mansion has a history of gracious service.

136 rooms. Restaurant, bar. Business center. Fitness center. Pool. Spa. $351 and up

★★★HYATT AT FISHERMAN'S WHARF
555 N. Point St., San Francisco, 415-563-1234; www.fishermanswharf.hyatt.com

Just a two-minute walk from Pier 39, this low-rise building is popular due to its location. But this touristy hotel offers another standout quality: great design. A recent refurbishing has given the lobby a bright, sophisticated look that extends to the chocolate-and-white room décor. (Unfortunately, the design stops short of reaching the bland, not-so-tough sports bar Knuckles at the Wharf.) An outdoor heated pool, a rarity in San Francisco, adds to the appeal of the 24-hour health club.

313 rooms. Restaurant, bar. Business center. Fitness center. Pool. $151-250

★★★HYATT REGENCY SAN FRANCISCO
5 Embarcadero Center, San Francisco, 415-788-1234; www.sanfranciscoregency.hyatt.com

A breathtaking, 17-story atrium is the centerpiece of this angular hotel, which sits across the street from the San Francisco Bay. After zooming up a few flights in a glass elevator, you'll be able to spread out in the understated, spacious rooms; perks like Portico bath products and granite bathrooms make your stay even more luxurious. Rooms offer vistas of the water or of the city; ask to be placed on a higher floor to escape some of the street noise below. The Eclipse Café offers standard salad-and-sandwich fare, but Eclipse Lounge amps up the sophistication along with providing views of the Embarcadero.

802 rooms. Restaurant, bar. Business center. Fitness center. $251-350

WHAT ARE THE BEST SAN FRANCISCO HOTELS FOR BUSINESS TRAVELERS?

Grand Hyatt San Francisco
A great Union Square location, plenty of work space in the contemporary rooms and 24-hour fitness center make this hotel a good choice for business travelers.

Le Méridien
You can practically roll out of bed and right to your meeting from this Financial District hotel, which also has high-speed wireless access and 24-hour room service.

★★★THE INN AT UNION SQUARE
440 Post St., San Francisco, 415-397-3510; www.unionsquare.com

A Lilliputian lobby belies the variety to be found within this European-style hotel. Standard rooms are on the petite side, so if you aren't traveling light, consider upgrading to a penthouse suite to enjoy an in-room fireplace and whirlpool tub. Either way, you'll revel in cozy red-and-gold rooms with classy touches such as damask duvets and Georgian-style chairs. A friendly staff aims to delight, taking care of little pleasures, from leaving fresh flowers on the desk to including chocolates with nightly turndown service. Guests get access to a nearby fitness center and pool.

30 rooms. Complimentary breakfast. Business center. $151-250

★★★INTERCONTINENTAL MARK HOPKINS SAN FRANCISCO
1 Nob Hill, San Francisco, 415-392-3434; www.markhopkins.net

Cable cars clatter by this San Francisco icon, and inside, the scene is as classic as ever. Rooms are traditionally styled in warm tan and brown shades and sleigh beds feature California king mattresses for extra sleeping space. A visit to the Intercontinental Mark Hopkins is incomplete without a stop at Top of the Mark. The lounge's legendary vistas may provide the city's best place to catch a sunset, and the bar's 100 Martinis menu is absolutely classic. The restaurant and bar serves breakfast, lunch and dinner.

380 rooms. Restaurant, bar. Business center. Fitness center. $251-350

★★★INTERCONTINENTAL SAN FRANCISCO
888 Howard St., San Francisco, 415-616-6500; www.intercontinentalsanfrancisco.com

On the outside, this 32-story hotel is a bold testament to steel and blue glass. Within its walls, the modern décor warms up to include floor-to-ceiling windows, large working desks and iPod docking stations in each room. Plasma TVs, a spacious 24-hour fitness center, and a full-service spa featuring Murad products offer plenty of ways to recharge. All of the suites have spectacular views of the city. The 2,000-square-foot Presidential Suite is on two floors and includes two terraces. Luce restaurant churns out well-done Italian fare in a beautiful, contemporary, high-ceilinged space off the lobby. The location, near the Moscone Center, is bound to draw convention-goers, but this spot offers just as much in the way of pleasure as it does for business.

550 rooms. Restaurant, bar. Business center. Fitness center. Pool. Spa. $251-350

★★★JW MARRIOTT SAN FRANCISCO UNION SQUARE
500 Post St., San Francisco, 415-771-8600; www.jwmarriottunionsquare.com

This Nob Hill hotel recently completed a top-to-bottom refurbishment. The effort has paid off and made this a stylish upscale business hotel. The sizable rooms feel fresh and modern, and thoughtful amenities include a one-touch button that summons a butler for all of your needs. The restaurant, Level Three, is brightly appointed in rich red and orange tones; head there to sample fancified takes on comfort food, such as macaroni and cheese with black truffle oil and Kobe beef sliders.

329 rooms. Restaurant, bar. Business center. Fitness center. Pets accepted. $251-350

★★★LE MÉRIDIEN
333 Battery St., San Francisco, 415-296-2900;
www.starwoodhotels.com

The cavernous Financial District isn't exactly the height of chic, but Le Méridien tries to add a dash of style to this big-business neighborhood. The former Park Hyatt has received a continental facelift, including streamlined rooms with contemporary furniture and décor in shades of taupe, red and brown. (Many rooms have balconies that offer views of the city or the Bay, so make your requests accordingly.) The classic décor at the Park Grill won't blow you away, so dine alfresco on the plant-filled terrace instead. For a comfortable room that's a little nicer than your average megachain, as well as a quick commute to your morning meeting, this hotel does the trick nicely.

360 rooms. Restaurant, bar. Business center. Fitness center. $251-350

★★★★MANDARIN ORIENTAL, SAN FRANCISCO
222 Sansome St., San Francisco, 415-276-9888;
www.mandarinoriental.com

Located on the upper floors of one of the city's tallest buildings, this luxury hotel offers sky-high views of the city—from the Golden Gate Bridge to the Transamerica Pyramid to the Bay Bridge. (Yes, binoculars are in every room.) Power lunches take place at the hotel restaurant, Silks, which incorporates California produce into Asian fusion cuisine; MO bar is more casual, offering great cocktails and small plates from the kitchen. While the rooms can feel spare—the gold and red accents perk up the subdued, contemporary furnishings, beige carpet and walls—the staff's warmth more than makes up for it. Asian-influenced hospitality extends from feng shui room design to complimentary jasmine tea service, making this Eastern-influenced location one of the most memorable stays in the West.

158 rooms. Restaurant, bar. Business center. Fitness center. Pets accepted. $351 and up

★★★OMNI SAN FRANCISCO
500 California St., San Francisco, 415-677-9494;
www.omnisanfrancisco.com

Built in 1926 and remodeled in 2002, the former Financial Center Building retains all of the richness of its past splendor. Sparkling chandeliers, polished brass and delicate ironwork dress up the lobby and the rooms are just as elegant. Though the furnishings

---

WHICH SAN FRANCISCO HOTELS HAVE THE BEST BEDS?

Four Seasons Hotel San Francisco:
The signature mattresses are swathed in layer upon layer of high-thread count linens and loaded with down pillows to make for a perfect slumber.

The St. Regis San Francisco:
Pillow-top mattresses, crisp white Pratesi linens and ample pillows combine to make sleeping here a transcendent experience.

are purely traditional, with colonial-style beds and armoires, and plenty of subdued fabrics, they've been updated with modern amenities such as Italian linens and iPod alarm clocks. There's even a children's suite with games, toys and kid-sized furniture. Don't be fooled by the casual name of Bob's Steak and Chop House—the atmosphere is upscale and the steaks are top-notch.

362 rooms. Restaurant, bar. Business center. Fitness center. Pets accepted. $61-150

★★★PALACE HOTEL

2 New Montgomery St., San Francisco, 415-512-1111; www.sfpalace.com

Originally built in 1875, this grand hotel has been restored to its Victorian grandeur, from crystal chandeliers to a sky-lit indoor pool. The rooms aren't the largest in town, but mahogany furniture and 14-foot-high ceilings make up for what they lack in space. Be sure to enjoy afternoon tea at the Garden Court restaurant, a historic landmark, which has a beautiful domed stained-glass ceiling; or for an upscale Japanese dinner, make a reservation at Kyo-ya, where the ambiance is more modern, but the service is equally refined.

553 rooms. Restaurant, bar. Business center. Fitness center. Pool. $251-350

★★★PARC 55 HOTEL

55 Cyril Magnin St., San Francisco, 415-392-8000; www.parc55hotel.com

This enormous 32-story tower attracts families and tour groups who love the hotel's proximity to major shopping areas and public transportation. The rooms are decorated in dark woods and deep earth tones, and although standard rooms can be small, they're laid out well. Dining options abound, including inexpensive curries at Siam Thai and surf-and-turf choices at the Cityhouse.

1,025 rooms. Restaurant, bar. Business center. Fitness center. Pets accepted. $151-250

★★★PRESCOTT HOTEL

545 Post St., San Francisco, 415-563-0303; www.prescotthotel.com

Many famous faces have passed through these doors, including cinema legends such as Robert Redford and Elizabeth Taylor, who made the hotel home while they were residing in the city. You'll be impressed by the Italian linens and cherry furniture, which give this boutique hotel a European flair. Although not all of the rooms have benefited from a recent renovation effort, beds through-out are comfortable and the linens are crisp. Room service is a delight; dishes are delivered from the onsite New American restaurant, Postrio. Located just a block from Union Square, you'll also find plenty of dining as well as shopping right outside your door. But don't leave without stopping by the hosted wine hour from the hotel's collection that is offered to all guests every evening.

164 rooms. Restaurant, bar. Business center. Fitness center. Pets accepted. $151-250

★★★★★THE RITZ-CARLTON, SAN FRANCISCO

600 Stockton St., San Francisco, 415-296-7465; www.ritzcarlton.com

Even the most blasé traveler would have to be impressed by this stately mansion atop Nob Hill. Built in 1909 as the headquarters of the Metropolitan Life Insurance Company, the hotel recently underwent a $12.5 million renova-tion that has restored its palatial polish, giving the opulent Old Europe design theme a little more gilt and sparkle. Club level suites feature options such as 1,000-thread-count sheets and a 1,200-square-foot private balcony. If you can't stay in the Presidential Suite, don't worry—the smaller rooms are only slightly less lavish, featuring a palette of butter cream and taupe, with walnut and mahogany furniture that adds warmth. You'll have excellent options for food, too: The Dining Room is frequently booked due to its excellent Asian fusion cuisine, and the Lobby Lounge is a great place to take in the skyline while eating from the raw bar and drinking from the farm-fresh Bloody Mary menu. Throughout the hotel, the legendary service is gracious whether you arrive by town car or by hopping off the cable car outside.

336 rooms. Restaurant, bar. Business center. Fitness center. Pool. Spa. Pets accepted. $351 and up

★★★SAN FRANCISCO MARRIOTT FISHERMAN'S WHARF
1250 Columbus Ave., San Francisco, 415-775-7555;
www.marriott.com

Other hotels may exude more character, but what this mid-range spot lacks in razzle-dazzle, it makes up for with tidy rooms, dependable service and a tourist-friendly location. Spada restaurant offers a chance to chow down on fresh-from-the-ocean seafood, but we recommend heading to one of the neighborhood's many eateries for a better taste of San Francisco.

285 rooms. Restaurant, bar. Business center. Fitness center. Pets accepted. $251-350

★★★SERRANO HOTEL
405 Taylor St., San Francisco, 415-885-2500; www.serranohotel.com

The Serrano nudges up next to the sketchy Tenderloin district, but it nonetheless delivers a reliable stay. The Spanish-inspired lobby is the setting for complimentary wine each night, and the guest rooms (though some fall on the small side) are clean and filled with light. The Ponzu restaurant serves Asian fusion fare and is surprisingly quiet on the weekends; it's better for a quick drink than a full meal. The hotel's attentive service—including a morning limousine ride to the Financial District—makes up for any dodgy dealings a few blocks away.

236 rooms. Restaurant, bar. Business center. Fitness center. Pets accepted. $151-250

★★★SHERATON FISHERMAN'S WHARF HOTEL
2500 Mason St., San Francisco, 415-362-5500;
www.sheratonatthewharf.com

Looking for a family-friendly, sunny spot? A $33 million renovation freshened the décor and amplified the amenities at this hotel. Pale woods, slanted windows and cheerful colors make for a vaguely nautical environment; a heated outdoor pool and close proximity to Pier 39 make this spot popular among visitors who eschew fussy hotels. Sol, a breakfast restaurant, will fuel you for a busy day; an outdoor seating area with fire pits will help you unwind at night.

531 rooms. Restaurant, bar. Business center. Fitness center. Pool. Pets accepted. $251-350

★★★★★THE ST. REGIS SAN FRANCISCO
125 Third St., San Francisco, 415-284-4000; www.stregissanfrancisco.com

Since opening in 2005, this hotel has been refining the concept of luxury, retaining the detail-oriented service focus, but removing any hints of stodginess. Rooms feature stylish contemporary décor in creams and dark woods, with standard features such as flat-screen TVs, crisp Pratesi linens and deep bathtubs that may inspire you to order from the hotel's Signature Bath menu.

The in-house Remède Spa is the pinnacle of extravagant pampering, while the ground-floor restaurant, Ame, offers Japanese-influenced fare. The hotel also offers a good dose of culture: The Museum of the African Diaspora is conveniently located within the hotel, while the renowned San Francisco Museum of Modern Art is right next door. When you go out, or venture beyond all the great shops outside your door, the staff will be happy to shuttle you to your destination—in a Bentley, of course.

260 rooms. Restaurant, bar. Business center. Fitness center. Pool. Spa. Pets accepted. $351 and up

★★★THE STANFORD COURT RENAISSANCE HOTEL
905 California St., San Francisco, 415-989-3500; www.marriott.com

This hotel stands at the former spot of railroad magnate Leland Stanford's mansion, but you're the one who'll feel at home. The décor is 20th century through and through, from the lobby's Tiffany dome to Baccarat crystal chandeliers brought over from the Grand Hotel in Paris. With a $35 million revamp in 2008, all rooms are new with luxurious bedding, large baths, plush bathrobes and, in deluxe view rooms, vistas of the bay and city. After spending a day downtown, enjoy a glass of wine at Aurea, the hotel's restaurant/bar, which serves seasonal Californian cuisine (or stop by during the day when it operates as a café).

367 rooms. Restaurant, bar. Business center. Fitness center. Pets accepted. $151-250

★★★W SAN FRANCISCO
181 Third St., San Francisco, 415-777-5300; www.whotels.com

Urban cool permeates this lively, stylish spot next to Yerba Buena Gardens. The hotel restaurant, XYZ, is almost always filled with a fashionable crowd enjoying the latest in California cuisine, and Bliss spa adds a dash of fun to your pampering experience. The bright white rooms are hypermodern, with light woods contrasting with the pops of colorful textiles. The black-clad staff aims to please, from the chauffeur service to the "pillow menu" that lets you choose exactly how to lay your head.

404 rooms. Restaurant, bar. Business center. Fitness center. Pool. Spa. Pets accepted. $251-350

★★★WESTIN SAN FRANCISCO MARKET STREET
50 Third St., San Francisco, 415-974-6400; www.westinsf.com

There's no big mystery behind this business-traveler mainstay, just a contemporary hotel with a great downtown location. Sometimes that's all you need, especially when the rooms are spacious and comfortable. Westin's legendary beds live up to their reputation for plush softness, and floor-to-ceiling windows let tons of light stream in while providing a chance to watch the bustling downtown traffic. Although the earth-toned décor isn't the most groundbreaking, it's quite the opposite at Ducca, where you can eat Venetian cuisine and kick back with a Peroni on the well-designed patio.

676 rooms. Restaurant, bar. Business center. Fitness center. Pets accepted. $251-350

★★★THE WESTIN ST. FRANCIS
335 Powell St., San Francisco, 415-397-7000; www.westinstfrancis.com

Part of the old guard of San Francisco lodging, this legendary hotel offers two wings with distinctly different experiences. The Historic Building is classic and sophisticated, offering Empire-style rooms painted in creams and powder blues. By contrast, the Tower Building's glass elevators show their 1970s origins, but the contemporary rooms—clean lines, cream-on-white coloring—are wholly modern. Chef Michael Mina's eponymous restaurant draws an epicurean crowd with its New American tasting menu, while the recently-opened Clock Bar offers smaller bites in a more casual environment. There's also a full-service spa and a large health club, and the location is just blocks from Union Square.

1,195 rooms. Restaurant, bar. Business center. Fitness center. Pool. Tennis. Spa. $151-250

RECOMMENDED

THE CRESCENT HOTEL
417 Stockton St., San Francisco, 415-400-0500; www.crescenthotelgroup.com

Located in the heart of historic Union Square within a restored Victorian building is this unique, modern hotel. Carefully designed rooms include 400 thread count Sateen linens, stylish furniture and marble bathrooms. The small touches that the owners incorporate, such as local delicacies in the mini-bars and wine from local wine makers, set this boutique hotel apart. Music lovers will appreciate the well-stocked iPod playlists that were carefully compiled by local and notable DJ's. Be sure to stop in The Burritt Room. Located on the second floor of the hotel, this bar and lounge is destined to be a classic. Like the rest of the hotel, the chic design—vintage and crystal chandeliers, exposed brick walls—is a welcome reprieve from the norm.

80 rooms. Bar. Complimentary breakfast. Business center. Spa. Pets accepted. $151-250

EXECUTIVE HOTEL VINTAGE COURT
650 Bush St., San Francisco, 415-392-4666; www.executivehotels.net

If you can't make it to Napa during your trip, stay at this wine-inspired hotel. Nightly wine tastings and a continental breakfast will fuel your adventures, while the décor's varying shades of green evoke visions of vineyards. It's just two blocks to Union Square and Chinatown, but once you spy the French offerings at the elegant (and excellent) Masa's Restaurant, you may want to stay put.

106 rooms. Restaurant, bar. Complimentary breakfast. Business center. Fitness center. $151-250

THE FITZGERALD HOTEL
620 Post St., San Francisco, 415-775-8100; www.fitzgeraldhotel.com

Low rates and a stellar location make this a frequent choice for value-conscious travelers. The room décor ranges from masculine brocades to Old World antiques, and a working gated elevator adds to the charm. Rooms are on the small side, even by city standards, but the Hidden Vine wine bar provides a place to stretch out with a full-bodied cabernet.

47 rooms. Complimentary breakfast. $61-150

HARBOR COURT HOTEL
165 Steuart St., San Francisco, 415-882-1300; www.harborcourthotel.com

Tucked away from the melee of Market Street, but close enough to the action of downtown, this boutique hotel serves up beautiful views of the Bay Bridge. Standard rooms, decorated in warm tones and colorful stripes, aren't enormous, but they're well-designed to offer as much space as possible. Although there is

no onsite fitness center, you can work it out at the next-door YMCA—or you may request a yoga mat from the front desk if the need to stretch strikes.
131 rooms. Pets accepted. $151-250

HOTEL BOHÈME
444 Columbus Ave., San Francisco, 415-433-9111; www.hotelboheme.com
Bohemian indeed, this tiny 15-room hotel is a wonderful mixed bag of Beat-era inspiration and nostalgia as cast-iron beds, yellowing newspaper clippings and antique furniture fill the space. Although the rooms are small, and the bathrooms may require some fancy footwork to fit two people at once, the accommodations are charming. Staying here is like stepping into a writer's nook—and in fact, if you luck into room 204, you'll rest where Allen Ginsberg once composed his poetry.
15 rooms. $151-250

HOTEL CARLTON
1075 Sutter St., San Francisco, 415-673-0242; www.jdvhotels.com
In one of the greenest cities in the country, it only makes sense to stay at an eco-friendly hotel. This one is partially powered by solar panels, cleaned with less-toxic detergents and certified green by the city. That doesn't mean you'll sacrifice comfort, though. The eclectic room décor blends Lucite lamps with Moroccan furniture, pulled together with a palette of persimmon, baby blue and teal. The onsite restaurant, Saha, dishes up a fusion of Arabic, European and American cuisines in a spicy, sexy setting. Note that it's a short walk to the Theater District and Union Square, and while the location is safe, heading a few blocks south can be dicey.
161 rooms. Restaurant. Pets accepted. $61-150

THE UNION STREET INN
2229 Union St., San Francisco, 415-346-0424; www.unionstreetinn.com
Set in an Edwardian home filled with antiques, this bed and breakfast features five distinctively decorated rooms. All are elegant without being stuffy, and some offer perks such as a private deck or Jacuzzi. Lovebirds should request the carriage house for more privacy. Within the main house, you'll enjoy lighting a fireplace in the maroon-walled New Yorker room. A beautiful garden patio shows off roses and lavender, and when the fog rolls in, you can head to the sitting room and feast on the always-available cookies and tea.
6 rooms. Complimentary breakfast. $151-250

WASHINGTON SQUARE INN
1660 Stockton St., San Francisco, 415-981-4220; www.wsisf.com
Tucked among the Italian restaurants of North Beach is this well-maintained, 16-room bed and breakfast. Best for solo travelers and couples, it's a quiet, homey place whose simple but elegant rooms have a continental influence. Afternoon tea and evening wine and cheese encourage guests to mingle, and the excellent location—across the street from the Saints Peter and Paul Church—may drag you out from your room if nothing else will.
16 rooms. No children under 12. Complimentary breakfast. $151-250

WHERE TO EAT

★★★ACQUERELLO
1722 Sacramento St., San Francisco, 415-567-5432; www.acquerello.com

Other Italian restaurants may see their names in food blogs and their chefs on TV, but Acquerello doesn't need all that razzmatazz, and probably doesn't want it. The restaurant's stately, white-linen ambience and its graciously formal service make all that attention seem a little vulgar. Here, you'll get a top-notch tasting menu complete with an amuse bouche and cheese cart; à la carte offerings done up Italian-style from antipasti (such as warm pancetta-wrapped figs with balsamic vinegar) to primi (risotto with apples and braised pork belly) to secondi (seared sea bass with piquillo peppers, capers and olive relish). Don't miss the Italian wine pairings; if you really like something, you'll get a free refill. Be sure to save room for desserts, especially the housemade biscotti.
Italian. Dinner. Closed Sunday-Monday. $36-85

★★★AME
The St. Regis San Francisco, 689 Mission St., San Francisco, 415-284-4040;
www.amerestaurant.com

A wall of flame between bar and dining room. A huge red center table. A dramatic open kitchen. All of this means you're entering a high-style zone. The menu at this contemporary spot is equally flawless, with food so sophisticated it's hard to describe. Think New American, with a strong Japanese influence and touches of French and Italian. Chef Hiro Sone is in charge of dinner (along with executive chef Orlando Pagan), which slinks elegantly from raw (pristinely cut sashimi, tartare or barely smoked fish) to cooked (anything from sake marinated cod to lamb two ways). His wife, Lissa Doumani, oversees the pastry duties, showcasing perfect seasonal fruit in tarts, pastries and ice creams. Order from an edited version of the menu, paired with deliciously intricate cocktails, in the also-stylish bar.
American. Dinner. $36-85

★★★AZIZA
5800 Geary Blvd., San Francisco, 415-752-2222; www.aziza-sf.com

Aziza's swirling Moroccan patterns, graceful arches and rich jewel tones contrast with the foggy Richmond District's soulless architecture. The food is equally dramatic: fresh, organic local ingredients with a deft, light Moroccan treatment. Basteeya, traditionally a pigeon pie, lightens up in a version pairing chicken and almonds with phyllo dough and confectioner's sugar. Fluffy couscous is topped with chicken, prawn, lambs or fresh vegetables; exotically scented spices like cardamom and Ras el Hanout work their way in everywhere from spectacular produce-based cocktails to can't-miss desserts such as watermelon granita with rose parfait.
Moroccan. Dinner. Closed Tuesday. $16-35

★★★BIG 4
The Huntington Hotel, 1075 California St., San Francisco, 415-474-5400;
www.big4restaurant.com

Dark wood, deep-green booths, lead-glass mirrors and lots of greenery give Big 4 a clubby feel. The restaurant is named for the old-boys' club of 19th-century railroad magnates C.P. Huntington, Charles Crocker, Leland Stanford and Mark Hopkins. Today, a modern-day old-boys' crowd packs in for lunch and happy hour, boosting the members-only atmosphere. A glowing fireplace and live piano music make this wonderfully old-school dinner date spot. Even the menu is timeless: Filet mignon, petrale sole, wild game (sometimes caribou, sometimes alligator!) and crab cakes are all well executed with touches like truffles, beautiful produce and a superior wine list.

American. Breakfast, lunch (Thursday-Friday), dinner, late-night. Bar. $36-85

★★★BIX

56 Gold St., San Francisco, 415-433-6300; www.bixrestaurant.com

You don't come to Bix for the food. That's not to say the food at this Jackson Square restaurant is not good—it is, and sometimes it's even great. It's just that this supper club emphasizes the "club" part of its concept, and you may remember the high-ceilinged Art Deco décor, live jazz, speakeasy alley location, snazzily dressed crowd, tableside service and top-notch cocktails more than the eats. The downstairs bar is often hopping; upstairs tables are quieter. No matter where you sit, you should try a cocktail from the ever-changing menu, with each expertly mixed using organic ingredients (though the place has such a jazz club vibe that a classic martini goes down easy, too). Traditional dishes are your best bet: mini lamb burgers, steak tartare, truffled french fries. The tastiest desserts make use of the kitchen's predilection for gooey goodness: The warm chocolate brioche bread pudding, bananas foster and fig and almond brown butter cake will remind you that clubby Bix also has a "supper" portion as well.

American. Lunch (Friday), dinner. $36-85

★★★BOULEVARD

1 Mission St., San Francisco, 415-543-6084; www.boulevardrestaurant.com

Boulevard is the grande dame of San Francisco dining: still sexy, not quite avant-garde, but gracious. She certainly impresses upon first sight with her delicate, pre-1906 earthquake, belle époque building, with an open kitchen (sit at the counter to watch the cooks in action), swirling peacock mosaic, art nouveau light fixtures and spectacular Bay views. And she's still up for a party: Business lunchers, couples, tourists and locals mingle here, whether dressed to the nines or sporting San Francisco casual (jeans are fine). The French-kissed American food is satisfying though a bit inconsistent. Your best bet is to order an appetizer or two (such as the dayboat sea scallops with pork belly, butternut squash and roasted chestnuts, topped with a picked squash relish) and then go for one of the grilled meats (the roasted rack of lamb with garlic and thyme is simplistic perfection). The superb wine list proves that like Boulevard, things often get better with age.

American. Lunch (Monday-Friday), dinner. $36-85

★★★★CAMPTON PLACE

Taj Campton Place, 340 Stockton St., San Francisco, 415-955-5555; www.camptonplacesf.com

Campton Place has a reputation for finding new talent (just google "Laurent Manrique," "Bradley Ogden," "Daniel Humm" or "Todd Humphries"). These rising-star chefs tend to move on quickly, but not much changes within the sedate dining room. Oversized banquettes and gleaming silver define Campton as upscale, with menu and service to match. Adroit waitstaff present dishes, from amuse bouche to petits fours, with a flourish. The food zooms in on high-end, locally sourced ingredients (even the foie gras is labeled "artisan") with trendy touches like foams dabbed here and there. Semi-celeb pastry chef Boris Portnoy trained his team well before he departed. Desserts are surprising, well-balanced little gems: English cucumber soup with pistachio, mint and yogurt sorbet sounds bizarre but tastes divine. Hotel guests rave about breakfast (malted walnut waffles; tiger prawn frittata).

American, Mediterranean. Breakfast, lunch (Monday-Saturday), dinner, Sunday brunch. $36-85

★★★COI

373 Broadway, San Francisco, 415-393-9000;
www.coirestaurant.com

Walking from the strip-club-heavy street into Coi's serene, earth-toned, windowless dining room is an unexpected transition. You know you're in for something different when the waiter presents a tiny concoction of grapefruit, ginger, tarragon and black pepper, neighbored by a dot of essential oils of the four ingredients, telling you to inhale before taking a bite: The aromas make the flavors explode. The journey continues through 11 tiny, intricate and surprising courses—one could be a griddled porcini mushroom with coconut tapioca, another might be a slow-cooked egg with morels and green garlic. The lounge serves tasty, but less interesting, à la carte dishes like udon noodles and suckling pig terrine. Nearly everything is housemade (butter, bread, some of the cheese) and locally-sourced (the left side of the menu serves as a bibliography to nearby farms, ranches and foragers). When not guiding you through the very good wine list, the sommelier brings out plates and advises on the menu along with the rest of the staff.

American. Dinner. Closed Sunday-Monday. $86 and up

★★★★★THE DINING ROOM AT THE RITZ-CARLTON

The Ritz-Carlton, San Francisco, 600 Stockton St., San Francisco, 415-773-6168; www.ritzcarltondiningroom.com

Dinner at the Ritz is a formal occasion, suitable for deal brokering, marriage proposals and all matters that require impressive surroundings. The city's only Five Star restaurant is known for service with a

---

WHAT ARE THE TOP CLASSIC RESTAURANTS IN SAN FRANCISCO?

Boulevard
Housed in a pre-quake Belle Epoque building, this restaurant oozes romance, and the menu delivers fresh, seasonal options that are just as alluring.

One Market
This Financial District mainstay, a favorite for power lunches and after-dinner powwows, has been serving farm-fresh new American food since 1993.

Tadich Grill
White-coated waiters serve fresh sourdough and cioppino to locals and tourists alike at this restaurant, which was established in 1849.

Zuni Café
The menu at this bistro has morphed from Mexican-influenced to seasonal organic French-Italian cuisine in its 30 years in business, but no matter what the kitchen is serving, you can be sure that it will be reliably satisfying.

WHAT ARE THE BEST NEIGHBORHOOD RESTAURANTS IN SAN FRANCISCO?

A16
You might have to wait for a table at this shoebox-sized Marina Italian restaurant, but it will be worth it when you taste the fresh-from-the-brick-oven pizzas and pastas.

Delfina
After a sunny day spent lounging around Delores Park, you can snag a table and devour a plate of fresh housemade pasta at this charming Mission bistro.

Spruce
Head to this Presidio Heights restaurant after hiking across the Golden Gate or frolicking around Crissy Field and dig into the sophisticated, fresh California cuisine.

quiet flourish amid lavish trimmings like shining silver carts carrying champagne, desserts or cheese. Every dish created by chef Ron Siegel is a shining, unique little jewel. He's known for haute French cuisine with Japanese touches—most evident in pairing subtle flavors like shiso and yuzu, and his delicate way with seafood. In the beautifully crafted nine-course tasting menu, a different meal is served to every other person at the table. An innovative recent menu played with the concept of "salt and pepper," using flavored salts (vanilla, ginger) and peppers (alepepo, Szechuan pepper) to set off abalone, foie gras and sorbet, among other ingredients. Spring for the wine pairing; the 12,000-bottle cellar is nothing short of astonishing.
French, Japanese. Dinner. Closed Sunday-Monday. $86 and up

★★★FIFTH FLOOR
Hotel Palomar, 12 Fourth St., San Francisco, 415-348-1555; www.fifthfloorrestaurant.com

Now under the direction of chef Jennie Lorenzo, the Fifth Floor's spare, chic, recently redesigned dining room is a comfortable space to sample creative, seasonal new American cuisine. Dig into dishes such as stuffed quail with asparagus and pea succotash, or roasted lamb sirloin with green beans and black olive tapenade. Master Sommelier Emily Wines—yep, that's really her name—knows her stuff, and has worked out a tasting menu with Lorenzo that pairs the hearty, satisfying menu with anything from sparkling to hand-crafted beers. It's a sure bet that any high-end restaurant renovation these days will include a casual lounge for bar-food nibblers and downturn diners. Fifth Floor doesn't disappoint, with croquettes and cocktails, beer and burgers, and a nice selection of wines by the glass.
American. Dinner. Closed Sunday. $36-85

★★★★FLEUR DE LYS
777 Sutter St., San Francisco, 415-673-7779; www.fleurdelyssf.com

The tented ceiling in the main dining room of this upscale eatery provides a little drama, setting off the posh flowers and gleaming tableware to deliver a grand first impression. The food arrives in small, appealing portions, with witty nods to hearty French tradition: Alsatian choucroute (sauerkraut) is served as soup, in strudel, and in fondant with caviar; boneless quail with roasted parsnips, leeks and foie gras. The wine list is thoughtful, offering pairing options with à la carte meals and with the omnivore or vegetarian tasting menus. Service, a Fleur de Lys hallmark, is classic and

professional, and the bar makes a cozy stop for pre- or post-dinner drinks.
French. Dinner. Closed Sunday-Monday. $86 and up

★★★HARRIS'
2100 Van Ness Ave., San Francisco, 415-673-1888; www.harrisrestaurant.com

If it weren't for the cityscape and bucolic California murals on the wall, you might not even remember Harris' is in San Francisco. The huge leather banquettes, traditional, dry martinis and classic dishes like steak Diane, Kobe rib-eye and prime rib (accompanied by sides like béarnaise sauce, baked potatoes and creamed spinach) make for tried-and-true steakhouse success, no matter where you are. The proudly touted "corn-fed Midwestern beef" is hardly California cuisine, but other local touches include a wine list that's enormous, California-heavy and very, very good.
Steak. Dinner. $36-85

★★★INCANTO
1550 Church St., San Francisco, 415-641-4500; www.incanto.biz

Chef Chris Cosentino is known for his love of offal, or those "nasty bits" of meat like kidneys, brains and trotters. If that isn't immediately appealing, consider that Cosentino has competed on *Iron Chef America* and *The Next Iron Chef* on the strength of that love. If offal sounds awful, there are a lot of other delicacies on Incanto's menu, particularly handmade pasta and house-cured pork salami. The rustic Italian stone arches throughout the dining room make for an ideal setting, and the nearly all-Italian wine list contains an impressive number of flights, half liters, and wines by the glass, so you can taste for yourself what best pairs with beef tongue ravioli.
Italian. Dinner. Closed Tuesday. $36-85

★★★JARDINIÈRE
300 Grove St., San Francisco, 415-861-5555; www.jardiniere.com

The name recalls traditional French vegetable stew, but the food at this extravagantly designed, pre-theater powerhouse by Traci Des Jardins skews more California, with American, Asian and French influences. All of it is nicely portioned and elegantly presented, with indulgent touches like foie gras and caviar. Couples looking to get cozy will appreciate the two-tiered, exposed-brick dining room with swerved metal balcony railings and a glowing fiber optic Lucite dome. Casual diners veer to the front of the space, where the J Lounge surfs the restaurant-lounge trend with everything from small plates (fried olives or duck meatballs with figs and olives) to full caviar service offered alongside cocktails crafted from high-end spirits such as Neisson Rhum Agricole and St. George absinthe.
American, French. Dinner. $36-85

★★★KOKKARI ESTIATORIO
200 Jackson St., San Francisco, 415-981-0983; www.kokkari.com

This huge, two-story taverna with an open rotisserie, wood-burning fireplaces and rough-hewn wood is equally popular with groups and couples. The food goes well beyond the Greek-American trinity of gyros, spanakopita and moussaka (though you can order delicious versions of the last two). Even better are whole grilled fish; tomato oven-baked beans; and the Kokkari Salad with arugula, cherry tomatoes and myzithra cheese. The kitchen's not afraid to keep it simple: The two best desserts are fresh fruit with mint and thick yogurt drizzled with honey and studded with walnuts. The wine list includes many interesting Greek bottles, and classic cocktails go down easy (graze on a limited menu in the lounge while you imbibe).

Greek. Lunch (Monday-Friday), dinner. Bar. $36-85

★★★KYO-YA
Palace Hotel, 2 New Montgomery St., San Francisco, 415-546-5089;
www.sfpalacerestaurants.com

Kyo-Ya is one of the Bay area's best kaiseki restaurants. An elaborate cuisine originating with tea ceremonies in 16th-century Kyoto, kaisekis are known for dainty presentation and delicate flavors delivered over many courses, moving from appetizers, soup, glowing sashimi and variously prepared savories to ages-old ochazuke (green tea over rice). If you can't commit to the time involved in such a lengthy meal, you can also order many of these dishes à la carte, or try master sushi chef Akifusa Tonai's beautiful sushi and sashimi. Some pieces are pristinely traditional, accompanied only by grated wasabi; others are posh and Western-style, incorporating ingredients such as sliced truffle, foie gras and gold leaf. The hushed, minimalist décor is appealing; at lunch (when you can order a delicious bento box), you'll likely sit alongside businessmen on expense accounts.

Japanese. Lunch, dinner. Closed Saturday-Sunday. $86 and up

★★★LA FOLIE
2316 Polk St., San Francisco, 415-776-5577; www.lafolie.com

La folie means "madness," and you shouldn't visit unless you're ready to lose your head a little. The luxe French menu, gigantic portions, heady wine list and lushly draperied décor will leave you giddy, if only from the spillover of excitement from the newly engaged couple at the next table. The richest dishes are best (standouts include a terrine of pigs' feet, lobster and sweetbreads; butter-poached lobster; cheese soufflé; and lots of black truffle). The vegetarian tasting menu is consistently flavorful, while desserts (preceded by a selection of complimentary petit fours and confections) lean to silky creations made out of chocolate. Service is some of the most affable and attentive in the city, down to congratulatory chocolates for the recently betrothed lovebirds.

French. Dinner. Closed Sunday. $86 and up

★★★★MASA'S
Executive Hotel Vintage Court, 648 Bush St., San Francisco, 415-989-7154;
www.masasrestaurant.com

San Francisco's most elegant dining room can be found at Masa's. White linen-swathed tables and toile d'Juoy-covered chairs contrast with rich chocolate walls, behemoth red lampshades suspended from the ceiling, an abundance of flowers and a dramatic bronze sculpture in the room's center. The 900-plus-bottle wine list and a variety of tasting menus aim for a night of lush comfort—and the French dishes, though not the most creative in town, don't disappoint. On the contrary, they are packed with flavor and often incorporate ingredients like caviar, crab or bone marrow. Dessert also comes in waves, with sorbet clearing the way for delights like chocolate soufflé and petits fours.

Perfect service, great wine, a romantic atmosphere and rich, spot-on flavors: Everything at Masa's is well executed.

French. Dinner. Closed Sunday-Monday. $86 and up

★★★NOPA

560 Divisadero St., San Francisco, 415-864-8643; www.nopasf.com

It isn't really "north of the Panhandle"—it's northeast. But the abbreviation is hip, and so is this restaurant. The buzz-word laden menu may put you off (what is "urban rustic food," exactly?), but you'll be in the minority. A cavernous, bi-level former bank, NoPa usually hums (loudly) with a sceney crowd who are there for the hipster art and cocktails as much as the food. You can always hang out at the bar, chance the no-reservations communal table or show up late—the kitchen's open until 1 a.m. Many of the hefty dishes (calamari with chorizo, chickpeas and endive; chicken with Romano beans) are roasted in the wood oven, and most ingredients are local and organic—a must-serve, of course, among hip eateries.

American. Dinner, late-night. $36-85

★★★ONE MARKET

1 Market St., San Francisco, 415-777-5577; www.onemarket.com

When he opened One Market in 1993, Bradley Ogden was a rising star with a quirky, pioneering take on farm-fresh New American food, as exemplified by a huge, witty à la carte menu. Over the years, said menu didn't change much, and so One Market settled into a reliably upscale destination for Financial District power diners. That is until Ogden's latest executive chef, Mark Dommen, arrived and updated the basic-and-fresh style with modern twists (think foie gras emulsions and smoked sea salt). He also added full plates, with sides specially made to go with the entrées. The enormous, efficient dining room isn't romantic, but the very good desserts are—especially the homemade ice cream and Ogden's signature butterscotch pudding.

American. Lunch (Monday-Friday), dinner. Closed Sunday. $36-85

★★★★QUINCE

470 Pacific Ave., San Francisco, 415-775-8500; www.quincerestaurant.com

Moving from the cozy Russian Hill location to a newer, larger and historic spot in the Jackson Square neighborhood was a brilliant move, as Quince is fresher than ever. It is also more accessible, with a full dining room, lively 12-seat bar and separate lounge, all of which serve the full menu. Chef/owner Michael Tusk's devotion to the lush seasonal ingredients that shape his daily changing Italian-focused menu hasn't changed, but the wine list is now much more extensive under new wine director David Lynch. The atmosphere has been upgraded as well, with luxurious Venetian chandeliers contrasting with the rustic exposed brick walls. Menus range from a la carte to two different five-course options. Recent highlights have included delicate squash blossoms with fresh crab, zucchini and fava beans, and spaghetti with clams, melon and espresso—an unusual combination for sure, but intriguing and satisfying. The cheese selection is well edited and desserts included chocolate beignets with cardamom ice cream.

American, Italian. Dinner. Reservations recommended. $86 and up

★★★RANGE
842 Valencia St., San Francisco, 415-282-8283; www.rangesf.com

The cocktail list at this chic eatery is as long as the dinner menu, though there's hardly room for a bar crowd in the tiny, hip (think Mid-Century modern crossed with industrial) space. The drinks are lovingly prepared, as is the contemporary American food. An ever-changing menu comes studded with intriguing ingredients like morels or wild nettles, and desserts (cornmeal crepes with huckleberries and nectarine ice cream, bittersweet chocolate-raspberry soufflé) are heavenly. Range is bar-like in its lack of elbow room and noise problem, so it won't set the mood for romance, but it definitely sees its share of scenesters sipping classic cocktails or smooth Belgian beers.

Contemporary American. Dinner. $36-85

★★★★RESTAURANT GARY DANKO
800 North Point at Hyde St., San Francisco, 415-749-2060; www.garydanko.com

Restaurant Gary Danko boasts the most tableside dazzle in town, including tea service, caviar service, cheese cart and flambéed desserts. The décor is theatrical, too, with large paintings, dim lighting, and a bathroom so large and luxurious it's practically a spa. It's not all looks and no substance: The tea is rare and steeped to perfection; and the cheeses are a kaleidoscope of different styles, animals and continents. The wine list may read like a dictionary, but your smart and very friendly server will happily guide you through it. The food is a blend of California, French and Mediterranean with dishes such as lobster risotto and quail stuffed with mushrooms, quinoa and foie gras; you can order three, four or five courses or go for the tasting menu. Everything's available at the bar, making Danko a smart stop for a swanky last-minute meal.

Contemporary American. Dinner. $86 and up

★★★★SILKS
Mandarin Oriental, San Francisco, 222 Sansome St., San Francisco, 415-986-2020; www.mandarinoriental.com

The antique kimono fabric displayed under glass on the walls at Silks says a lot about the ambience: classic and elegant. This is a spot for ladies who lunch, power brokers and guests of the luxe Mandarin Oriental hotel in which the restaurant is hidden. Gleaming silver, heavy linen, attentive service and a hushed atmosphere lay claim to tradition. But the Asian-inflected food dreamed up by executive chef Rick Bartram is innovative: roasted local halibut with Forbidden fried rice, spiced carrot purée and spring vegetables, and Colorado lamb with almond and apricot couscous. After dinner, slink into the nearby MO bar for a nightcap or linger at the table over coffee and petite fours.

American. Breakfast, lunch (Monday-Friday), dinner (Wednesday-Saturday). $36-85

★★★★SPRUCE
3640 Sacramento St., San Francisco, 415-931-5100; www.sprucesf.com

A revamped auto barn with black décor, overstuffed leather seats, an imposing backlit bar and a glowing wine cabinet, Spruce feels like an updated steakhouse. The dry martini has been replaced by fancier quaffs, and the American menu boasts far more than beef—but the self-satisfied, no-surprises vibe is the same. The food is downright delicious (buttered Maine lobster with golden potato gnocchi; duck-fat-fried potatoes), and the kitchen and service are polished and confident. Come for the scene and the staggering wine list, which is so amazing that there's a page for each vinification of a single grape from a single country (for example, riesling and Germany). Spruce is great for lunch, if you're willing to travel to the sleepy neighborhood, shell out $14 for a tasty burger, and avoid a third glass of wine, should you have things to do later in the day.

American. Lunch (Monday-Friday), dinner. Bar. $36-85

★★★TOWN HALL

342 Howard St., San Francisco, 415-908-3900; www.townhallsf.com

When they helmed the staid but classy Postrio, the Rosenthal brothers must have been itching to mix things up. Town Hall's two-story building is a former ship engine manufacturing plant reconceived with New England schoolhouse elements; lots of brick and large windowpanes are juxtaposed with a huge mirror and chandeliers, and there's a nice heated patio outside. The seasonal menu is a zingy take on New American (read: Southern with a few regional specialties). Tempura squash blossoms with four-cheese stuffing and pesto are so succulent you won't want to share; gumbo is a favorite when it shows up on the menu. The ballpark-adjacent spot swells to capacity at lunch, pre-weekend and during home games, but quiets down on weeknights.

American. Lunch (Monday-Friday), dinner. $36-85

RECOMMENDED

A16

2355 Chestnut St., San Francisco, 415-771-2216; www.a16sf.com

Most people will tell you A16's pizza is all about the blistery crust and chewy heft of the dough, made in a wood-fired oven that is the centerpiece of the kitchen. Of course, there are folks who'll say it's all about the tripe. Or the Southern Italian wine list. Or the cured meats, like prized San Daniele prosciutto and house-cured salame. Or the amazing braised romano beans, or the toothy housemade maccaronara noodles. Nearly everything's outstanding at this small, noisy, casual, always-hopping spot. The restaurant takes its name from the highway that circles Naples. From the chef's certification as a pizzaiolo focusing on the Neapolitan-style pizzas to the intense wines grown in the rich soil of Pompeii, this place aims to be rustic and authentic—and, judging by the crowd, is also very hip.

Italian. Lunch (Wednesday-Friday), dinner. $36-85

BAR CRUDO

655 Divisadero St., San Francisco, 415-409-0679; www.barcrudo.com

If you're not a seafood lover, consider yourself warned: There's not much else on the menu here. People who hate to wait should also take notice: Service to the eight tables in this minuscule, loft-like space can be agonizingly slow. Everyone else, prepare to be blown out of the water by the delicious seafood menu. A cold raw bar platter might include marinated Olde Salt clams, Nova Scotia mussels and sweet Dungeness crab—all clean-flavored and simple. The rest of the menu is more dressed-up—creamy burrata cheese, sweet Banyuls vinaigrette and pistachio oil paired with lobster and beets seems over the top, but it's divine, while the rich, bacon-laced, seafood-packed chowder

WHAT ARE THE BEST OVERALL RESTAURANTS IN SAN FRANCISCO?

The Dining Room at the Ritz-Carlton
A decidedly dressed-up affair, a meal here is a culinary journey that ignites all the senses. Exquisite, almost-too-beautiful to eat French-influenced cuisine is created by chef Ron Siegel and served by a charming, polished staff.

Fleur de Lys
The dining room at this restaurant is swathed in rich, red fabric that draws the eye to the tented ceiling, making a dramatic and romantic setting for the equally impressive French food created by chef Hubert Keller.

Masa's
With its appealing, chocolate brown dining room and extensive multi-course menus, this temple of French-influenced California cuisine has been a San Francisco mainstay for more than 25 years.

Silks
An attractive dining room with a vague hint of the Orient is the perfect setting for the sophisticated Pacific Rim cuisine served at this restaurant at the Mandarin Oriental.

is a cold-weather joy. The Belgian-focused beer list is almost as impressive as the wonderful, world-spanning whites on the wine list.
Seafood. Dinner. Closed Monday. $16-35

BETELNUT PEJIU WU
2030 Union St., San Francisco, 415-929-8855; www.betelnutrestaurant.com
Food trends come and go, and in San Francisco, pan-Asian screams mid-'90s—but Betelnut is still proudly continent-skipping. The menu references India, Hawaii, Mongolia, Hunan, Shanghai, Szechwan, Korea, Taiwan, Indonesia, Japan, Thailand, Vietnam and even Sri Lanka. The busy red lacquer/dark wood/bamboo décor (filled with fans and lanterns) is either overly dramatic and kitschy or witty and cool, depending on your taste (or possibly how many drinks you've had). The food isn't completely authentic, but it's consistent and flavorful. Spicy Szechwan green beans, minced chicken with lettuce cups, and "little dragon" dumplings of pork and shrimp with ginger vinegar are especially tasty, and the small plates go nicely with strong tropical cocktails and beer (pejiu wu translates to "beer house," so you'll have to order the house specialty). If you're not in the mood to outshout the crush of young Marina-dwellers swilling and spilling outside to the sidewalk tables, order anything on the menu for takeout.
Pan-Asian. Lunch, dinner. $16-35

BOCADILLOS
710 Montgomery St., San Francisco, 415-982-2622; www.bocasf.com
The Financial District's worth would plummet like the Dow without Bocadillos, the go-to casual breakfast and lunch destination. Suits line up in the morning for hard-boiled eggs and toast, Greek yogurt with honey or eggs with Catalan sausage; lunchers go for tiny (three-bite), flavorful sandwiches such as chorizo with walnuts and BLTs. In the evenings, the minuscule spot loosens its tie and morphs into a mellow tapas joint. Even with the warm woods and brick wall there's a lunch-counter feel, but the food is exceptional. After a glass of sherry and a few hearty tapas (think housemade chorizo or braised tripe "basquaise"), you'll realize the worth of this dream child of Piperade chef Gerald Hirigoyen.
Tapas. Breakfast (Monday-Friday), lunch (Monday-Friday), dinner. Closed Sunday. $16-35

CANTEEN
817 Sutter St., San Francisco, 415-928-8870; www.sfcanteen.com

You might be perplexed by Canteen. This tiny space with eclectic diner décor offers a brief menu and only a few seatings per night. Go just once and you'll understand: It may be cramped, but the food defies the surroundings. Chef Dennis Leary (not the actor) used to helm upscale Rubicon; here, he can't be bothered with trappings like space, décor and service. Leary's too busy reinventing flavor combinations on the daily-changing menu, including duck breast with a ragout of butter beans, pork and thyme. Brunch might include blueberry French toast topped with coffee. It's like a fine dining experience, without obsequious service, but certainly without any fuss. Tip: You have to request dessert up front when you order dinner (another one of Leary's quirks), but it's worth it, especially for the wonderfully fragrant vanilla soufflé.
American. Lunch (Wednesday-Friday), dinner (Tuesday-Wednesday, Friday-Saturday; prix fixe dinner Tuesday), Saturday-Sunday brunch. Closed Monday. $36-85

COCO500
500 Brannan St., San Francisco, 415-543-2222; www.coco500.com

The fried green beans chef-owner Loretta Keller perfected when this spot was a French bistro called Bizou are still on the menu, and they pair dazzlingly with the drinks now that the space has been reimagined as a moody after-work hangout. Some might remember the quieter bistro with nostalgia, but times (and neighborhoods) change. Keller has the trendy-cocktail thing down with small-batch spirits, organic drink ingredients and a lovely teak bar. The American food skews French (duck liver terrine, salt-cod brandade), but the local produce is called "California dirt" on the menu. The well-crafted nonalcoholic "sober cocktails" (including a "no-jito") are great options for lunch, when the place is less noisy.
American. Lunch, dinner. Closed Sunday. $36-85

DELFINA
3621 18th St., San Francisco, 415-552-4055; www.delfinasf.com

Spilling out onto the sidewalks of the Mission with its hipster servers, loud music, slick beams-and-mirrors décor and trendy Neapolitan pizzas, Delfina defines San Francisco Cal-Italian. It seems the city can't get enough: Ten years after it ushered in a huge trend with its organic and housemade ingredients (pasta, sausage, gelato), Delfina still requires reservations well in advance. Maybe it's Craig Stoll's 2008 James Beard Award win, or maybe it's the primo location. Most likely, it's the food. Whether a complex mixed grill of rabbit, sausage and sweetbreads, or simple spaghetti with dead-ripe plum tomatoes and subtly aromatic olive oil, it's hauntingly good.
American, Italian. Dinner. $36-85

FIREFLY RESTAURANT
4288 24th St., San Francisco, 415-821-7652; www.fireflyrestaurant.com

Low amber lights and mismatched décor screams "flash-in-the-pan quirky neighborhood spot," but Firefly has been going strong since 1993 for its dependable food. Service is so friendly you may think your waiter might pull up a chair, but it's attentive. The seasonal, expertly cooked California fare is worth seeking out even if you're nowhere near this sleepy corner of Noe Valley.

HIGHLIGHT

WHAT ARE THE CITY'S BEST GOURMET FOOD SHOPS?

At her Berkeley restaurant Chez Panisse, Alice Waters changed the world in the '70s (at least for foodies) with a simple pursuit of the best ingredients: locally sourced, organically grown, as fresh as possible, artisanal. As Waters proved, you don't have to sacrifice flavor in pursuit of healthy eating, and the Bay Area shows how to do it right.

To sample San Francisco's best organically grown eats, go where Waters herself shops, the waterfront Ferry Building Marketplace at the end of Market Street. The stalls are filled with bounty, ranging from tea to produce to gelato, with a small Tuesday and huge Saturday farmers' market. **Boulettes Larder** (*Shop No. 48, 415-399-1155; www.bouletteslarder.com*) prettily presents housemade ingredients, such as preserved lemons and prepared food, like potato focaccia. **Cowgirl Creamery** (*Shop No. 17; 415-362-9354; www.cowgirlcreamery.com*) sells cheeses made at its dairy in nearby Point Reyes Station—try the luscious, triple-cream Red Hawk. **Boccalone Salumeria** (*Shop No. 21, 415-433-6500; www.boccalone.com*), pet project of Incanto chef Chris Cosentino, offers "tasty salted pig parts" like pâté and salami handcrafted from sustainably-raised porkers at family farms. Try one of the fabulous sandwiches, such as capocollo bursting with herbs and coupled with sweet plum and fresh arugula.

In the Mission, **Ritual Roasters** (*1026 Valencia St., 415-641-1024; www.ritualroasters. com*) brews fair-trade coffee from places like Indonesia and Panama, minimally roasted onsite. Stop at **Mission Pie** (*2901 Mission St., 415-282-4743; www.missionpie.com*), which is run by the nonprofit Pie Ranch, where urban high-schoolers learn new foodways. The all-pie menu may include fragrant apricot frangipane or juicy peach olallieberry. **Bi-Rite Creamery** (*3692 18th St., 415-626-5600; www.biritecreamery.com*) churns sustainably and packages biodegradably with seductive ice cream flavors like salted caramel and orange cardamom. Worker-run cooperative **Rainbow Grocery** (*1745 Folsom St., 415-863-0620; www.rainbowgrocery.org*) is the city's hippiest store, with dazzling displays of produce, vegan cookies, old-school health food and coffee, wine and cheese.

Across the Bay Bridge is Berkeley, where Waters also shops. Cheese freaks should visit **The Cheese Board Collective** (*1504 Shattuck Ave., Berkeley, 510-549-3183; www.cheeseboardcollective.coop*), whose helpful owner-staff all love the fermented dairy products and insanely good breads baked onsite (oh, those corn-cherry scones!). Organic French takeout **Grégoire** (*2109 Cedar St., Berkeley, 510-883-1893; 4001B Piedmont Ave., Oakland, 510-547-3444; www.gregoirerestaurant.com*) offers addictive potato puffs and a menu that might see a house-smoked lamb sandwich or California white bass over ratatouille. Then there's the mighty **Berkeley Bowl** (*2020 Oregon St., Berkeley, 510-843-6929; www.berkeleybowl.com*), with 8,000 of its 40,000 square feet dedicated solely to produce. The meat and fish counters rival the best independent butchers and mongers, and a full kitchen dishes up burritos, pan-Asian takeout, sushi and sandwiches. If you want someone else to do the cooking, avoid shopping altogether and go to the original: Waters's **Chez Panisse** (*1517 Shattuck Ave., 510-548-5525; www.chezpanisse.com*). The single prix-fixe menu is based on seasonal availability and changes nightly, or order à la carte from the café for lunch or dinner. But, plan ahead—reservations are required for the restaurant and recommended for the café. After dining here, you'll forget that organic and local food is good for you and instead remember that it just tastes good.

Seafood pot stickers burst with the sweet taste of the ocean, and Concord grape sorbet with coconut tapioca is a surprising hot and cold contrast. Of the entrées, two are usually vegetarian; carnivores will breathe a sigh of relief after reading the menu's tagline: "All our meat comes from happy, never mad, drug-free animals; no hormones, antibiotics or crack cocaine."
American. Dinner. $16-35

FOREIGN CINEMA
2534 Mission St., San Francisco, 415-648-7600; www.foreigncinema.com
The walk down the long hall to Foreign Cinema's impressive indoor-outdoor space leads you far away from the Mission's hustle and bustle. In the covered, heated patio, the restaurant screens moody foreign movies (anything from Fellini classics to *The Diving Bell and the Butterfly*) against a concrete wall. Inside, a huge fireplace makes the dining room as cozy as 20-foot ceilings and salvage-chic décor gets. Focus instead on the consistently rewarding food, by Zuni Café vets (and spouses) Gayle Pirie and John Clark. Try fried eggs deglazed with balsamic vinegar for brunch, or beef carpaccio so thoroughly spattered with horseradish sauce, fried herbs, capers and waffle chips that it appears to move on the plate (and that's a good thing). Wine and cocktails are both solid, and there are even kids' and between-meals menus.
American, Mediterranean. Dinner, Saturday-Sunday brunch. $16-35

FRINGALE
570 Fourth St., San Francisco, 415-543-0573; www.fringalesf.com
When Gerald Hirigoyen and J.B. Lorda opened Fringale in 1991, its Basque-accented French bistro fare was new and terribly exciting. Flash forward to today: Hirigoyen is gone, Lorda is retired, Basque food is everywhere (partly due to Hirigoyen's Piperade and Bocadillos) and the towering, ring-molded presentation recalls the '90s. It's surprising, then, that Fringale is still so tasty. Substantial French classics like the salad of frisée, bacon and poached egg and duck confit with little Puy lentils are still a treat. Bonus: The whole menu is available for takeout.
French. Lunch (Tuesday-Friday), dinner. $36-85

GREENS
Fort Mason Center, San Francisco, 415-771-6222; www.greensrestaurant.com
Diehard carnivores envy Greens' prime location in historic Fort Mason with its glorious Bay views—the former waterfront military base is a cool combination of piers, parks and little museums. Good thing that even meat-lovers are bound to like Greens' greens. Annie Somerville has dished out upscale vegetarian fare since 1979, and like most chefs who specialize in California cuisine, she lets her produce sing—matching it to local wines (Greens' list consistently wins awards), specialty teas and organic coffees. Brunch is particularly nice (try potato-scallion cakes with cheddar or any baked good), while mung dal fritters are a must at dinner. Some dishes are available vegan; you can also buy many of them from the takeout counter and make use of the prime location. Order sandwiches (or pastry and coffee) to go, grab a seat on Fort Mason's benches and take in the salty air while you enjoy your tasty vegetarian meal.
Vegetarian. Lunch (Tuesday-Saturday), dinner, Sunday brunch. $36-85

HELMAND PALACE

2424 Van Ness Ave., San Francisco, 415-345-0072; www.helmandpalace.com

Don't be put off by the description of Helmand Palace's most famous appetizer, kaddo. Candied pumpkin with ground beef sauce and garlic yogurt may sound odd, but it's a delicious sweet-savory balance. Order it with the mantwo—beef-filled pasta, misrepresented on the menu as "pastry," with addictive split pea sauce. Everything's interesting at this quiet, low-lit Afghani spot, including the many vegetarian options. Whatever you order will be preceded by pillowy, warm flatbread and a trio of cilantro, pepper and yogurt sauces. If there's room after the hearty portions, go for dessert: ice cream, rice pudding, custard and baklava are all delicious with a shot of potent Turkish coffee.

Afghani. Dinner. $16-35

HOG ISLAND OYSTER COMPANY

Ferry Building Marketplace, Market Street and the Embarcadero, San Francisco, 415-391-7117; www.hogislandoysters.com

The few tables at Hog Island Oyster Company are always crowded on nice days (especially during Monday and Thursday happy hours, when the oysters are $1 and pints are $3.50). They're less packed and more fun in the fog, when the Bay view is so very San Francisco and you can try a grilled cheese with three melted cheeses from nearby Cowgirl Creamery paired with a light, smoky Sweetwater oyster stew. This restaurant serves the fruits of the renowned Hog Island oyster farm in Tomales Bay to the north, which has been sustainably culturing delicious Pacific, Sweetwater, Kumamoto and Atlantic bivalves since 1983. The oysters are treasured by local and not-so-local chefs, and are definitely worth the perpetually long wait in the Ferry Building halls.

Seafood. Lunch, dinner (closes at 6 p.m. Saturday-Sunday). $16-35

IDEALE RESTAURANT

1315 Grant Ave., San Francisco, 415-391-4129; www.idealerestaurant.com

It's not the city's best Italian—that's a tall order—but Ideale Restaurant is hands-down the best Italian in North Beach, a district rich in Little Italy ambience, but bereft of decent chow. At this eatery, the welcome is as warm as the brightly painted walls and as pleasing as the mostly Roman food and moderate prices. Standouts include raw zucchini with truffle oil and shaved Parmigiano-Reggiano. The thin-crust pizza is crispier than the very hip Naples-style versions elsewhere, but it's authentic to Rome; hollow bucatini all'amatriciana pasta is simply soulful. The wine list isn't much to write home about, but it's thankfully free of any straw-skirted bottles of chianti.

Italian. Dinner. $16-35

JAI YUN

680 Clay St., San Francisco, 415-981-7438

This place does authentic Chinese in Chinatown—we're talking a chef (albeit a local-celebrity one) who doesn't speak English, doesn't serve from a menu, and uses ingredients like pork knuckle and chicken knees. Even if you're already familiar with Shanghaiese dining, Jai Yun is an adventure, and a worthwhile one: Every dish is impeccably prepared, with contrast in texture as important as the flavor. When you make your reservation, you'll be asked how much you want to spend, from $45 to $60 or more for special dishes, and you'll be treated to some 10 courses depending on the night and party size. You don't have a say in the menu: You could get tofu cubes with cilantro; hot, thinly sliced abalone with egg white foam; wok-fried noodles with salty pork; crispy, tender fried eggplant; housemade pickles or sausage. Portions are small, and the dull fans-and-screens décor doesn't begin to match the food, but they're part of the charm.

Chinese. Lunch (Monday-Friday), dinner. $36-85

KISS SEAFOOD
1700 Laguna St., San Francisco, 415-474-2866

With just three tables and a bar, dining at Kiss feels more like visiting someone's home than a restaurant. Just as you would at a dinner party, let your host make the choices, with one of two omakase (chef's choice) meals. One offering is $42 and the other is $60, and you'll get five or six bang-up plates for your buck from chef Naka San. Everything is exquisite. The sushi at this Japantown joint is consistently pristine, but the poetic soups made of cherry blossoms or delicate clams swimming in miso boggle the mind and go way beyond dinner-party fare.

Japanese. Dinner. Closed Sunday-Monday. $36-85

LA MAR
Embarcadero Pier 1 1/2, San Francisco, 415-397-8880; www.lamarcebicheria.com

Grab a table on the outdoor patio, order a bloody lorcho made with pisco, homemade Bloody Mary mix and octopus, and prepare for a tantalizing treat. Inspired by the cebicherías found throughout Peru, the food and drink served at the first U.S. outpost of this waterfront restaurant (other locations include Lima, Santiago and Panama) are refreshingly satisfying. Start with one of the ceviches which are marinated in lime juice and peppers, and which come in different varieties (or try them all in the sampler). Or order one of the delicate causas, a traditional Peruvian delicacy consisting of whipped potato with ají amarillo (a yellow chili pepper that is often used in Peruvian dishes) and seafood or vegetarian toppings (the wonderful causa limeña has crab, avocado purée, quail egg and cherry tomatoes). Everything is meant to be shared, including main dishes. Desserts include traditional favorites such as picarones (warm pumpkin and sweet potato fritters with spiced Chancaca honey), but you're likely to be perfected sated from your sweet and savory meal.

Peruvian. Lunch, dinner. $16-35

LA TAQUERIA
2889 Mission St., San Francisco, 415-285-7117

In the city that invented the Mission burrito, debate over the perfect version of it is as hot as the bottles of picante sauce on La Taqueria's benches. You can easily find cheaper, bigger meals elsewhere, but here, what a burrito lacks in size it makes up for in flavor and quality. Juicy, salty carnitas (pork confit) or carne asada (steak) share tortilla space with well-seasoned pinto beans and hot-as-Hades salsa. You're allowed to add jack cheese or chunky fresh avocado, if you wish, but diehards will argue that that's not a real burrito. The breezy tiled patio is the perfect place to cool down with a watermelon aqua fresca or a Mexican beer—both of which are indisputably refreshing.

Mexican. Lunch, dinner. $15 and under

PIPERADE

1015 Battery St., San Francisco, 415-391-2555; www.piperade.com

Piperade, with its amber lighting and cozy dining room, isn't particularly trendy but is somehow still sexy, the kind of place filled with happy regulars. The food, by Basque chef Gerald Hirigoyen, is hearty and a little unusual—very salty, very piquant, very satisfying. Start with small plates like house-cured salt cod set off by oyster tartare and lemon crème fraîche. Entrées include steamed Pacific snapper with spinach and fried garlic vinaigrette, as well as pipérade itself—fried peppers and Serrano ham with a poached egg served in a skillet. A different "Basque classic" is served each day at a reasonable fixed price. The wine list includes an "Unusual Suspects" category with bottles from the Basque regions of France and Spain, and desserts (such as cornmeal cake with strawberry compote and crème fraîche, or turron mousse cake with roasted almonds) are so luscious they'll have you pondering a trip to Hirigoyen's homeland to see if they can be as good as Piperade's.

French, Basque. Lunch (Monday-Friday), dinner. Closed Sunday. $36-85

RN74

301 Mission St., San Francisco, 415-543-7474 www.RN74.com

Named for the vineyard-lined highway that snakes through Burgundy, RN74 certainly has an extensive wine list. The focus is on wines from the Burgundy region, but the tome of a wine list also spans the globe. You could spend hours leafing through the massive list (there are more than 50 wines by the glass). But the best deals are on the vintage train station-inspired flip-letter boards, which reveal last bottles and special deals for the evening. The menu is divided into first, second and "anytime" courses. The first courses (think pork belly with stuffed squash blossom, soft-shell crab with celery leaf remoulade) are the most enjoyable while second courses might feature a risotto with English peas or roasted chicken with cornbread and figs. Order a bottle from the board and enjoy a variety of small bites from the anytime menu (which you can also do in the bar area) before jetting off to wherever it is you're headed to next.

French, American. Lunch (Monday-Friday), dinner. Bar. Reservations recommended. $86 and up

SEBO

517 Hayes St., San Francisco, 415-864-2122; www.sebosf.com

If you're looking for a California roll or rice made by a Japanese sushi master, Sebo's not your place. But if you're fishing for super-high-quality seafood, stop by this small, skylit, no-reservations restaurant with glowing backlit screens and a laidback minimalistic atmosphere. It attracts restaurateurs and other off-duty sushi chefs, as well as locals wanting to experience the exclusivity of the tiny 20-seated joint. The friendly American chef-owners fly the fish in daily: It's usually wild, typically from Japan and always unexpected. Hokkaido scallops, giant clams, blue-banded sprats, horse mackerel and other deep-sea delights are best tried omakase-style, meaning it's the sushi chef's choice of what you'll be dining on each visit. Dishes run the gamut from sashimi to sunomono (vinegared salads) to nigiri to maki rolls. On Sunday nights, go for the Izakaya menu of rustic bar snacks such as simmered pork belly and grilled fish collar. Top it off with some sake, which is also expertly selected.

Japanese. Dinner. Closed Monday. $36-85

THE SLANTED DOOR

1 Ferry Building, Market Street and the Embarcadero, San Francisco, 415-861-8032; www.slanteddoor.com

A mix of tourists, foodies and executives converge behind the Slanted Door—some attracted by mesmerizing views of the Bay and bridge, others by cocktails, but most by owner Charles Phan, who has a reputation as the city's best Vietnamese chef. Snake past the glamorous revelers who jam-pack the long bar and low-slung cocktail couches (try one of the brightly colored drinks like The Last Word, a combination of gin, Maraschino and green chartreuse, and you'll know why they're here). The place is comfy despite its stark, gray granite décor. Food includes crispy imperial rolls, caramelized catfish claypot and tender shaking beef—nothing you couldn't get elsewhere for much less money, until you factor in the top-notch local ingredients, smart waitstaff, deliciously balanced desserts, lovely wine list heavy on German and Austrian riesling and unparalleled tea service.

Vietnamese. Lunch, dinner. $16-35

SLOW CLUB

2501 Mariposa St., San Francisco, 415-241-9390; www.slowclub.com

The Slow Club's moniker is a misnomer because your wait is rarely long, and besides, time flies at the glowing, backlit bar, where delicious cocktails are mixed from intriguing ingredients like blackberry brandy. Once you're seated, service is efficient to the point of abrupt. If you're hungry, you'll appreciate the efficiency, and the large portions and American flavors kill pangs quickly. Grilled flatbread with lots of melted cheese and salty ham is a perfect cocktail foil; hand-cut fresh pappardelle is tender and topped with a rich ragu; the $12.50 hamburger lives up to its price (if you don't appreciate pre-applied condiments, ask for them on the side). The bread pudding is legendary. It's an odd menu for the industrial-chic/trendy-drink Potrero Hill space, but it works (even if the restaurant's name doesn't).

American. Breakfast (Monday-Friday), lunch (Monday-Friday), dinner (Monday-Saturday), Saturday-Sunday brunch. $16-35

SWAN OYSTER DEPOT

1517 Polk St., San Francisco, 415-673-1101

Swan doesn't take reservations, it doesn't accept credit cards, the line always spills out the door, and the servers can be gruff. It's all part of the semi-rowdy, old-time San Francisco atmosphere (which is much more authentic than the versions found at Fisherman's Wharf). Nimble-fingered shuckers prep oysters for locals and tourists alike. Cool off on a hot day with cold, cracked Dungeness crab, or warm up on a foggy night with satisfyingly creamy clam chowder—either way, wash it all down with a frosty Anchor Steam beer. Or pick up an ice-packed order of fresh seafood to take to your own party (they're open for takeout daily at 8 a.m.).

Seafood. Lunch. $15 and under

TADICH GRILL

240 California St., San Francisco, 415-391-1849; www.tadichgrill.com

Can a place be both tourist-friendly and authentic? Tadich can. It's a last bastion of old-school San Francisco, from white-coated waiters to sourdough on the tables to the roll of the dice to see who's paying—a nearly lost tradition. Tadich doesn't take reservations, but pre-dinner martinis and people-watching at the bar are part of the fun. Service is hurried but jovial, and the more local and simply prepared the dish, the better. Best bets are pan-fried sand dabs, cioppino (tomato-based seafood soup), calf's liver steak with onions, broiled petrale sole filet, oysters Rockefeller and Dungeness crab Louie. Go in a group of six to snag a booth, sample more food and decrease your odds of losing the dice roll. *Seafood. Lunch, dinner. Closed Sunday. $16-35*

YANK SING

49 Stevenson St., San Francisco, 415-541-4949; 101 Spear St. (inside Rincon Center), SOMA, 415-957-9300; www.yanksing.com

If you're a dim sum purist, know this: Yank Sing's signature Shanghaiese xiao long bao (soup-filled dumplings) may be untraditional, but they're delicious—as is everything that arrives on the cart at San Francisco's most upscale dim sum palace. Dumplings are a highlight, especially sweet and savory shrimp-based har gau and shiu mai. Fried soft-shell crabs, flaky curry chicken puffs, and sticky rice packets are also delicious. The second location, inside the historic Rincon Center, has its ups (great murals in the building, outdoor atrium seating, allegedly better weekend selection and a takeout counter) and its downs (a food court ambience indoors, compared to the Stevenson location's elegant maroon dining room). Both have immense dining areas that manage to fill up with office crowds on weekdays and brunchers on the weekend. *Dim Sum. Lunch, Saturday-Sunday brunch. $36-85*

ZUNI CAFÉ

1658 Market St., San Francisco, 415-552-2522; www.zunicafe.com

The liquor bottles stacked against the floor-to-ceiling bar window face out to busy Market Street and add to Zuni's dazzle, along with exposed brick walls, the open kitchen and a copper bar. Though it had a snooty heyday, the scene now is less see-and-be-seen than see-and-devour-the-chicken—Zuni's roasted bird for two is justly famous for its crisp-skinned juiciness (plus it's organic, as is all of the meat here). Other favorites include Caesar salad, wood-fired pizza and a much-debated burger (some love the juicy patty served on focaccia; others think it's pretentious and soggy) and fries (some adore the crispy matchstick haystack; others complain there's not enough potato). Less famous, but often better, are house-cured anchovies, ricotta gnocchi or grill specials. *French. Lunch, dinner. Closed Monday. $36-85*

SPAS

★★★NOB HILL SPA

The Huntington Hotel, 1075 California St., San Francisco, 415-345-2860; www.nobhillspa.com

Trudge uphill to one of the city's classic hotels, and you'll be rewarded with a posh spot for top-notch pampering. The bi-level space offers 10 treatment rooms, an indoor pool, saunas and steam rooms, fireplaces and a workout area—all of which are overseen by friendly, but unobtrusive staffers. Indulge in a High Skin Refiner Facial, which helps smooth out wrinkles and lines, or the Ultimate Massage—a 110-minute customized blissfest in which you're kneaded with aromatherapeutic oils and hot stones that'll leave you so relaxed you may need a ride home. Or try the spa's newest treatment, an 80-minute detox ritual that promises to eliminate toxins and blanket skin with vital nutrients to leave your skin feeling firmer and softer. The treatment begins with a seaweed body scrub during which an essential oil scalp and neck massage is performed. After this, the entire body is wrapped in organic muslin and cocooned in a thermal blanket. Before you head out, take some time to compose yourself by ordering a light lunch (Nob Hill is one of the rare spas to offer more than cucumbers and water on its spa menu) while taking in the city views from the balcony patio.

★★★★REMÈDE SPA

The St. Regis San Francisco, 125 Third St., San Francisco, 415-284-4060; www.stregis.com

If heaven has a spa, it must look like this: pristine ivory walls with dark wood accents, a glassy infinity pool with views of the city, plush velour sofas and a staff that entices you with truffles and champagne. Since it's in the posh St. Regis hotel, the service is as refined and gracious as you'd expect—and the services are as luxurious as they are effective. You can't go wrong with the Remède Customized Facial, which tops off thorough pore cleansing and a customized face mask with a decadent essential-oil scalp massage and skin-softening mud-and-paraffin wraps for hands and feet. It's an experience that's so lavish and pampering it's almost sinful. The same goes for The Stillness Ritual. You can have a regular massage anywhere. Here, treat yourself to this signature massage, which begins with a calming herbal bath followed by a 90-minute Swedish massage that combines craniosacral work and foot reflexology.

WHERE TO SHOP

826 VALENCIA

826 Valencia St., San Francisco, 415-642-5905; www.826valencia.org/store

After writing his best-selling novel *A Heartbreaking Work of Staggering Genius*, Dave Eggers opened a tutoring center to help children develop their writing skills. To fund the effort, he opened the city's premiere (probably only) pirate-supply emporium in the storefront of the tutoring center. Practice your arrrs before browsing eye patches, spy glasses and souvenir tees—and of course, books from Eggers' publishing arm, *McSweeney's*—and support this nonprofit in the process.

Daily noon-6 p.m.

AB FITS

1519 Grant Ave., San Francisco, 415-982-5726; www.abfits.com

When you can't find a pair of jeans that fits quite right, see the denim doctors at AB Fits. Not only do they have a large selection of traditional and trendy dungarees, they also dole out honest feedback on which pair flatters most. Contemporary T-shirts, casual dresses and accessories round out the selection at this homey North Beach boutique.

Tuesday-Saturday 11:30 a.m.-6:30 p.m., Sunday noon-6 p.m.

AGENT PROVOCATEUR

54 Geary St., San Francisco, 415-421-0229; www.agentprovocateur.com

Luxurious, seductive and unapologetically naughty, this London-based lingerie brand offers upscale underpinnings coveted by celebs and civilians alike. Here, it's all about the full get-up: seamed stockings, old-fashioned garters, negligees and more. Sizes begin at A and go up to F, giving the petite and buxom equal opportunity to seduce.
Monday-Saturday 11 a.m.-7 p.m., Sunday noon-5 p.m.

AMBIANCE SAN FRANCISCO

1458 Haight St., San Francisco, 415-552-5095; 3985 & 3989 24th St., San Francisco, 415-647-7144; 1864 & 1858 Union St., San Francisco, 415-923-9797; www.ambiancesf.com

Situated in the Haight-Ashbury neighborhood within the Western Addition area, this popular little shop features everything from dresses to wear out to your latest special event to vintage-inspired pieces for more casual affairs to funky accessories that go with everything. The wide variety of brands includes Plenty, LA Made, Joe's Jeans, Michael by Michael Kors, Betsey Johnson, Catherine Malandrino and Diane von Furstenberg. Check the website for special events; there are regular late-night shopping events with champagne and brownies to make shopping decisions more fun.
Monday-Saturday 10 a.m.-7 p.m., Sunday 11 a.m.-7 p.m.; Monday-Saturday, until 8 p.m. from Memorial Day-Labor Day.

AMOEBA RECORDS

1855 Haight St., San Francisco, 415-831-1200; www.amoeba.com

One of the country's last great record stores, Amoeba is home to tens of thousands of LPs, CDs, DVDs and obscure music magazines. The warehouse-like space in Haight-Ashbury—a former bowling alley—stocks everything from upcoming indie-rock albums to vintage records. Touring artists, such as M.I.A. and Jamie Lidell, frequently stop by to play a few tunes, but even on a slow day, you'll see that vinyl is still very much alive.
Monday-Saturday 10:30 a.m.-10 p.m., Sunday 11 a.m.-9 p.m.

THE ARCHIVE

317 Sutter St., San Francisco, 415-391-5550; www.archivesf.com

Don't be put off by the high-concept window displays, which often cause passers-by to roll their eyes. (Gas masks on mannequins?) There isn't a pleated pair of Dockers to be found in this haute men's clothing

boutique, but it's not as cutting edge as you'd think. The Archive special-izes in dashing ensembles for the tall, slim and impeccably dressed—picture weathered leather jackets, dapper wingtips and slim suits. International designers such as Rick Owens and Balmain provide sleek, urban looks for those genetically blessed enough to pull it off.
Monday-Saturday 10:30 a.m.-6:30 p.m.

ARIA

1522 Grant Ave., San Francisco, 415-433-0219

We love poring over the curiosities at this fascinating repository of long-gone culture. The proprietor splits his time between San Francisco and Paris (be sure to call before planning a visit, as the shop closes for five months every year while he's abroad), scouring both cities to find ephemera and relics of decades past. Some might call his eclectic finds antiques, but they're more unusual, more special, than the typical doilies-and-Tiffany-glass items you might expect. Look for oversized flora and fauna lithographs, faded photographs, weathered domino sets and dioramas—and don't be afraid to haggle a little if you can't leave without taking some of them home.
Tuesday-Saturday 11 a.m.-6 p.m., Sunday noon-5 p.m.

ARTHUR BEREN

222 Stockton St., San Francisco, 415-397-8900; www.berenshoes.com

In an era of nearly extinct customer service, the clerks at this two-story shoe store suggest otherwise. They're happy to unearth hard-to-find sizes and widths, and they offer services such as stretching and waterproofing to boot. Cole Haan, Bruno Magli, Ferragamo and Mephisto are just a few of the lines you'll find for men and women, with none of the crowding you'd expect of the location.
Monday-Friday 9:30 a.m.-7 p.m., Saturday 9:30 a.m.-6 p.m., Sunday noon- 6 p.m.

BARE ESCENTUALS

Westfield San Francisco Centre, 865 Market St., San Francisco, 415-357-9804; www.bareescentuals.com

Leslie Blodgett's cult collection of mineral makeup is headquartered in San Francisco, and its boutique is constantly filled with women swirling, tapping and buffing their way to a brighter complexion. This outpost is almost always packed on weekends—so stop by early to see what the hype is all about.
Monday-Saturday 10 a.m.-8:30 p.m., Sunday 10:30 a.m.-7 p.m.

BASTILLE

66 Kearny St., San Francisco, 415-951-0210; www.ilovebastille.com

The store's sleek design—white and gray walls, simple silver clothing racks, wooden tables—makes the clothing the main focus. Bastille carries designers such as Paul Smith, Theory, James Perse, Band of Ousiders and G-Star, as well as a large selection of the popular Swedish brand Filippa K for both men and women. Men will love the selection of loafers from Band of Outsiders and women will snatch up breezy dresses from Filippa K and James Perse. Check out the blog on Bastille's website for store events such as trunk shows with free drinks and live DJs. Even if you don't purchase anything, you're sure to be inspired.
Monday-Saturday 11 a.m.-7 p.m., Sunday noon-6 p.m.

BEAUTYLAND

180 O'Farrell St., San Francisco, 415-989-1818

If you're having a beauty emergency, this local apothecary has a convenient location just off busy Market Street. Its high-quality tools and supplies draw professional stylists and beauty junkies who love its well-edited selection of shampoos, nail lacquers and cosmetics. It's not as flashy as its corporate competitors—think simple displays rather than infinite makeup testers—but its knowledgeable staff gladly guides shoppers to what they need most.

Monday-Friday 9:30 a.m.-7 p.m., Saturday 10 a.m.-7 p.m., Sunday 11:30 a.m.-6 p.m.

BELLJAR

3187 16th St., San Francisco, 415-626-1749; www.belljarsf.com

Contrary to the connotations of its Plathian name, this new boutique isn't even remotely depressing. The owner, a former art director, has created an eclectic collection of clothes, trinkets and housewares. Printed Eskell dresses hang alongside vintage birdcages, near which Moroccan leather poufs and botanical bath products intermix. Everything has an intriguing stuck-in-the-past charm to it, and there's just enough darkness (mounted deer heads, framed anatomical drawings) to balance the softness of the flowy frocks on the racks.

Monday-Thursday noon-7 p.m., Friday-Saturday noon-8 p.m., Sunday noon-6 p.m.

BENEFIT

2219 Chestnut St., San Francisco, 415-567-1173; 2117 Fillmore St., 415-567-0242;
www.benefitcosmetics.com

San Francisco is home to this fun-loving makeup brand, and of its many retro-tinged beauty boutiques, this one is the most enchanting. Floor-to-ceiling windows let you see how your makeup looks in daylight, and the Hollywood Regency décor is unabashedly girly. Pop in to try the brand's famous Benetint lip and cheek stain, or opt for a no-appointment-necessary brow shaping or eyelash tint. No matter what you choose, you'll be charmed by the staff's unstoppable enthusiasm and the brand's all-ages appeal.

Monday-Wednesday 10 a.m.-7 p.m., Thursday-Friday 9:30 a.m.-7 p.m., Saturday 9 a.m.-6:30 p.m., Sunday 10 a.m.-6 p.m.

CAMPER

39 Grant Ave., San Francisco, 415-296-1005; www.camper.com

Quirky and colorful, these Spanish shoes are heralded for their rubber-soled comfort. Generally, they're closer to the hip side of things than the orthopedic, but you won't find a dainty kitten heel in sight. Instead, check out the TWS collection (the left shoe's design is different from the right) and the so-cute offerings for kids.

Monday-Saturday 10 a.m.-7 p.m., Sunday 11 a.m.-6 p.m.

CARROTS

843 Montgomery St., San Francisco, 415-834-9040; www.sfcarrots.com

This chilled-out, light-filled store is near the edge of the staid Financial District, but it's more stylish than its location suggests. The focus is on high-quality, well-tailored clothing from European and American designers, including Vanessa Bruno, Proenza Schouler and California native Alexander Wang. The men's collection is slightly less formal than the women's offerings, but no less

fashionable. In case you're wondering, the name of the boutique is due to the owners' family business as the world's largest producer of carrots.
Tuesday-Saturday 11 a.m.-6 p.m.

CITY LIGHTS BOOKSTORE

261 Columbus Ave., San Francisco, 415-362-8193; www.citylights.com

Browse three floors of tightly packed stacks at this Beat Generation bookshop. A must-see for all literature lovers, City Lights Bookstore was co-founded by poet Lawrence Ferlinghetti in 1953 as the country's first paperback-only bookseller. In 1955, Ferlinghetti started City Lights Publishers, perhaps best known for publishing Allen Ginsberg's groundbreaking *Howl & Other Poems* in 1956, which led to Ferlinghetti's arrest on obscenity charges. The shop now carries a wide range of both paper and hardback titles. Reflecting the free-speech interests of its founders, it caters to those outside-the-mainstream voices, with books on progressive politics and social issues, works from small presses and an entire room devoted to poetry. Although the staff members are extremely knowledgeable, they also have a reputation for being a bit prickly with those they deem less informed. While you shouldn't let their attitude stop you from shopping here, you may want to think twice about asking where to find the latest Danielle Steel novel.
Daily 10 a.m.-midnight.

COTTON SHEEP

572 Hayes St., San Francisco, 415-621-5546

Wabi-sabi—the Japanese aesthetic of finding beauty in imperfection—is in full bloom at this large, high-ceilinged emporium of Japanese cotton goods. Uneven wood floors and rustic displays put the focus on the imported clothing and accessories, including organic-fabric basics for adults and adorable animal-shaped socks for kids. Unusual finds such as hand-dyed Kapital jeans (with 14k gold rivets, no less) will make you rethink your definition of what cotton can be.
Monday-Saturday 11 a.m.-7 p.m., Sunday 11 a.m.-6 p.m.

CRIS

2056 Polk St., San Francisco, 415-474-1191

Some of the city's best-dressed women consign their closet castaways here, and bargain hunters are all the better for it. You'll typically find high-end items from Marc Jacobs, Chanel, Yves Saint Laurent, Christian Dior and Manolo Blahnik. A pair of Jimmy Choo sling-backs can be had for less than a third of their original price, for instance, and good-as-new handbags are at least 40 percent off. Don't be surprised if you find original tags dangling from a few items; someone else's overstuffed wardrobe is your gain.
Monday-Saturday 11 a.m.-6 p.m.

CROSSROADS TRADING CO.

2123 Market St., San Francisco, 415-552-8740;
www.crossroadstrading.com

This chain of consignment stores has locations across the city, but the Castro outpost gets the best blend of merchandise. The hit-or-miss selection demands that you wade through piles of last year's H&M, but you'll be rewarded with the occasional high-end find that's sinfully underpriced (like a Miu Miu dress for

$35). Patience and a willingness to browse almost always pay off, so carve out an hour for best results.
Monday-Thursday 11 a.m.-7 p.m., Friday-Saturday 11 a.m.-8 p.m., Sunday noon-7 p.m.

DIPTYQUE
171 Maiden Lane, San Francisco, 415-402-0600;
www.diptyqueparis.com
Francophiles love this bi-level outpost of the Parisian fragrance company, just one of less than a dozen in the world. Its scented candles start at $60, but the high concentration of essential oils means they'll last longer than their less-pricey counterparts. Start exploring with a cult favorite such as the best-selling Baies (black currant and rose essence), or the Philosykos, which captures the fragrance of fig leaves.
Monday-Saturday 10 a.m.-6 p.m., Sunday noon-5 p.m.

ECO CITIZEN
1488 Vallejo St., San Francisco, 415-614-0100; www.ecocitizenonline.com
San Francisco would not be San Francisco without the many fair trade and eco-conscious stores, including this one. The shop is filled with items that are fair trade, organic and sustainable. Browse the racks and you'll find a large selection of women's organic clothing from designers such as Josh Podoll, Edun and Covet; a few things for men including Tom's burlap shoes; beautiful handmade jewelry; onesies for babies with phrases like "Save the Planet"; and even a selection of environmentally-friendly bridal gowns from Leila Hafzi.
Tuesday-Saturday 11 a.m.-7 p.m., Sunday noon-6 p.m.; Monday by appointment only.

FERRY BUILDING MARKETPLACE
1 Ferry Building, the Embarcadero, San Francisco, 415-983-8000;
www.ferrybuildingmarketplace.com
Foodies the world over (including chef Alice Waters) come to browse the gourmet offerings at this restored transportation hub, and with good reason: It showcases the best locally produced meat, eggs, vegetables, bread and cheese in the area. On Tuesday and Saturday, locals pack the place while browsing the farmers' market, but other days have a more subdued atmosphere. (The market is also open on Thursday with street food vendors and a small handful of farm stands). Treat yourself to a rose geranium macaroon at pastry shop Miette, browse exotic morels at Far West Fungi, or sample blood orange olive oil at Stonehouse Olive Oil. Dine-in restaurants abound, but we like grabbing an Acme Bread baguette and some Red Hawk cheese from Cowgirl Creamery's Artisan Cheese Shop, then snacking outside while watching traffic zip by on the Bay Bridge.
Monday-Friday 10 a.m.-6 p.m., Saturday 9 a.m.-6 p.m., Sunday 11 a.m.-5 p.m.

FRESH
301 Sutter St., San Francisco, 415-248-0210; www.fresh.com
Stepping into this bright and airy boutique is like getting a blast of, well, freshness. The brand creates unusual, natural, beautiful perfumes and skin-care products—brown sugar polish, sake bath oil—that practically beg to be eaten. Ask for a complimentary quickie facial; the sweet staffers are happy to oblige.
Monday-Wednesday, Friday-Saturday 10 a.m.-7 p.m., Thursday 10 a.m.-8 p.m., Sunday 11 a.m.-6 p.m.

GIMME SHOES

416 Hayes St., San Francisco, 415-864-0691; 2358 Fillmore St., 415-441-3040; www.gimmeshoes.com

If you're a shoe junkie, prepare to bliss out upon seeing this supremely well-edited collection of heels, sandals, boots and handbags. Sleek styles from Dries Van Noten and Paul Smith come straight from the runway, while leather boots from Loeffler Randall and Repetto ballet slippers will fulfill your footwear fix.
Monday-Saturday 11 a.m.-7 p.m., Sunday 11 a.m.-6 p.m.

GREEN APPLE BOOKS

506 Clement St., San Francisco, 415-387-2272; www.greenapplebooks.com

This neighborhood shop smells of old pages and aging cloth covers—just as you would hope from an independent bookstore. Specializing in new releases, as well as used books, Green Apple has shelves that stretch from the floor to the ceiling, with tomes overflowing everywhere. A good selection of DVDs and independent music rounds out the selection, making this a quieter alternative to bookstore megachains.
Sunday-Thursday 10 a.m.-10:30 p.m., Friday-Saturday 10 a.m.-11:30 p.m.

THE GROCERY STORE

3625 Sacramento St., San Francisco, 415-928-3615

If your shopping list calls for sophisticated, crisp and of-the-moment women's clothing, get yourself over to this industrial-chic store. Packed with high-end finds from Miu Miu, Jeremy Lang, Dsquared2 and The Row, it caters to a coolly well-dressed crowd that chooses tailored luxury over gaudy labels. The staffers know their fashion—they're almost too helpful with their guidance—and they'll help you check off your list in no time.
Monday-Friday 10:30 a.m.-6:30 p.m., Saturday 10:30 a.m.-6 p.m.

HEIDISAYS

2426 Fillmore St., San Francisco, 415-749-0655; www.heidisays.com

Filled with contemporary wear from Milly, Twelfth Street by Cynthia Vincent and Trina Turk, this PacHeights boutique always has a flirty date-night dress or an outfit-perfecting accessory. Its nearby sister store, HeidiSays Casual *(2146 Fillmore St.)*, offers soft tees and curve-hugging jeans, while the shoe boutique *(2105 Fillmore St.)* caters to a similarly well-heeled crowd.
Monday-Saturday 11 a.m.-7 p.m., Sunday noon-6 p.m.

HOUSE OF HENGST

924 Valencia St., San Francisco, 415-642-0841; www.houseofhengst.com

Susan Hengst may not be a household name, but to Bay Area fashionistas, she's the crème de la crème. Starting out as a vintage buyer, she learned how to sew from her grandmother. Hengst draws liberally from the past for her designs—think disco-era halter tops and Fitzgerald-heroine smocks—but imbues her clothing with a contemporary sensibility that won't leave her a secret for much longer. Hengst's designs are also sold at small boutiques across the country (and one in Paris), but phone orders are welcome. You may even run into Hengst here—so you can say you knew her when.
Monday-Saturday noon-7 p.m., Sunday noon-6 p.m.

JAPAN CENTER
Webster and Geary streets, San Francisco, 415-567-4573; www.sfjapantown.org

Japan Center isn't the most aesthetically pleasing building in town, but what's inside is a delight. Kimonos, books, collectibles and other imported goods draw busy weekend crowds to this wonderfully unusual mall. Most stores are worth a peek, but a few stand out: Kinokuniya Stationery and Gift stocks twee stationery and magazines, some in English as well as Japanese. For wasabi peas and Kewpie-doll-logoed mayonnaise, wheel your shopping cart down the aisles of Nijiya Market. Bypass the Denny's for Mifune Don, whose ramen is worlds away from the stuff you used to eat in college.

Hours vary.

JEREMY'S
2 S. Park St., San Francisco, 415-882-4929; www.jeremys.com

First things first: The staff at this outlet couldn't care less that you're there, so don't expect a warm welcome. Do, however, expect to gasp at the price tags—in a good way. Jeremy's routinely receives overstock from retailers such as Barneys and Bergdorf Goodman, and the result is obscenely inexpensive designer wear. Time your visit right, and you could walk out with jaw-dropping deals such as $6 for a pair of Costume National trousers, or $250 for a Chloé handbag.

Monday-Saturday 11 a.m.-6 p.m., Sunday 11 a.m.-5 p.m.

JOHN FLUEVOG
1697 Haight St., San Francisco, 415-436-9784; www.fluevog.com

If you demand comfort and quirkiness from your shoes, Fluevog's your man. His shoes are often retro, usually funky and always unusual. While some styles can look costumey if you're not an active participant in musical subcultures, others work perfectly for a more conservative look. Be sure to peek at CBC, a line of leather-free shoes, suited for the PETA activist in all of us.

Monday-Saturday 11 a.m.-7 p.m., Sunday noon-6 p.m.

KRYOLAN
132 Ninth St., San Francisco, 415-863-9684; www.usa.kryolan.com

Take a cue from professional makeup artists and head to this unassuming showroom. Kryolan manufactures its own cosmetics line in the same building, which means that all of the products are right off the line. The highly pigmented makeup is often as inexpensive as its drugstore counterparts, but don't be fooled; Kryolan also manufactures products for a few pricey beauty brands found at high-end department stores.

Monday-Friday 9 a.m.-5 p.m., first Saturday of every month 10 a.m.-4 p.m.

LONDON SOLE
19 Maiden Lane, San Francisco, 415-397-8088; www.londonsole.com

Modern-day Audrey Hepburn types love this feminine boutique for its seemingly endless supply of that style staple, the ballet flat. Available in almost any color, fabric or pattern you can imagine, these comfortable shoes are favored by locals who have to climb hills to get home. These are investment-quality flats, not toss-after-one-season shoes, and if you're like us, you'll want to pick them up like candy.

Monday-Saturday 10 a.m.-6 p.m., Sunday noon-5 p.m.

METIER

355 Sutter St., San Francisco, 415-989-5395; www.metiersf.com

It's essentially impossible to find even one less-than-beautiful item at this women's boutique, which focuses on clothing and jewelry by buzzed-about designers, including Isabel Marant, Alexander Wang, Phillip Lim, Rag and Bone, and many others. Owner Sheri Evans has an eye for edgier pieces, which she uses for her own tossed-off chic look. The long, deep space incorporates light woods and flattering lighting, so it's hard not to feel fabulous while twirling around in the spacious fitting rooms.

Monday-Saturday 10 a.m.-6 p.m.

MY ROOMMATE'S CLOSET

3044 Fillmore St., San Francisco, 415-447-7703; www.myroommatescloset.com

Looks are deceiving at this Marina boutique: It looks like a chic shop, and it's filled with contemporary designer clothing, but the prices are all relatively low. That's because the "closet" features overstock and samples from local designers and boutiques, shaving 50 percent or more off the retail price. Unlike other discount shops in the city, this one has charm and warm service; the only thing it's short on is a high markup.

Monday-Friday 11 a.m.-6:30 p.m., Saturday 11 a.m.-6 p.m., Sunday-Monday noon-5 p.m.

MY TRICK PONY

742 14th St., San Francisco, 415-861-0595; www.mytrickpony.com

Taking customization to the next level, this small, off-the-beaten-path shop can transfer your vision to T-shirts, ties, even baby onesies. The service goes beyond merely affixing iron-on letters; instead, the Pony people create screen-printed, spray-painted and airbrushed designs to your specifications. Shirts cost about $35 and are usually done in less than an hour, making this a one-trick pony with a particularly impressive trick.

Tuesday-Saturday 11:30 a.m.-7 p.m., Sunday noon-5 p.m.

NANCY BOY

347 Hayes St., San Francisco, 415-552-3636; www.nancyboy.com

Metrosexuality may be passé, but don't let that stop you from exploring this shop's excellent line of naturally derived grooming products. Even though the focus is on keeping men fresh and clean, women

WHAT IS THE BEST STORE IN SAN FRANCISCO FOR VINTAGE CLOTHING?

Ver Unica
There is a treasure trove of vintage finds packed in the racks at this shop, so come prepared to dig for it. You may just walk away with a pristine Dolce and Gabbana suit, or a Hermès scarf.

will find plenty to love, too. The tongue-in-cheek shop name belies the breadth of its offerings, from shaving creams to lavender-geranium laundry soap. Here's an insider tip: Sign up for the mailing list to receive 15 percent off right away.
Monday-Friday 11 a.m.-7 p.m., Saturday-Sunday 11 a.m.-6 p.m.

NIDA

544 Hayes St., San Francisco, 415-552-4670

Equally divided between men's and women's European designers, this long, narrow space is filled with whatever's on the pages of *Numéro* or *Paris Vogue*. Labels such as Cacharel, Vanessa Bruno and Isabel Marant attract women building a grown-up wardrobe, while men delight in slim-fit shirts and trousers from the likes of Steven Alan and Issey Miyake. For all the serious fashion going on, the staff is among the nicest in town, providing styling advice for the sartorially challenged.
Monday-Saturday 11 a.m.-7 p.m., Sunday noon-6 p.m.

OOMA

1422 Grant Ave., San Francisco, 415-627-6963; www.ooma.net

The name stands for Objects of My Affection, and considering the local girls who swarm the shop on weekends, it's a well-loved place indeed. The cotton-candy-colored environment provides a festive atmosphere for browsing colorful dresses from Orion London and beautiful Italian resin bracelets from local line Bellissima. The shop carries a great selection of on-trend pieces and accessories that have the ability to transform an outfit. The staff is especially helpful and well-dressed, so don't be shy about asking for style advice.
Tuesday-Saturday 11 a.m.-7 p.m., Sunday noon-5 p.m.

PARK LIFE

220 Clement St., San Francisco, 415-386-7275; www.parklifestore.com

Contemporary works from up-and-coming artists fill the back room of this boutique, and its retail offerings are similarly hip. The loft-like space offers silk-screened tees from local designers, hard-to-find design books and unusual objects, such as ceramic pistol-shaped vases. The selection of goods from international designers is worth a look, and while you can drop $200 on an (admittedly cool) alarm clock, there's plenty of fun to be had for less than $20, too—such as ceramic eggs with seeds inside that sprout when you water them.
Monday-Thursday noon-8 p.m., Friday-Saturday 11 a.m.-9 p.m., Sunday 11 a.m.-7 p.m.

PAXTON GATE

824 Valencia St., San Francisco, 415-824-1872; www.paxtongate.com

This wonderfully weird florist-cum-boutique has a beautiful take on the natural sciences, as exemplified by the taxidermic animals that rest near tea supplies, delicate jewelry and gardening implements. The esoteric selection—incorporating Japanese garden tools, and pen and ink sets—is a little Victorian, a little odd and completely worth the trip.
Daily 11 a.m.-7 p.m.

PERCH

654 Chenery St., San Francisco, 415-586-9000; www.perchsf.com

This adorable gift and home furnishings shop features items that anyone would be happy to receive as a present. With a new selection of goods delivered weekly, you're sure to find something unique, from fun books, candles and vintage tea sets to leather wrist cuffs made from vintage belts and dog tags. The unique assortment includes locally-made items as well as trinkets from around the globe. Stay and browse for as long you like; the owners want you to feel welcomed to "perch" a while.

Monday-Saturday 11 a.m.-7 p.m., Sunday noon-5 p.m.

PHILANTHROPIST

3571 Sacramento St., San Francisco, 415-441-1750; www.philanthropistboutique.com

This pretty store looks like any other high-end boutique with its sparkling chandeliers, cow-hide rug, metallic flower wallpaper and rows of designer clothing. But there's a twist: Unlike at any other store, 100 percent of the profits go to a different poverty-fighting local charity each season. That's right. Owners Jessica Moment and Sally Fowler decided to marry their love of fashion and their philanthropic interest and it's a win-win for shoppers. Not only do you benefit from their generosity (help others while shopping) but from their great taste. This is a good place to scoop up staple pieces from designers such as Alice & Olivia, Jason Wu, Derek Lam, Catherine Malandrino, Paul & Joe, Rachel Roy and Zac Posen, among others.

Monday-Saturday 11 a.m.-6 p.m., Sunday by appointment only.

RAG CO-OP (RESIDENTS APPAREL GALLERY)

541 Octavia St., San Francisco, 415-621-7718; www.ragsf.com

A one-stop shop for locally designed apparel and accessories, this fashion co-op features creations from more than 70 Bay Area designers. Women's clothing and jewelry dominate the homey space, but there's plenty for men and children, too. Don't miss 4fifteen's graphic tees, especially the "I hella heart SF" design, which tweaks the iconic tourist logo with a bit of local slang.

Wednesday-Saturday noon-7 p.m., Sunday noon-6 p.m.

RARE DEVICE

1845 Market St., San Francisco, 415-863-3969; www.raredevice.net

There's no sign out front, but you'll recognize this design-centric shop by the geometric shapes that hover above its blue doorway. Walk inside to discover unusual home goods and gifts, such as custom-made dishware and silk-screened totes. The walls overflow with paintings and prints by local artists; the installations change monthly, but like the retail offerings, they have a drawn-by-hand charm to them.

Tuesday-Saturday noon-7 p.m., Sunday noon-6 p.m.

SCHEIN & SCHEIN

1435 Grant Ave., San Francisco, 415-399-8882; www.scheinandschein.com

This dealer of antique maps and prints looks like the library of a learned man, and its staff is happy to help your home look the same. Rare books line the shelves, and wooden flat-file cabinets roll out to reveal maps reaching back as far as the 17th century. Husband and wife Jim and Marti Schein have an encyclopedic knowledge of their offerings, so along with your purchase, you'll receive a quick lesson about its history.

Tuesday-Saturday 11 a.m.-7 p.m.

WHAT'S A GREAT
CHILDREN'S
STORE IN SAN
FRANCISCO?

Small Frys
Stop in for a quick toy
and you'll be playing
for hours thanks to a
seemingly endless collec-
tion of colorful baubles.
We particularly loved
the selection of green
toys, made from recycled
milk jugs.

WHAT'S A GREAT
BOUTIQUE
FOR WOMEN'S
CLOTHING?

Heidisays
Suits, cocktail dresses,
the perfect brooch.
You'll find it all here in
a well edited collection
of designer clothes from
Catherine Malandrino,
Diane von Furstenberg
and Tory Burch, among
others.

WHAT IS THE BEST
SHOP FOR LUXURY
BEAUTY GOODS?

Shu Uemura
The late Japanese
makeup artist
revolutionized the way
women put on their
faces. Women swear by
the legendary eyelash
curler. Be sure to indulge
in a few faux eyelashes
from the Tokyo Lash Bar
before you go.

SELF EDGE

714 Valencia St., San Francisco, 415-558-0658; www.selfedge.com

To enter this shop is to reach a denim mecca in the city that created jeans in the first place. Known internationally for its selection of hard-to-find designer denim, Self Edge delivers the most premium and obscure brands possible: Sling & Stones, Sugar Cane and Skull are just some of the jean lines available. Be prepared to examine the wonders of gold rivets, Japanese and raw denim—and to drop $300 or so to take a pair home.
Monday-Saturday noon-7 p.m., Sunday noon-5 p.m.

SHU UEMURA

1971 Fillmore St., San Francisco, 415-395-0953;
www.shuuemura.com

The late Japanese makeup artist Shu Uemura was a cosmetics pioneer, and his brand continues to create groundbreaking products. If you've never tried the legendary eyelash curler, the staff at this slickly designed store—one of only three in the U.S.—will help you clamp and curl until you're positively doe-eyed. For extra drama, buy a pair of faux lashes at the Tokyo Lash Bar; you'll leave batting your eyes at everyone who passes by.
Monday-Saturday 10:30 a.m.-7:30 p.m., Sunday 11 a.m.-6 p.m.

SMALL FRYS

4066 24th St., San Francisco, 415-648-3954; www.smallfrys.com

Tie-dyed onesies, organic-cotton-stuffed animals, wooden toys—there's not much you won't find for babies at this fairytale store. Put Junior in a Bob Marley tee, or plop him in wee penny-loafer booties for a relatively formal look. The offerings are playful and fun, and the staff is happy to ship packages for a nominal fee.
Monday-Thursday, Saturday 10 a.m.-6 p.m., Friday 10 a.m.-7 p.m., Sunday 11 a.m.-5:30 p.m.

SMOKE SIGNALS

2223 Polk St., San Francisco, 415-292-6025

You can find *Vogue* or *Newsweek* anywhere, but what about *Vogue India* or the latest edition of *Le Monde*? At this small, packed-to-the-brim newsstand, you'll unearth hundreds, if not thousands, of hard-to-find periodicals. Whether your interest lies in Italian fashion glossies, British journals or Chinese newspapers, you'll have your pick of a wide swath of obscura here, along with a range of tobacco products.
Monday-Saturday 8 a.m.-7:30 p.m., Sunday 8 a.m.-5:30 p.m.

SUSAN

3685 Sacramento St., San Francisco, 415-922-3685

Serious fashion fiends will find all of the clothing from *Vogue* and *Bazaar* at this high-end boutique. Chloé, Lanvin, Marni, Balenciaga—the biggest names in fashion are all here. The best part: All the pieces are chosen with an eye toward longevity, which means you won't find many in-today, out-tomorrow items that you might regret later.

Monday-Friday 10:30 a.m.-6:30 p.m., Saturday 10:30 a.m.-6 p.m.

TED BAKER

80 Grant Ave., San Francisco, 415-391-1256; www.tedbaker.com

You might be offered a martini upon entering this men's and women's clothing emporium, and then you'll drink in the styles from this London-based designer. Ted Baker is known for its menswear, and deservedly so; the suits are well-tailored and fresh, even if some of the collared shirts work better at a booming club than at the office. Women's clothes and accessories are upscale interpretations of trends seen on U.K. high streets, from sequined silk tunics to smart wool overcoats.

Monday-Wednesday 10 a.m.-7 p.m., Thursday-Saturday 10 a.m.-8 p.m., Sunday 11 a.m.-6 p.m.

THOMAS PINK

255 Post St., San Francisco, 415-421-2022; www.thomaspink.com

Who says haberdashery is dead? It's thriving at this London-based purveyor of dress shirts, ties and natty accoutrements. Here, the focus is on proper fit, from the width of the collar to the tailoring of the waist. The accessories and cufflinks are stylish without being flashy, and the more casual offerings for men—striped shirts, patterned ties—will help you spin the color wheel without clashing even once.

Monday-Friday 10 a.m.-7 p.m., Saturday 10 a.m.-6 p.m., Sunday 11 a.m.-6 p.m.

THE URBAN NEST

3927 24th St., San Francisco, 415-341-0116; www.theurbannestsf.com

Saunter into this well-appointed gift store and you'll find a charming Parisian flea-market vibe. While Edith Piaf croons on the stereo, explore the slightly rustic, often French ceramics, wall hangings and plush robes. You can pick up Damask lunch bags and garden-gnome cereal bowls—it's these quirky takes on everyday items that make The Urban Nest so irresistible.

Sunday-Monday 11 a.m.-6 p.m., Tuesday-Friday 11 a.m.-7 p.m., Saturday 10 a.m.-7 p.m.

VER UNICA

437B Hayes St., San Francisco, 415-431-0688

There's vintage, and then there's Ver Unica. The packed-to-the-brim store specializes in the best pre-loved dresses, shirts and more from decades past. (Think 1974 Yves Saint Laurent.) While there aren't many bargains lurking among the racks, you'll be pleased to find plenty of perfectly preserved pieces that retain their wow factor. Don't be surprised if you spot neo-folk singer Joanna Newsom browsing Jessica McClintock sundresses; the well-maintained clothing is key to San Francisco's bohemian style revival that she helped start.

Monday-Saturday 11 a.m.-7 p.m., Sunday noon-6 p.m.

THE BAY AREA

Believe it or not, there's tons to do in the Bay Area outside of San Francisco. Perched on a gorgeous stretch of California coastline, Half Moon Bay has a charming, well-preserved historic downtown. The close proximity to San Francisco (only 28 miles away) and many upscale restaurants, galleries and resorts make this town a popular choice for weekend visits. With mild temperatures, visitors can take in local beaches, parks and golf courses.

Set in the middle of Silicon Valley, free-roaming wildcats indigenous to the Santa Cruz Mountains inspired the name La Rinconada de Los Gatos, which means "the cat's corner." Today, it's shortened to Los Gatos and two 8-foot sculptured cats, Leo and Leona, guard the town entrance at Poet's Canyon. Look for the cats as you head into the small, upscale downtown for some antique shopping. The downtown of Los Gatos acts as a model for other communities and is listed on the National Register of Historic Places.

One of the most progressive cities in the nation, Berkeley is home to the flagship campus of the University of California and a population of well-heeled, aging hippies who want to enjoy the good life organic-style, even as they yearn for their politically radical pasts.

Located north of San Francisco in Marin County, the seaside town of Inverness is one of the villages that surround the beautifully rugged Point Reyes National Seashore and Tomales Bay. It is a popular area for hiking and exploring, and the town is filled with quaint restaurants and bed and breakfasts.

The charming Bay Area suburb of Mountain View, located south of San Francisco, is famous for being the world headquarters of search engine phenomenon Google, Inc. It's also home to many other Silicon Valley businesses, including Microsoft and AOL. The main downtown area is filled with shops, cafés and restaurants. There is also a superb farmers' market that is open all year.

Once a small farm town, San Jose has always had grand ambitions. The state capital before California even became a state, it is now the nerve center of the computer and high-tech industries and known as the capital of Silicon Valley.

Nicknamed the "Mission City," Santa Clara may sound placid, but it's located in the heart of Silicon Valley and is home to Great America, an amusement park that packs enough thrills to make you appreciate some tranquility.

Santa Cruz is a trip—and lots of people don't mean that literally. It's a lefty/counter-culture/free-thinker haven whose tree-lined streets are shared by hippies sporting tie-dyed ensembles, activists fighting for everything from veganism to medical marijuana, beach bums and surfers, nature types enjoying the great outdoors and tourists taking it all in. They're all drawn to the hushed redwoods and dramatic beaches, migrating whales and butterflies, historic attractions and Victorian houses and, most of all, the laidback vibe. This is a town where stores proudly sell T-shirts and stickers reading "Keep Santa Cruz Weird." Most of

BEST ATTRACTIONS

WHAT ARE SOME OF THE BEST PLACES FOR OUTDOOR FUN?

SNIFF AROUND THE BERKELEY ROSE GARDEN
Considered the best rose garden in Northern California, this Berkeley spot blooms with more than 3,000 bushes of the fragrant flower.

WALK AROUND JACK LONDON SQUARE
Find some writerly inspiration at this square, where author Jack London lived and worked. Visit Heinold's First and Last Chance Saloon, where he wrote some of his most famous novels.

EXPLORE SAN JOSE'S JAPANTOWN
This is one of the last remaining urban neighborhoods of its kind to survive the Japanese internment during World War II. Check out the great shops, eateries and galleries.

GET ACTIVE IN BIG BASIN REDWOODS STATE PARK
Big Basin is a good place for outdoorsy types. It's especially known for being the top spot for windsurfing, but you can also do hiking and horseback riding here.

PLAY AROUND ON THE SANTA CRUZ BEACH BOARDWALK
At California's oldest beachside amusement park, hop on the wooden roller coaster or ride the carousel, if that's more your speed. Then gorge on fried boardwalk fare.

the action is on Pacific Avenue, where street musicians, students, panhandlers, tourists and locals mingle amid a mix of quirky restaurants, indie shops and chain stores. There are 29 miles of public beaches and a boardwalk that retains its early 20th-century charms.

WHAT TO SEE

BERKELEY
BERKELEY ART MUSEUM & PACIFIC FILM ARCHIVE
2626 Bancroft Way, Berkeley, 510-642-0808; www.bampfa.berkeley.edu
Founded in 1963, this UC Berkeley campus museum contains paintings by Abstract Expressionist Hans Hofmann and many important historical and contemporary art works, including those by artists Jackson Pollock, Paul Gauguin and Joan Brown. There is also an outdoor sculpture garden, museum

store, cafe and the Pacific Film Archive Library and Film Study Center. The museum showcases temporary exhibitions, which explore international art.

Gallery admission: adults $8, non-UC Berkeley students, senior citizens, disabled persons, young adults 13-17 $5, UC Berkeley students, faculty and staff, children 12 and under free. Admission: adults $9.50, non-UC Berkeley students, UC Berkeley faculty and staff, seniors, disabled persons, children 17 and under $6.50, UC Berkeley students, BAM/PFA members $5.50. Additional feature $4. Show times may vary. First Thursday of every month free. Wednesday-Sunday 11 a.m.-5 p.m.

BERKELEY MARINA
201 University Ave., Berkeley, 510-981-6740; www.ci.berkeley.ca.us/marina

The Berkeley marina's public fishing pier, at 3,000 feet long, juts out into 52 acres of water for those who want to fish (no license required) or enjoy the view. The marina also includes restaurants, an adventure playground for children and a nature center with a 100-gallon saltwater aquarium.

Daily sunrise-sunset.

BERKELEY REPERTORY THEATRE
2025 Addison St., Berkeley, 510-647-2949; www.berkeleyrep.org

This Tony-award winning theater has garnered respect for its outstanding theatrical productions and talented, reputable actors, directors and playwrights since it opened in 1968. It is also home to the Berkeley Repertory School of Theatre, which provides theater education for children and adults. Each season consists of various plays and schedules; and in the past three years, it sent five of its hit plays to Broadway, including *Eurydice, Bridge & Tunnel* and *Taking Over.*

BERKELEY ROSE GARDEN
1200 Euclid Ave., Berkeley, 510-981-5150; www.ci.berkeley.ca.us

Opened in 1937, this historic rose garden consists of 3,000 rose bushes with 250 varieties. The best time to visit the garden is in mid-May, when most of the roses are in full bloom.

Daily sunrise-sunset.

BOTANICAL GARDEN
200 Centennial Drive, Berkeley, 510-643-2755; www.botanicalgarden.berkeley.edu

The University of California at Berkeley's Botanical Garden has many unusual plants from all over the world, including Asia, Australia and South America, along with many native California plants. The garden spans 34 acres and includes 12,000 varieties.

Admission: adults $7, seniors and children 13-17 $5, children 5-12 $2, children under 5 free. First Thursday of every month free. Daily 9 a.m.-5 p.m.; closed first Tuesday of every month. Tours: Thursday, Saturday-Sunday 1:30 p.m.

FREIGHT & SALVAGE COFFEEHOUSE
1111 Addison St. Berkeley, 510-548-1761; www.thefreight.org

Since 1968, Freight & Salvage Coffeehouse has operated as a non-smoking, alcohol-free all-ages coffee house and performance venue. Over time, with changes in its location and owner, it still acts as a nonprofit community resource for traditional music from many different cultures. On a given night, you might find musicians performing traditional blues, bluegrass, world-beat, gospel, jazz or folk. You can pick up some coffee, tea and a snack at the Freight food counter and kick back and enjoy the diverse music.

TILDEN PARK GOLF COURSE

10 Golf Course Drive, Berkeley, 510-848-7373; www.tildenparkgc.americangolf.com

Tilden Park isn't very long (a few yards under 6,300), but the many challenging tees require careful club selection. Several holes dogleg, and most are lined with large trees likely to swallow errant drives. Three of the four par-threes measure longer than 200 yards and provide perhaps the biggest overall challenge to the layout. The course is usually very crowded (about 75,000 rounds are played there each year), so arrive early and hope that you play behind someone who is fast.

Daily 6 a.m.-9 p.m.

TILDEN REGIONAL PARK

2501 Grizzly Peak Blvd., Berkeley, 510-843-2137, 888-327-2757; www.ebparks.org

The park's 2,079-acre recreational area offers plenty of outdoor recreation, including a beach, nature trails for hiking and biking, an 18-hole golf course, an old-fashioned carousel, steam train rides and a botanical garden of native California plants. The park connects with East Bay Skyline National Trail at Inspiration Point.

Daily 5 a.m.-10 p.m. Carousel: Saturday-Sunday.

UNIVERSITY OF CALIFORNIA, BERKELEY

2200 University Ave., Berkeley, 510-642-5215; www.berkeley.edu

More than 35,000 students attend this vast campus in the foothills of the east shore of San Francisco Bay. Founded in 1873, it is the oldest of the 10 University of California campuses and later became the system's flagship institution. The university's white granite buildings are surrounded by groves of oak trees and its 307-foot tower, known simply as the "Campanile," can be seen from a distance. The campus is known for its high-ranked public research library, discoveries in research, and the history that surrounds the city of Berkeley and the free thinkers who have lived there over the years. UC Berkeley boasts many famous alumni including newspaper publisher William Randolph Hearst; co-founder of Apple Steve Wozniak; actor Gregory Peck; author Jack London; chef and author Alice Waters; and MySpace co-founder Tom Anderson, to name a few.

WILLIAM RANDOLPH HEARST GREEK THEATRE

Gayley Road and Hearst Road, Berkeley, 510-809-0100; www.apeconcerts.com

Located on the University of California Berkeley campus, this theater was a gift from newspaper tycoon William Randolph Hearst (a UC Berkeley alumnus) to the university in 1903. This intimate outdoor amphitheater features regular performances from leading pop and jazz artists and has hosted performances

by the likes of Bob Dylan, Grateful Dead, Phish, Dave Matthews Band, as well as speakers including Theodore Roosevelt and the 14th Dalai Lama. Nestled in the foothills, this legendary theater overlooks the San Francisco Bay with views of the Golden Gate and Bay Bridges.
May-October.

HALF MOON BAY
HALF MOON BAY GOLF CLUB
2 Miramontes Point Road, Half Moon Bay, 650-726-1800; www.halfmoonbaygolf.com
Just off historic Highway 1 on the Pacific Ocean, this golf club has two courses, the Old Course and the Ocean Course, which vary slightly in their makeup. The Old Course resembles Pebble Beach with its traditional American design, while the Ocean course lets wild grasses overtake the rough and looks more like a links layout. A cart is included (walking is not permitted).

INVERNESS
COWGIRL CREAMERY AT TOMALES BAY FOODS
80 Fourth Street, Point Reyes Station, 415-663-9335; www.cowgirlcreamery.com
These cowgirls whip up around 3,000 pounds of their four soft aged cheeses and three fresh cheeses every week from their headquarters in Point Reyes Station. Visit the original creamery in the barn where owners and founders Sue Conley and Peggy Smith first started making their famous cheese in 1997. A viewing window into the kitchens allows you to see the cheeses being made. You can also take a tour of the facility, which includes a tasting. Purchase the cheese in the gift shop, which also sells books, knives, boards and condiments, or find the goods at the Cowgirl Creamery at the Ferry Plaza in San Francisco.
Admission: $5, Friday 11:30 a.m. Creamery: Wednesday-Sunday 10 a.m.-6 p.m.

HOG ISLAND OYSTER COMPANY FARM
20215 Highway 1, Marshall, 415-663-9218; www.hogislandoysters.com
The Hog Island Oyster Company has farmed top-notch West Coast oysters in the Tomales Bay since 1983. Thanks to the bay's plankton-rich seawater, the beds produce more than 3 million oysters annually. The farm is also a leading advocate of sustainable and responsible aquaculture. Visitors can buy fresh oysters to go or to shuck and slurp onsite. The farm provides waterfront picnic tables, shucking knives and barbecue grills for a small fee and reservations are required for weekends and holidays.
Daily 9 a.m.-5 p.m.

POINT REYES NATIONAL SEASHORE
1 Bear Valley Road, Point Reyes Station, 415-464-5100; www.nps.gov/pore
A 20-mile-long peninsula of pastoral beachfront jutting into the Pacific, Point Reyes National Seashore is a hodgepodge of active ranchland, dramatic sea cliffs, dense forests and pristine beaches. Visitors can enjoy hiking, sea kayaking, biking, whale-watching (January-April) and bird watching (more than 45 percent of all bird species in North America have been sighted here at one time or another). A lighthouse is located at the peninsula's northernmost

point. Pick up fresh oysters from Johnson's Oyster Farm.

Point Reyes Lighthouse: Thursday-Monday 10 a.m.-4:30 p.m. Bear Valley Visitor Center: Monday-Friday 9 a.m.-5 p.m., Saturday-Sunday 8 a.m-5 p.m.

STINSON BEACH

Highway 1, Stinson Beach, 415-868-1444; www.stinsonbeachonline.com

Only 20 miles from San Francisco, Stinson Beach has three and a half miles of sand, and is popular with surfers, swimmers and sunbathers. If you want to surf, there are shops in the area that provide rentals. Lifeguards are on duty from April through September. A park adjacent to the beach has more than 100 picnic tables and some grills, and the area also includes restrooms, showers and a snack bar, which is open during summer months.

Daily sunrise-sunset.

TOMALES BAY STATE PARK

1208 Pierce Point Road, Inverness, 415-669-1140; www.parks.ca.gov

Forty miles north of the Golden Gate Bridge, this state park is filled with virgin groves of Bishop pine trees in the Jepson Memorial Grove and more than 300 species of plants which grow on 2,000 acres. The four beaches of Tomales Bay are perfect for swimming, fishing, hiking, biking and picnicking.

LOS GATOS

BYINGTON VINEYARD AND WINERY

21850 Bear Creek Road, Los Gatos, 408-354-1111; www.byington.com

If you like a good cabernet, Byington Vineyard and Winery is at the top of its game. Perched at the summit overlooking the vast valley below, Byington—with its ivy-covered stone façade, outdoor patio and bocce ball court—looks like it was transported from the European countryside. Enjoy a glass of wine on the second-story terrace as well as the lawn—all have views of the valley below. Before you depart, take a short spiral pathway to Wedding Hill, where brides and grooms exchange vows surrounded by jasmine and overlooking vineyards, redwood forests and the Monterey Bay.

Tastings: $5. Daily 11 a.m.-5 p.m.

LOS GATOS CREEK TRAIL

Lexington Reservoir, Los Gatos; www.losgatosca.gov

Covering 10 miles of Los Gatos from Lexington Reservoir to Meridian Avenue in San Jose, this trail takes you through portions of Los Gatos and is a perfect outdoor activity for hikers and bicyclists.

Daily 7 a.m.-half hour after sunset.

OLD TOWN

50 University Ave., Los Gatos; www.losgatoschamber.com

The historic downtown area of Los Gatos is a charming place. Take a walking tour to see sites such as the Lyndon Plaza (where John Steinbeck, John Ford and Charlie Chaplin met for drinks at the Lyndon Hotel); the Los Gatos Theatre, which was a silent movie house when it was built in 1915; Ford's Opera House;

Los Gatos Creek Trail; and the Fretwell Building. There are shops, restaurants, art galleries and flowered garden walkways dating back to 1923.

MOUNTAIN VIEW
SHORELINE AT MOUNTAIN VIEW
3070 N. Shoreline Blvd., Mountain View; www.ci.mtnview.ca.us

Part of the Shoreline Regional Wildlife and Recreation Area, this park offers plenty to see and do. The Shoreline Amphitheatre, operated by Live Nation, hosts different types of musical acts for outdoor concerts (the majority of the amphitheatre is covered but the outdoor lawn seats are better to lounge and dance under the stars). Tour the oldest house in Mountain View, the Rengstorff House, built in 1867. There are large wildlife habitats at Shoreline where you can hike along ponds, marshland and hills to spot a variety of animals. Bike, jog or hike through one of Shoreline's seven miles of trails that wind through the area. Rent pedalboats, rowboats, canoes or kayaks to take out on Shoreline Lake or take a windsurfing, sailing or kayaking lesson. Or spend the day on the 18-hole golf course, and stop in afterwards for a meal at Michael's, the clubhouse for Shoreline Golf Links.

OAKLAND
ANTHONY CHABOT REGIONAL PARK & LAKE CHABOT
9999 Redwood Road, Castro Valley, 510-569-0213, 888-327-2757; www.ebparks.org

This East Bay regional park covers over 5,000 acres of land for hiking and horseback riding, biking, camping and golf. There are 31 miles of hiking trails along the East Bay Skyline National Trail. Fishing, boating facilities, bicycle trails and picnic areas are available at Chabot Family Campground, which overlooks Lake Chabot. The Willow Park Golf Course is also nearby, which includes a restaurant.

Daily 7 a.m.-10 p.m.

CAMRON-STANFORD HOUSE
1418 Lakeside Drive, Oakland, 510-874-7802; www.cshouse.org

This house, built in 1876, now serves as a museum with authentic period furnishings, sculpture and paintings. Once home to the notable Camron and Stanford families, the building served as the Oakland Public Museum from 1910 to 1967.

Admission: adults $5, seniors $4, children 12-18 $3, children 11 and under free. Third Wednesday afternoon of each month from 1-5 p.m., also by appointment.

CHABOT SPACE AND SCIENCE CENTER
10000 Skyline Blvd., Oakland, 510-336-7300; www.chabotspace.org

Built in 1883, this 86,000-square-foot complex includes the nation's largest public refracting telescope, a state-of-the-art planetarium, a MegaDome theater and hands-on science exhibits. The center also includes a six-acre environmental education area and nature trail.

Admission: adults $14.95, seniors & students $11.95, children 3-12 $10.95.

Wednesday-Thursday 10 a.m.-5 p.m., Friday-Saturday 10 a.m.-10 p.m., Sunday 11 a.m.-5 p.m.; call or visit the website for telescope viewing and holiday hours.

CHILDREN'S FAIRYLAND

Lakeside Park, 699 Bellevue Ave., Oakland, 510-452-2259; www.fairyland.org

This 10-acre park contains a child-sized fairyland, with tiny buildings depicting various fairy tales. Kids can play on sets of their favorite fairytales and stories. The grounds include a carousel, Ferris wheel, train and trolley rides, children's bumper boats and a puppet theater.

Admission: $7, children under 1 free. Hours change seasonally; check website for information.

JACK LONDON SQUARE

311 Broadway, Oakland; www.jacklondonsquare.com

This famous square is surrounded by Clay Street, Franklin Street, Embarcadero and the Oakland Estuary. Jack London lived and worked in this colorful waterfront area, spending most of his time writing his most famous novels in the still-operating Heinold's First and Last Chance Saloon at the foot of Webster Street. Several restaurants and the reconstructed cabin in which the author weathered the Klondike winter of 1898 reflect characters and situations from his life and books. Adjacent is Jack London Village at the foot of Alice Street, which has shops, restaurants and a marina area.

Daily.

JOAQUIN MILLER PARK

3300 Joaquin Miller Road, Oakland, 510-238-3187; www.oaklandnet.com

This 500-acre park contains the 68 acres of estate that once belonged to author Joaquin Miller, otherwise known as the "Poet of the Sierras." He had monuments built, some of which are on display, and managed the planting of 75,000 trees in an effort to create an artist's retreat. One of these structures is the Abbey, which was built in 1889 by Miller and today is a Registered National Historic Landmark. The park is also the site of Woodminster Amphitheater, the setting for the Woodminster Summer Musicals. There are hiking and picnic areas, community centers and the Sequoia Horse Arena.

Daily.

LAKESIDE PARK, LAKE MERRITT AND LAKE MERRIT WILDLIFE REFUGE

Bellevue and Grand avenues, Oakland, 510-238-2196; www.oaklandnet.com

Lakeside Park, located in downtown Oakland, welcomes visitors who come to see the many amenities this park has to offer including gardens, bandstands, a nature center, the Children's Fairyland and more. Within Lakeside Park is Lake Merritt, the largest city-bound natural body of saltwater in the world, surrounded by drives and handsome buildings. The Wildlife Refuge located here is North America's oldest wildlife refuge and is a National Historic Landmark. It features nature and conservation exhibits, a boating center with kayak rentals, tennis courts, a golf course, hiking and walking trails, and more.

Daily.

OAKLAND-ALAMEDA COUNTY COLISEUM

7000 Coliseum Way, Oakland, 510-569-2121; www.coliseum.com

Oakland's professional baseball team, the Athletics, otherwise known as the "A's," play ball in the Oakland-Alameda County Coliseum. It's also home to the professional football team, the Oakland Raiders. The A's have featured plenty of all-stars over the years including Tony LaRussa, Mark McGwire, Jose Conseco and Jason Giambi.

OAKLAND MUSEUM OF CALIFORNIA

1000 Oak St., Oakland, 510-238-2200; www.museumca.org

The only museum dedicated exclusively to California's history, art and natural sciences, the Gallery of California Art traces the work of California artists from the 1800s to today. The museum features several temporary exhibitions each year, ranging in subject matter from fashion to photography to archaeology.

Admission: adults $8, seniors and students $5, children under 6 free. Wednesday-Saturday 10 a.m.-5 p.m., Sunday noon-5 p.m.

OAKLAND ZOO

9777 Golf Links Road, Oakland, 510-632-9525; www.oaklandzoo.org

Situated on 525 acres, the zoo houses 440 native and exotic animals, a children's petting zoo and a lion habitat with a pride of six lions, along with an African Savannah filled with animals native to Africa, among much more. The zoo also includes rides for children and picnic areas.

Admission: adults $10.50, seniors and children 2-14 $7, children under 2 free. Daily 10 a.m.-4 p.m.

PARAMOUNT THEATRE

2025 Broadway, Oakland, 510-465-6400; www.paramounttheatre.com

This restored 1931 Art Deco movie palace, designed by architect Timothy L. Pflueger, is now home to the Oakland Ballet, the Oakland Symphony and a variety of musical performances.

Admission: $5. Tours take place the first and third Saturday of each month and start at 10 a.m. at the Box Office entrance. Box Office Hours: Tuesday-Friday 11 a.m.-5:30 p.m., Saturday 11 a.m.-3 p.m.

USS POTOMAC

Franklin D. Roosevelt Pier, Jack London Square, 540 Water St., Oakland, 510-627-1215; www.usspotomac.org

Once Franklin D. Roosevelt's "Floating White House" and now a fully restored, floating museum, the 165-foot steel vessel was built in 1934 as the Coast Guard cutter *Electra*. Take a narrated two-hour educational cruise around San Francisco Bay from May through November.

Dockside tours: Mid-January-mid-December, Wednesday, Friday, Sunday; groups by appointment only. Reservations are required for cruises; see website for information.

PALO ALTO
JUNIOR MUSEUM & ZOO
1451 Middlefield Road, Palo Alto, 650-329-2111; www.cityofpaloalto.org

The Palo Alto Junior Museum and Zoo features displays that encourage children's interest in art, science, history and anthropology through a variety of hands-on exhibits and workshops. The zoo features more than 50 exotic and native animals.

Admission: $3 (suggested donation). Tuesday-Saturday 10 a.m.-5 p.m., Sunday 1-4 p.m.

HOOVER TOWER
434 Serra Mall Stanford, Stanford, 650-723-2053; www.stanford.edu

Part of the Hoover Institution on War, Revolution and Peace research center, which was founded by President Herbert Hoover during World War I, the Hoover Tower is a landmark of Stanford University. Hoover was part of the graduating class at Stanford in 1895 and as an alumnus, he gave a gift to build and start this institution. Ride the elevator up to the 14th floor of this 250-foot tower for a panoramic view of campus and the peninsula from the carillon platform.

Admission: adults $2, seniors and children 12 and under $1. Daily 10 a.m.-4:30 p.m. (closed during finals and academic breaks).

STANFORD UNIVERSITY
450 Serra Mall, Stanford, 650-723-2300; www.stanford.edu

Located in the center of Silicon Valley, between San Francisco and San Jose, the world-renowned Stanford was founded in 1891 by Senator and Mrs. Leland Stanford in memory of their only son who died at 15 of typhoid fever. It is said that the Stanfords hoped that "the children of California shall be our children." Designed by Frederick Law Olmsted, Stanford has become one of the world's leading universities.

THOMAS WELTON STANFORD ART GALLERY
419 Lasuen Mall, Stanford, 650-723-2842; art.stanford.edu

This gallery is used as a venue for Stanford and Bay Area communities as well as a teaching resource for the Department of Art and Art History. Changing exhibits feature artwork from students in the M.F.A. program and focus on contemporary art.

Admission: Free. Tuesday-Friday 10 a.m.-5 p.m., Saturday-Sunday 1-5 p.m.

WINTER LODGE
3009 Middlefield Road, Palo Alto, 650-493-4566; www.winterlodge.com

The only outdoor ice rink in the U.S. located west of the Sierra Nevada Mountains, Winter Lodge offers daily public skate sessions as well as group lessons. There are also skate rentals and an outdoor picnic area. Check website for updated schedule information.

Admission: $8. Skate Rental: $3. Late September-mid-April, Monday 3-5 p.m.; Tuesday and Thursday 8-10 a.m., 3-5 p.m.; Wednesday and Friday 8-10 a.m., 3-5 p.m., 8-10 p.m.; Saturday 3-5 p.m., 8-10 p.m.; Sunday 3-5 p.m., 5:30-7:30 p.m.

SAN JOSE

ALUM ROCK PARK
16240 Alum Rock Ave., San Jose, 408-277-2757

These 720 acres are known as "Little Yosemite" and are named for a giant rock boulder once thought to be aluminum. You can go hiking, bicycling and riding on the many bridle trails. There are picnic grounds and a playground.
Daily.

CHILDREN'S DISCOVERY MUSEUM
180 Woz Way, San Jose, 408-298-5437; www.cdm.org

This museum's hands-on exhibits explore the relationships between the natural and created worlds and the people who live in them. Exhibits include "Streets," a 5/8-scale replica of an actual city, with streetlights, parking meters and fire hydrants, and "Waterworks," in which pumps and valves move water through a reservoir system.
Tuesday-Saturday 10 a.m.-5 p.m., Sunday noon-5 p.m.

HAPPY HOLLOW PARK & ZOO
1300 Senter Road, San Jose, 408-277-3000; www.happyhollowparkandzoo.org

Since 1961, this park within Kelley Park has been keeping kids and parents busy and happy. There's a new education center, animal care facility, retail shop, animal barn, new rides and exhibits, public art and a greener design.
Monday-Friday 10 a.m.-5 p.m., Saturday-Sunday 10 a.m.-6 p.m.; no admittance during last hour open.

JAPANTOWN SAN JOSE
Jackson and Sixth streets, San Jose, 408-298-4303; www.japantownsanjose.org

One of the few remaining urban districts of its kind to survive the Japanese internment during World War II, this district has a rich history that dates back to the first Japanese immigrants who settled here in 1900. Centered on the intersection of Sixth and Jackson streets, modern Japantown is home to a mix of businesses and merchants. The area includes an abundance of Asian groceries and eateries, art galleries, martial arts studios and gift shops, a number of which were first established in the early 1900s. On Sunday mornings, there is a farmers' market.

J. LOHR WINERY TASTING ROOM
1000 Lenzen Ave., San Jose, 408-288-5057; www.jlohr.com

Visit the home of J. Lohr wines, known for its chardonnay, cabernet sauvignon, syrah, white riesling, valdiguié and merlot. J. Lohr is committed to keeping their vineyards sustainable and organic. Stop by for a free tasting.
Tasting room: Daily 10 a.m.-5 p.m.

MUNICIPAL ROSE GARDEN
Naglee and Dana avenues, San Jose, www.sjparks.org

More than 4,000 rose plants take up these six acres, blooming in a rainbow of colors. The best time to visit the garden is in May when they're at full bloom. There are picnic areas and walking paths.
Daily. 8 a.m.-sunset.

OVERFELT GARDENS PARK

368 Educational Park Drive, San Jose, 408-251-3323; www.sjparks.org

This 33-acre botanical preserve includes extensive natural areas and wildflowers, a formal botanic garden and a wildlife sanctuary. Migratory waterfowl and other wildlife inhabit three lakes. The Chinese Cultural Garden has a bronze and marble statue of Confucius overlooking a reflecting pond, an ornate Chinese gate and three Chinese pavilions—all gifts from the Chinese community.

RAGING WATERS SAN JOSE

2333 S. White Road, San Jose, 408-238-9900; www.rwsplash.com

Stop by this park to cool off on a hot summer day with the kids. This water-themed amusement park has 23 acres of slides and attractions, including a 350,000-gallon wave pool.

Admission: adults $30.99, seniors and children under 48 inches $22.99. Adult prices may be lower online; visit the website for more information. Mid-June-late August, Daily; mid-May-mid-June, late August-September, Saturday-Sunday.

ROSICRUCIAN EGYPTIAN MUSEUM & PLANETARIUM

1664 Park Ave., San Jose, 408-947-3636; www.egyptianmuseum.org

This museum holds one of the largest collections of Egyptian antiques west of the Mississippi, including human and animal mummies, an exhibit on the Egyptian afterlife and a full-scale replica of a nobleman's tomb with images of daily life in the Nile Valley.

Admission: adults $9, students and seniors $7, children 5-10 $5 and children under 5 free. Monday-Friday 9 a.m.-5 p.m., Saturday-Sunday 11 a.m.-6 p.m.

SAN JOSE MUSEUM OF ART

110 S. Market St., San Jose, 408-271-6840; www.sjmusart.org

This downtown facility is best known for its permanent collection of contemporary works from the 20th and 21st centuries, with a focus on those by West Coast artists. Often edgy and abstract, these pieces run the gamut from oil paintings to room-sized installations and together comprise one of the top collections of modern art in the area, rivaling that of San Francisco's better-known MOMA. High-quality showcases for regional contemporary artists and high-concept, themed exhibitions dominate the calendar.

Admission: adults $8, students and seniors $5, children under 6 free. Tuesday-Sunday 11 a.m.-5 p.m.

THE TECH MUSEUM OF INNOVATION

201 S. Market St., San Jose, 408-294-8324; www.thetech.org

See how a microchip is made, design a roller coaster or make a movie in the Digital Studio at this 132,000-square-foot facility with 240 interactive exhibits. The Hackworth IMAX Theater, which has a dome that has become a landmark in the San Jose skyline, screens films in a larger-than-life setting with ground-breaking computer graphics and technology.

Admission: $8. Daily 10 a.m.-5 p.m.

WINCHESTER MYSTERY HOUSE
525 S. Winchester Blvd., San Jose, 408-247-2101; www.winchestermysteryhouse.com

Construction began on this architectural oddity in 1884 at the command of eccentric widow Sarah Winchester (of the Winchester Rifle family). Without the guidance of any overall blueprint, it went on until Winchester died in 1922. By then her home had grown to 160 rooms—with 47 fireplaces, 17 chimneys, 950 doors, staircases that go nowhere and cabinets that are the sole entry to entire wings. The grounds also feature two museums, including one dedicated to the Winchester Rifle, and extensive gardens.

Check website for hours and prices.

SANTA CLARA
GREAT AMERICA
4701 Great American Parkway, Santa Clara, 408-988-1776; www.cagreatamerica.com

This 100-acre park offers theme park thrills in an array of rides, live stage shows and entertainment for kids of all ages. Some of the most thrilling rides include the FireFall, where you're raised up to 60 feet and then taken on a 360-degree journey of twists, turns and spins through fire and water effects. There are also family rides, a Nickelodeon-themed playland with rides, and more.

Admission: adult $54.99, children and seniors $35.99. April-October, days and times vary; call or visit website for schedule.

INTEL MUSEUM
2200 Mission College Blvd., Santa Clara, 408-765-8080; www.intel.com/museum

Have you ever wondered how computer chips are made? Or how micro-processors work? If so, consider visiting this 10,000-square-foot museum, located in the main lobby of Intel's corporate headquarters. Surf the Internet or play computer games in the Application Lab, where a huge microprocessor simulates the brain of a computer.

Admission: Free. Monday-Friday 9 a.m.-6 p.m., Saturday 10 a.m.-5 p.m.

SANTA CRUZ
AÑO NUEVO STATE RESERVE
New Year's Creek Road, Highway 1, Pescadero, 650-879-0227; www.parks.ca.gov

This wild, windswept coastal reserve is where thousands of massive elephant seals come to mate and give birth each winter. You can experience this and the undeveloped area by making reservations for a guided walk (which is the only way to see this reserve).

Mid-December-March, daily 8 a.m.-sunset.

BARGETTO WINERY
3535 N. Main St., Soquel, 831-475-2258; www.bargetto.com

Located in the Santa Cruz Mountains, Bargetto Winery has been producing wines at this family vineyard since 1933. For $5, you can taste five wines and enjoy the scenic courtyard. Tours are available by appointment.

Daily noon-5 p.m.

BIG BASIN REDWOODS STATE PARK
Santa Cruz Mountains, 831-338-8860 www.bigbasin.org

Hikers and horseback riders congregate at one of the state's most popular parks—and its first redwood preserve—for 80 miles of trails over the 18,000 acres. Established in 1902, this state park is one of California's oldest and a great place to see wildlife in their natural habitat, from mountain lions to coyotes to quail and woodpeckers. There are also waterfalls and canyons. Waddell Creek, located within Big Basin, has a beach and is well-known as one of the best spots for windsurfing; however, due to the strong winds and often heavy surf, it's not recommended for the novice wind surfer.

Daily 6 a.m.-10 p.m.

MYSTERY SPOT
465 Mystery Spot Road, Santa Cruz, 831-423-8897; www.mysteryspot.com

Discovered in 1939, this 150-foot-long area defies conventional laws of gravity and perspective—it's where balls roll uphill and trees grow sideways. You have to see this mystery to believe it.

Admission: $5, children 3 and under free. Guided tours: Memorial Day-Labor Day, Daily 9 a.m.-7 p.m.; Labor Day-Memorial Day, Daily 10 a.m.-5 p.m.

NATURAL BRIDGES STATE BEACH
2531 W. Cliff Drive, Santa Cruz, 831-423-4609; www.parks.ca.gov

This state beach is well-known for its Monarch Grove, where more than 100,000 monarch butterflies migrate to each winter. The beach has a natural bridge (an ocean-formed sandstone arch) from where you can view sealife below. There are areas for fishing, picnicking and nature trails.

Daily 8 a.m.-sunset.

SANTA CRUZ BEACH BOARDWALK
400 Beach St., Santa Cruz, 831-423-5590; www.beachboardwalk.com

The town's emblem and the best and oldest remaining California beachside amusement park offers good old fashioned fun. Ride the 1920s-era Giant Dipper, a still-thrilling wooden rollercoaster, and take a whirl on the preserved carousel from 1911. Once you've maxed out on rides, air hockey and guilty-pleasure fair food like fried artichoke hearts (from nearby artichoke capital Castroville), kick back on the beach and watch the kites loop through the air. There is also a bowling alley, arcades, numerous restaurants and souvenir shops and a concert venue, Cocoanut Grove, which has been a cornerstone of the park since it opened. Annual events held here include a clam chowder cook-off in February and free Friday concerts during the summer.

Memorial Day-Labor Day.

SANTA CRUZ MISSION STATE HISTORICAL PARK
144 School St., Santa Cruz, 831-425-5849; www.parks.ca.gov

Constructed from 1822 and 1824, Casa Adobe (Neary-Rodriguez Adobe) is the only remaining building of the old Santa Cruz Mission. Located in downtown Santa Cruz, it's hard to miss.

Thursday-Sunday 10 a.m.-4 p.m.

SANTA CRUZ WHARF

Pacific Avenue and Beach Street, Santa Cruz, 831-420-5270;
www.santacruzparksandrec.com

One of few piers of this type to permit auto traffic, the Santa Cruz pier has plenty of restaurants, shops, fish markets and boat rentals. It's also a huddle spot for honking sea lions. From April to November, keep an eye out for the flashing flippers of a humpback. Beach Street turns into the two-mile West Cliff Drive, with cliffs on one side and stately Victorian mansions (many now bed and breakfasts) on the other.

SEACLIFF STATE BEACH

Highway 1, Santa Cruz, 831-685-6442; www.parks.ca.gov

This fishing pier leads to "The Cement Ship," (it's real name is the *Palo Alto*) which was purposely sunk here in 1929 to serve as an amusement center. This is a popular swimming beach, with seasonal lifeguards. You can fish off the pier, but because the ship is unsafe, it's closed to the public. There are picnicking areas and campsites.

Daily 8 a.m.-sunset.

WHERE TO STAY

BERKELEY

★★★THE CLAREMONT HOTEL CLUB & SPA

41 Tunnel Road, Berkeley, 510-843-3000, 800-551-7266; www.claremontresort.com

Set on 22 acres of lush gardens in Berkeley's Oakland Hills, this country retreat is only 12 miles from San Francisco and just a glance from a bay view. The hotel recently underwent a renovation that left the cheerful rooms stocked with down-duvet topped beds and flat-screen TVs. With two pools, 10 tennis courts, a comprehensive fitness center and a full-service spa, there's plenty to do. The resort's three restaurants turn out Pacific Rim and American dishes. The Meritage at the Claremont, a contemporary-casual dining room, offers a menu that focuses on food and wine pairings, while the Paragon Bar & Cafe has a café-style menu with amazing views of the San Francisco bay and live music four nights a week.

279 rooms. Restaurant, bar. Business center. Fitness center. Spa. Pets accepted. $251-350

HALF MOON BAY

★★★MILL ROSE INN

615 Mill St., Half Moon Bay, 650-726-8750, 800-900-7673; www.millroseinn.com

Just two blocks from the center of Half Moon Bay and many shops, restaurants and art galleries, this handsome inn's stylish interiors are matched by its well-manicured grounds and blooming gardens. Each room or suite has a private entrance, European antiques, a hand-painted fireplace, claw-foot tub, a complimentary stocked refrigerator, wireless Internet access and a Japanese dressing robe. A free gourmet breakfast is served daily, either in your room, in the dining room or outdoors in the garden courtyard. The morning meal features housemade breads, crêpes, omelets and quiche.

6 rooms. Complimentary breakfast. $251-350

★★★★THE RITZ-CARLTON, HALF MOON BAY

1 Miramontes Point Road, Half Moon Bay, 650-712-7000; www.ritzcarlton.com

From its cliff-top setting to its shingled architecture, this hotel looks like a slice of Scotland on the Northern California coast. While the windswept dunes and emerald links hint of a foreign land, this exquisite resort—only 30 miles from San Francisco—has a decidedly West Coast flavor. The guest rooms and suites are the essence of relaxed sophistication, with soft colors, floral or striped fabrics and nautical artwork. Golfers will develop a soft spot for the resort's 36 oceanfront holes, while others can go horseback riding on the secluded beach or play volleyball, basketball or croquet. Navio restaurant serves coastal California cuisine with fresh local seafood in a romantic setting. For a more casual atmosphere, try the Conservatory Lounge, which has floor-to-ceiling windows with ocean views. Or stop in ENO, a wine, chocolate and cheese cellar where you can get a flight of wine or cheese and try unique chocolates. Pets are welcome in the resort's guesthouses; they'll be spoiled with dog bones served on silver trays.

261 rooms. Restaurant, bar. Pool. Pets accepted. $351 and up

INVERNESS

★★★MANKA'S INVERNESS LODGE

30 Callendar Way, Inverness, 415-669-1034; www.mankas.com

Though a fire destroyed much of the main lodge and restaurant in 2006, the lodge was reopened and is as wonderfully quirky and rustic as ever. Surrounded by national park land, the old-time lodge sits in the hills above a small coastal village. Manka's is made up of three different properties offering unique types of lodging, from individual rooms in the main hunting and fishing lodge to cabins from the early 1900s to the luxurious Boathouse, sitting above Tomales Bay, with private bathrooms, a galley kitchen, a library and more. Regardless of where you stay, rooms are cozy and warm with comfortable bedding, fireplaces, deep reading chairs, oversized baths, and windows that have views of the bay or the woods. The restaurant features fresh seafood and other local ingredients.

18 rooms. Restaurant. Pets accepted. $251-350

LOS GATOS

★★★THE TOLL HOUSE HOTEL

140 S. Santa Cruz Ave., Los Gatos, 408-395-7070, 800-238-6111; www.tollhousehotel.com

Fine dining is within walking distance of this European-style hotel set among picturesque low hills. Spacious rooms are appointed with comfortable beds, complimentary Internet access, a choice of a daily paper and turndown service among other amenities. A business center features everything you would need to take care of work on the road. Three Degrees Restaurant and Bar provides a menu filled with local, organic fresh produce with seafood, chicken, pork chops, rib-eye, short ribs and more. The Sunday brunch prix fixe menu offers options such as blueberry white chocolate pancakes, a Cajun chicken omelet and corned beef hash. Enjoy your meal on the large outdoor patio.

115 rooms. Restaurant, bar. Business center. Fitness center. Pets accepted. $151-250

OAKLAND
★★★WATERFRONT PLAZA HOTEL
10 Washington St., Oakland, 510-836-3800, 800-729-3638, 888-842-5333;
www.waterfrontplaza.com

Having recently undergone a renovation in 2008, this hotel offers upgraded guestrooms, a new restaurant and more. Just a short ferry ride from San Francisco and blocks from shops and entertainment, the hotel sits in Jack London Square on the Oakland Harbor. Settle into a suite and take in the water views from a private balcony. The onsite restaurant, Miss Pearl's Jam House, features island cuisine (jerk chicken, sweet fried plantains) and Caribbean-inspired cocktails.

145 rooms. Restaurant, bar. Fitness center. Pool. $151-250

PALO ALTO
★★★DINAH'S GARDEN HOTEL
4261 El Camino Real, Palo Alto, 650-493-2844, 800-227-8220; www.dinahshotel.com

This tranquil oasis in the midst of Silicon Valley is richly appointed with 8 acres of gardens featuring lagoons, waterfalls and art sculptures. Guest rooms are decorated uniquely with influences from all over the world. For larger more private rooms, rent the Asian Sunset Signature Suite, which has two bedrooms, two and a half baths, a dining table as well as a kitchen with granite countertop, dishwasher, utensils and dishware. The hotel features two swimming pools, a fitness center with a sauna, and Trader Vic's restaurant, which has an international menu with Polynesian décor.

*148 rooms. Restaurant, bar. Complimentary breakfast. Business center. Fitness center. Pool.
$61-150*

★★★★FOUR SEASONS HOTEL SILICON VALLEY AT EAST PALO ALTO
2050 University Ave., East Palo Alto, 650-566-1200; www.fourseasons.com

Built in 2006, this 10-story, 190,000-square-foot luxury hotel's contemporary rooms have marble bathrooms with deep-soaking tubs, separate glass-enclosed showers, flat-screen TVs, DVD/CD players, a spacious work area with desk and floor-to-ceiling windows. Work out in the state-of-the-art fitness center—exercise machines have their own audiovisual monitors and wireless headsets—or pick up a map of nearby jogging and biking trails. Enjoy the rooftop pool and whirlpool and have lunch in a private poolside cabana with umbrellas and lounge chairs. You can even get some work done while by the pool—the area has a television, telephones and Internet access. Relax with a spa treatment at the full-service spa, which has seven treatment rooms. The hotel's contemporary dining room Quattro serves up Italian-influenced California cuisine and a wine list of international vintages. The sophisticated bar is the perfect place to have a cocktail. The contemporary spa has seven treatment rooms and offers everything from Thai massage to shiatsu.

200 rooms. Restaurant, bar. Business center. Fitness center. Pool. Spa. $351 and up

★★★GARDEN COURT HOTEL

520 Cowper St., Palo Alto, 650-322-9000, 800-824-9028; www.gardencourt.com

This hotel is located in the heart of Silicon Valley near Stanford University, shopping and restaurants. Sunlit rooms overlook a courtyard full of flowers and have four-poster beds, down comforters and Aveda bath products. Most guest rooms also feature either a whirlpool, fireplace, breakfast nook or private balcony. Complimentary coffee and tea and breakfast pastries are available each morning while port and cookies are put out each evening.

62 rooms. Complimentary breakfast. Fitness center. Pets accepted. $251-350

★★★SHERATON PALO ALTO HOTEL

625 El Camino Real, Palo Alto, 650-328-2800, 888-625-5144; www.sheraton.com

Surrounded by flower gardens, koi ponds and fountains, this resort-like hotel stands at the entrance to Stanford University, near the Stanford Shopping Center. Guest rooms have Sheraton Sweet Sleeper beds (and dog beds are available, too), bathrobes, flat-screen televisions, and generous workstations with ergonomic chairs. An outdoor heated pool, fitness facility and in-room massage treatments from the hotel's Thermae Spa, are available to aid in fitness and relaxation. The Cardinal Club Lounge is a great place to grab a cocktail, and the Poolside Grill serves a delicious breakfast buffet and a lunch and dinner menu with California cuisine.

346 rooms. Restaurant, bar. Complimentary breakfast. Business center. Fitness center. Pool. Pets accepted. $151-250

★★★THE WESTIN PALO ALTO

675 El Camino Real, Palo Alto, 650-321-4422, 800-937-8461; www.westin.com

Located near Stanford University, this contemporary hotel is spread over five Mediterranean-style buildings. Comfortable rooms have luxury bedding and bathrooms, as well as flat-screen televisions and iPod docking stations. Restaurant Soleil features Californian and Mediterranean cuisine and serves breakfast, lunch and dinner. Luna Lounge is a great spot to sip a martini after dinner. There is an outdoor heated pool and whirlpool to enjoy and a fitness center to get in a workout. Pick up a jogging map to take advantage of the surrounding Palo Alto area.

184 rooms. Restaurant, bar. Business center. Fitness center. Pool. Pets accepted. $151-250

SAN JOSE

★★★CROWNE PLAZA HOTEL

282 Almaden Blvd., San Jose, 408-998-0400, 800-972-3165; www.crowneplaza.com

Palm trees line the street in front of this downtown San Jose hotel situated across from the Center for the Performing Arts, the San Jose McEnery Convention Center, and the Tech Museum of Innovation. Modern guest rooms feature tones of crimson, beige and mahogany, and include flat-screen TVs and beds topped with fluffy pillows. The hotel is easily accessible to major freeways and approximately three miles from the airport.

239 rooms. Restaurant, bar. Business center. Fitness center. Pets accepted. $151-250

★★★THE FAIRMONT SAN JOSE

170 S. Market St., San Jose, 408-998-1900, 800-441-1414;
www.fairmont.com

This 20-story twin-tower complex has spacious accommodations, a well-equipped business center and an in-house spa. The four onsite restaurants offer something for every palate, from the Grill on the Alley's steaks and seafood to the Chinese dishes of Pagoda. The hotel's spa, Tova Day Spa, offers a variety of different treatments from massages to facials. Guests will also find an outdoor heated pool and a full 24-hour fitness center.
808 rooms. Restaurant, bar. Business center. Fitness center. Pool. Spa. Pets accepted. $151-250

★★★HILTON SAN JOSE

300 Almaden Blvd., San Jose, 408-287-2100, 800-774-1500;
www.sanjose.hilton.com

This hotel, which is connected to the McEnery Convention Center in downtown San Jose, rises 18 stories above the Silicon Valley. It is located minutes from the San Jose International Airport and multiple Fortune 500 companies. Rooms feature pillow-top mattresses, refrigerators and large desks. The City Bar and Grill serves reliable American cuisine.
354 rooms. Restaurant, bar. Business center. Fitness center. Pool. Pets accepted. $61-150

★★★HOTEL DE ANZA

233 W. Santa Clara St., San Jose, 408-286-1000, 800-843-3700;
www.hoteldeanza.com

This beautifully restored 1931 Art Deco hotel, listed on the National Register of Historic Places, has quirky, colorful rooms with amenities that include two TVs, CD and DVD players and large work desks. Fruit, cookies, coffee and bottled water are offered throughout the day. Restaurant options include the Hedley Club, a popular spot for cocktails and wine. La Pastaia Restaurant offers rustic Italian cuisine, suitable for a more romantic occasion.
Restaurant, bar. $251-350

★★★HOTEL VALENCIA SANTANA ROW

355 Santana Row, San Jose, 408-551-0010, 866-842-0100;
www.hotelvalencia.com

From the faux mink bed cover to the toiletries provided by California apothecary Lather, this hotel is made for those seeking high-tech luxury on the Row. Wireless Internet is accessible anywhere on the property and high-speed hook-ups are available at the room desks,

bedside and through large flat-screen TVs. Citrus specializes in steaks, while Vbar and Cielo Wine Terrace & Bar are among the most popular spots in town.
212 rooms. Restaurant, bar. Complimentary breakfast. Business center. Fitness center. Pool. Spa. $151-250

★★★THE SAINTE CLAIRE
302 S. Market St., San Jose, 408-295-2000; www.thesainteclaire.com

This National Historic Landmark in downtown San Jose has been restored to its 1926 elegance. The lobby features high ceilings, chandeliers and intricate, decorative woodwork, while spacious guest rooms offer many contemporary amenities. Beds are topped with multiple down pillows and thick duvets. Il Fornaio restaurant offers authentic Italian cuisine and serves freshly baked Italian artisan breads from its bakery, Panetteria.
170 rooms. Restaurant, bar. Business center. Fitness center. $151-250

★★★SAN JOSE MARRIOTT
301 S. Market St., San Jose, 408-280-1300, 800-314-0928; www.sanjosemarriott.com

Business travelers and vacationers will appreciate the Marriott San Jose's convenient downtown location in the heart of Silicon Valley. It is connected to the San Jose McEnery Convention Center, three miles from the San Jose International Airport, and in close proximity to area attractions. Vibrantly decorated guest rooms feature flat-screen TVs, work desks and beds with pillow-top mattresses and triple sheeting. Dine at chef Michael Mina's Arcadia, where you'll enjoy innovative American cuisine and top-notch wine. There's a heated outdoor pool and whirlpool as well as a full fitness center.
506 rooms. Restaurant, bar. Business center. Fitness room. Pool. $251-350

★★★SHERATON SAN JOSE HOTEL
1801 Barber Lane, Milpitas, 408-943-0600, 800-325-3535; www.starwoodhotels.com

Recently renovated, this hotel is a good choice for business travelers. This conveniently located hotel is situated just four miles from the San Jose International Airport in Milpitas. Request a room overlooking the pool's tropical courtyard, featuring gardens, waterfalls and palm trees. Mountain-view rooms and rooms with balconies are also offered. Whichever view you choose, rooms are outfitted with Internet access, the Sheraton Sweet Sleeper Bed, bathrobes, and flat-screen TVs.
229 rooms. Restaurant, bar. Business center. Fitness center. Pool. $61-150

SANTA CLARA
★★★HYATT REGENCY SANTA CLARA
5101 Great America Parkway, Santa Clara, 408-200-1234; www.santaclara.hyatt.com

This contemporary, sprawling hotel underwent a recent renovation that produced stylish rooms with Mid-Century modern furnishings, wireless Internet, flat-screen TVs and iPod docks. The resort-like outdoor pool and fitness center are just some of the onsite activities. Tresca, the hotel's main restaurant, features innovative American cuisine.
501 rooms. Restaurant, bar. Fitness center. Pool. $61-150

★★★SANTA CLARA MARRIOTT
2700 Mission College Blvd., Santa Clara, 408-988-1500, 800-228-9290; www.marriott.com

This recently renovated hotel has rooms with wireless Internet access, flat-screen TVs and private balconies. Parcel 104, the onsite restaurant that is under the direction of chefs Bradley Ogden and Robert Sapirman, is a local favorite for fresh, seasonally inspired California cuisine. The large patio and fire-pit make for comfortable outdoor dining in warm weather. The hotel's fitness center is stocked with cutting-edge equipment, and the grounds include a palm-tree lined outdoor pool.

748 rooms. Restaurant, bar. Fitness center. $151-250

SANTA CRUZ
★★★CHAMINADE
1 Chaminade Lane, Santa Cruz, 831-475-5600, 800-283-6569; www.chaminade.com

This beautiful contemporary Spanish mission-style hotel sits on a mountain ridge and offers guests panoramic views of Monterey Bay. Rooms are bright and stylish with plush down duvets, microfiber bathrobes and granite bathrooms. Guests choosing to stay on the grounds can opt for a relaxing spa treatment or a dip in the heated pool, a game of tennis, volleyball or badminton, or a workout in the fitness center. End the day with a meal at one of the two onsite restaurants. Sunset features beautiful views and buffets and a Sunday champagne brunch. Linwood's Bar and Grill serves California cuisine with a colorful dining room, fireplace and outdoor patio.

156 rooms. Restaurant, bar. Fitness center. Pool. Spa. $251-350

RECOMMENDED

BERKELEY
HOTEL DURANT
2600 Durant Ave., Berkeley, 510-845-8981; www.jdvhotels.com

This green-certified boutique hotel underwent a major renovation in 2008. With its Spanish Mediterranean architecture and decor, it offers not only comfortable guest rooms, but also luxurious amenities and a prime location. Each room has organic bathrobes, 300-thread count linens, 37- or 42-inch flat-screen televisions, an honor bar and complimentary Internet access.

144 rooms. Restaurant, bar. Business center. Pets accepted. $151-250

INVERNESS
BLACKTHORNE INN
266 Vallejo Ave., Inverness, 415-663-8621; www.blackthorneinn.com

Located in a wooded canyon, this rustic inn resembles a tree house with four levels of decks. Each room is individually decorated; stays come with breakfast served from a large buffet each morning.

5 rooms. Complimentary breakfast. $251-350

OLEMA INN

10000 Sir Francis Drake Blvd., Olema, 415-663-9559; www.theolemainn.com

This country inn was built in 1876 and is loaded with antiques. Rooms feature down comforters, Ralph Lauren linens and antique furniture. The onsite restaurant serves local, organic and sustainable ingredients, including oysters, mussels, sea bass, halibut, duck breast and New York steak. The wine list features unique wines from surrounding wineries.

6 rooms. Restaurant, bar. Complimentary breakfast Pets accepted. $151-250

SANTA CRUZ
DREAM INN SANTA CRUZ

175 W. Cliff Drive, Santa Cruz, 831-426-4330, 800-716-6199; www.dreaminnsantacruz.com

Renovated in 2008, this contemporary hotel is the only beachfront hotel along the Santa Cruz Monterey Bay coastline and overlooks the Santa Cruz Beach Boardwalk. Each room has a private balcony or patio, flat-screen TV, iPod docking station and bathrobes. Guests can walk to the beach or enjoy the outdoor heated pool.

165 rooms. Restaurant, bar. Business center. Pool. Beach. $151-250

WHERE TO EAT

BERKELEY
★★★CHEZ PANISSE AND CAFÉ

1517 Shattuck Ave., Berkeley, 510-548-5525; www.chezpanisse.com

Chez Panisse is celebrity chef Alice Waters' finest creation, and one of the best arguments anywhere for relying on organic, locally grown meat and produce. The charming, long-standing restaurant pioneered the farm-to-table movement, with an ever-changing menu of Mediterranean dishes that make the most of whatever is in season. A casual upstairs café serves an à la carte menu. Make reservations several weeks in advance for the prix fixe menu offered in the formal downstairs dining area.

American, Mediterranean. Lunch, dinner. Closed Sunday. Reservations recommended. $36-85

★★★SKATES ON THE BAY

100 Seawall Drive, Berkeley, 510-549-1900; www.skatesonthebay.com

From two levels of tables, you can sample creative California cuisine paired with stellar views through large picture windows that frame the bay, Golden Gate Bridge, Bay Bridge and San Francisco skyline. The menu features steaks, seafood and fresh oysters, and the extensive wine list includes flights. Take a seat at the bar for happy hour and try the Smoky Martini, made with vodka and garnished with a slice of pepperoni and a blue cheese-stuffed olive.

Steak, seafood. Lunch (Monday-Friday), dinner, Saturday-Sunday brunch. Reservations recommended. Children's menu. Bar. $36-85

HALF MOON BAY
★★★CETRELLA BISTRO & CAFÉ

845 Main St., Half Moon Bay, 650-726-4090; www.cetrella.com

With a dedication to fresh, local and seasonal ingredients, this restaurant serves flavorful yet simple Mediterranean-inspired food. Executive chef Sylvain Montassier confidently creates dishes such as wood-oven baked grouper with wild mushroom rice and broth, or honey-glazed Berkshire pork chop with brussels sprouts fricassée, lentils and bacon broth. With over 400 wines to choose from, the friendly staff can suggest the perfect wine to accompany your meal.

Mediterranean. Dinner, Sunday brunch. Closed January-April. $36-85

★★★NAVIO
The Ritz-Carlton, Half Moon Bay, 1 Miramontes Point Road, Half Moon Bay, 650-712-7000; www.ritzcarlton.com

A classic and romantic dining room with views of the ocean, this restaurant inside the Ritz-Carlton, Half Moon Bay serves California cuisine with a focus on fresh seafood. In order to provide the freshest catch, the menu changes daily. Dishes may include local butterfish with braised shiitake mushrooms, baby bok choy and shiitake broth; crispy salmon with melted cabbage, caramelized apples and fried celery root; or herb roasted beef tenderloin with Yukon Gold potato gratin, spinach, oyster mushrooms and red wine sauce. The Sunday brunch is a local favorite.

American, seafood. Breakfast, lunch, dinner, Sunday brunch. $36-85

INVERNESS
★★★MANKA'S INVERNESS LODGE
30 Callendar Way, Inverness, 415-669-1034; www.mankas.com

Strictly devoted to fresh, local ingredients, the kitchen creates simple California cuisine, with dishes that change nightly but may include lamb grilled in the fireplace and served with duck confit hash. On weekends, a five- or seven- course prix fixe menu is offered; the rest of the week, you can choose a la carte dishes from the menu as well.

California. Dinner. $36-85

LOS GATOS
★★★★MANRESA
320 Village Lane, Los Gatos, 408-354-4330; www.manresarestaurant.com

This intimate restaurant is the showcase for chef David Kinch's daring and inventive French- and northern Spanish-influenced cuisine, which is heavy on local ingredients, many from an exclusive garden in the Santa Cruz Mountains. The exquisitely presented dishes are served in a provincial dining room. Guests may choose a three- or four-course meal or the tasting menu. Dishes might include mussels braised in butter, avocado and smoked bread, roasted monkfish with braised pearl onions with bone marrow and light chervil cream, and beef short ribs with roasted shallots. Desserts such as cherry blossom mousse with toasted almond meringue kisses, chicory ice cream and rhubarb consommé make for an exquisite finish.

French. Dinner. Closed Monday-Tuesday. Bar. $86 and up

MOUNTAIN VIEW
★★★CHEZ TJ
938 Villa St., Mountain View, 650-964-7466; www.cheztj.com

Once the residence of a town council member, this green-painted Victorian-style house is now home to fans of fine dining looking for upscale California cuisine in an intimate atmosphere. Chez TJ supports local farms and producers, getting much of their ingredients at local markets to create dishes such as milk-fed veal tenderloin with crispy sweetbread, sweet onions and butter lettuce jus, and duck breast with a foie gras tartine and green tomato jam. The wine list boasts the bounty of Mountain View's neighboring vineyards, with each selection carefully chosen to pair with dishes on the menu.

American. Dinner. Closed Sunday-Monday. Reservations recommended. $86 and up

OAKLAND
★★★BAY WOLF
3853 Piedmont Ave., Oakland, 510-655-6004; www.baywolf.com

Thriving since 1975 in an early 1900s Victorian, Bay Wolf serves food influenced by the food of Tuscany, Provence and the Basque country with a California twist. Dine on the heated veranda or in one of two small dining rooms. The menu changes regularly but may include salt-baked duck breast, housemade herbed ravioli with spring vegetables and wild mushroom broth, or cumin-crusted roasted rack of pork with grilled asparagus and sherry. The wine list also features regional wines from the Mediterranean.

American, Mediterranean. Lunch, dinner. Reservations recommended. Outdoor seating. Bar. $16-35

★★★OLIVETO CAFÉ & RESTAURANT
5655 College Ave., Oakland, 510-547-5356; www.oliveto.com

Known for its authentic Italian cuisine, Oliveto specializes in organic housemade pastas, and serves fresh-milled corn polenta, a selection of housemade salumi and fresh baked desserts and pastries. The menu changes almost daily, but you'll find dishes such as pappardelle with braised rabbit; ravioli filled with wild nettles, green garlic and new potatoes; fresh-milled polenta with spring vegetables and chanterelle mushrooms; spit-roasted leg of lamb with fried asparagus and young onions; and wild striped bass with spinach, potatoes and artichoke-Moroccan olive relish. The simple and sleek restaurant showcases artwork from local artists, while garden flowers and plenty of windows bring the outdoors in. A downstairs café is available for more casual dining.

Italian. Lunch (Monday-Friday), dinner. Bar. $36-85

PALO ALTO

★★★EVVIA ESTIATORIO

420 Emerson St., Palo Alto, 650-326-0983; www.evvia.net

A roaring fireplace, handmade pottery, copper pots and pans, and an open kitchen give this Greek restaurant a warm, rustic feel. The menu focuses on classic Greek dishes such as saganaki, moussaka and souvlaki. Other entrées include braised lamb shank with aromatic spices on orzo and myzithra cheese; and lemon-oregano chicken with roasted sweet onions and potatoes. For dessert, there's traditional baklava to enjoy with a shot of strong Greek coffee. Dishes are made with fresh and seasonal local ingredients.

Greek. Lunch (Monday-Friday), dinner. Bar. $36-85

★★★TAMARINE

546 University Ave., Palo Alto, 650-325-8500; www.tamarinerestaurant.com

Small plates are the standard at this contemporary, vegetarian-friendly Vietnamese restaurant, which encourages sharing. Entrées such as seared scallops with green curry and lemongrass bass are mixed with a choice of seven different types of rice, from jasmine to coconut to black and short grain rice with citrus butter. Specialty cocktails, including the signature mojito with mango and a ginger mint martini, are crowd pleasers. Designed by a top design firm, the walls of the restaurant are covered in rich colors and fine art from Vietnam. Emerging artists from Vietnam exhibit their artwork in the restaurant's gallery.

Vietnamese. Lunch, dinner. Reservations recommended. Bar. $16-35

★★★★THE VILLAGE PUB

2967 Woodside Road, Woodside, 650-851-9888; www.thevillagepub.net

About 30 minutes from San Francisco and San Jose, this upscale pub emphasizes the use of local artisanal and organic ingredients, including produce cultivated at the restaurant's partner farm in the nearby Santa Cruz Mountains. The two dining rooms are quaint and charming, and there is an outdoor veranda for private parties. The seasonal menus feature contemporary American dishes with French and Mediterranean influences such as bacon wrapped trout with braised sauerkraut and riesling butter sauce; and seared duck breast with huckleberry duck jus, braised leeks and scarlet turnips. Diners craving more traditional pub fare will find burgers, steaks and fries. Desserts feature decadent options such as walnut cake with mascarpone mousse and fruit; and opera cake with mocha buttercream and chocolate ganache. The ample wine list includes a number of reasonably priced selections along with half-bottles and a variety of by-the-glass options.

American. Lunch (Monday-Friday), dinner. Reservations recommended. Bar. $36-85

SAN JOSE

★★★EMILE'S

545 S. Second St., San Jose, 408-289-1960; www.emilesrestaurant.com

Emile's has served European-influenced Californian cuisine since 1973. Hand-sculpted brass work and fresh flowers on every table complement the cuisine at this San Jose fixture. Choose a dish from the a la carte menu, the tasting menu or a three-course prix fixe menu. You'll enjoy items such as sautéed veal medallions with morel mushroom sauce; and scallops, lobster and prawns in a lobster sauce served in a puff pastry shell along with fresh vegetables. Desserts include rhubarb soufflé, warm apple tart with caramel sauce and pistachio ice cream, as well as house-made sorbets.

French. Dinner. Closed Sunday-Monday. Bar. $16-35

★★★LA PASTAIA

Hotel De Anza, 233 W. Santa Clara St., San Jose, 408-286-8686; www.lapastaia.com

Located within the downtown Hotel De Anza, La Pastaia serves contemporary, rustic Italian dishes. The charming dining room features a fireplace, Italian posters and colorful tiled floors. Appetizers include salumi, grilled portobello mushrooms and calamari. The dinner menu features dishes such as chicken breast sautéed with chestnuts, and dried figs with soft polenta. The lunch menu also includes tasty panini.

Lunch, dinner. Outdoor seating. $16-35

RECOMMENDED

BERKELEY

AJANTA

1888 Solano Ave., Berkeley, 510-526-4373; www.ajantarestaurant.com

With a menu that constantly changes, there is always something new to try at this green-certified restaurant. The kitchen offers a prix fixe menu for both lunch and dinner. A meal arrives with plenty of accompaniments, including naan, mango chutney and basmati rice. Dishes are creative and come from a variety of regions in India; the artwork that adorns the walls was inspired by caves in Ajanta.

Indian. Lunch, dinner. Reservations recommended. $16-35

CAFÉ ROUGE

1782 Fourth St., Berkeley, 510-525-1440; www.caferouge.net

Cafe Rouge features a meat market and oyster bar, so it's no surprise that the menu here focuses on fresh organic meats and housemade charcuterie. The menu changes every two weeks, with dishes such as grilled flat-iron steak with marble potatoes, and the half-pound Rouge burger with fries making regular appearances.

Mediterranean, American. Lunch, dinner (Tuesday-Sunday), Sunday. brunch. Outdoor seating. Bar. $35-85

CÉSAR

1515 Shattuck Ave., Berkeley, 510-883-02222; www.barcesar.com

Located in the "gourmet ghetto" of Berkeley, César serves fresh Spanish tapas, and offers an extensive list of wines, beers and spirits. Chef Maggie Pond continues to travel through Spain every year to find new ingredients and recipes to bring back to incorporate into her menu. A few of the most popular dishes are salt cod and potato; toasted palacios ham and cheese sandwich; and to complete the meal, bread pudding with orange-caramel sauce.

Spanish. Lunch, dinner, late night. Outdoor seating. Bar. $16-35

HENRY'S PUB

Hotel Durant, 2600 Durant Ave., Berkeley, 510-809-4132; www.henrysberkeley.com

Although this is a gastropub, you won't find typical bar food here. The menu is inspired by chef Eddie Blyden's childhood in West Africa, and his formal training from New York to Switzerland and the British West Indies. He also follows the slow-food movement, using locally grown produce and organic, free-range meats. The addicting fare includes spiced lemongrass-garlic frites with aromatic mayo, lamb sliders with roasted red peppers, olive tapenade and harissa aioli, and housemade BBQ wings with herbed sour cream.

International. Breakfast, lunch, dinner, late-night, Saturday-Sunday brunch. Bar. $15 and under

LALIME'S

1329 Gilman St., Berkeley, 510-527-9838; www.lalimes.com

This two-level restaurant housed in a cottage serves organically produced fruits and vegetables from local farmers. Chef Brian White's menu features tasty options such as halibut with mushroom vinaigrette and buttermilk mashed potatoes, and roasted rack of lamb with onion marmalade, beet green pesto and spiced yogurt. Special event meals include menus crafted with wines or beers.

American, Mediterranean. Dinner. Bar. $36-85

O CHAMÉ

1830 Fourth St., Berkeley, 510-841-8783

For those who enjoy Japanese fare, O Chamé combines a subtle Californian influence that's just right. A popular dish is the udon noodles with a choice of topping, from Monterey squid to pork tenderloin to grilled grouper. The menu is paired with an extensive wine list and plenty of sake options.

Japanese. Lunch, dinner. Outdoor seating. $16-35

HALF MOON BAY
HALF MOON BAY BREWING COMPANY

390 Capistrano Road, Half Moon Bay, 650-728-2739; www.hmbbrewingco.com

This oceanfront restaurant and brewing company is located about four miles north of Half Moon Bay on Pillar Point Harbor in Princeton-by-the-Sea. The restaurant and brewpub features ocean views, live music and dancing. It also serves sustainable seafood, like a Portuguese fisherman's stew with fish, shellfish and linguica simmering in a garlic broth. The eight brews are tasty and refreshing with a light ale, amber ale, hefeweizen, and more.

American. Lunch, dinner. Outdoor seating. $16-35

OAKLAND
SCOTT'S SEAFOOD

2 Broadway, Oakland, 510-444-3456; www.scottseastbay.com

Located in the center of Jack London Square, the menu here features fresh seafood such as Dungeness crab, ahi tuna, swordfish, halibut, grilled sole, baked scallops and vegetable risotto. Stop in on Sunday for the New Orleans-inspired champagne jazz brunch, when you can sit outside and listen to a live jazz trio.

Seafood. Lunch, dinner, Sunday brunch. Outdoor seating. Bar. $16-35

SAN JOSE
O'FLAHERTY'S IRISH PUB
25 N. San Pedro St., San Jose, 408-947-8007; www.oflahertyspub.com

If you're looking for a traditional Irish pub experience, head to this spot near downtown San Jose. Fish and chips, chowder, and tasty sandwiches and salads grace the menu, and traditional, live Irish music provides entertainment on Tuesdays and Saturdays. Enjoy your meal with a refreshing Guinness, Smithwick's, Bass or Harp.

Irish. Lunch (Monday-Friday), dinner, late-night. Outdoor seating. Bar. $16-35

SPAS

HALF MOON BAY
★★★★THE RITZ-CARLTON SPA, HALF-MOON BAY
The Ritz-Carlton, Half Moon Bay, 1 Miramontes Point Road, Half Moon Bay, 650-712-7040, 800-241-3333; www.ritzcarlton.com

Golfers will be taken in by the 36-hole oceanfront course at this resort, but its 16,000-square-foot spa is equally impressive. Wind down with a co-ed, candlelit Roman mineral bath, lounge in the oceanfront Jacuzzi or enjoy the steam and sauna facilities. The signature pumpkin body peel delivers the nourishing benefits of this local treat. The well-equipped fitness center overlooks the ocean and the gazebo lawn, which also includes a heated yoga studio or you can take a pilates class, water aerobics or Tai-Chi.

WHERE TO SHOP

BERKELEY
AMOEBA RECORDS
2455 Telegraph Ave., Berkeley, 510-549-1125; www.amoeba.com

Since it opened in 1990, this independent record shop has offered music lovers an array of tunes from top 40 to indie rock, underground rock and hip-hop, world music and much more. Since then, Amoeba has opened stores in San Francisco and Hollywood. With new and used music filling the racks, you can find pretty much anything you want to listen to. Unlike larger music chains, Amoeba focuses on creating a community for independent musicians and music lovers. Located on Telegraph Avenue, Amoeba is at the center of free-spirited Berkeley.

Monday-Saturday 10:30 a.m.-10 p.m., Sunday 11 a.m.-9 p.m.

BERKELEY FARMERS' MARKETS
Center Street and Martin Luther King Jr. Way, Berkeley, 510-548-3333; www.ecologycenter.org

At this pair of outstanding farmers' markets, held year-round on Tuesday, Thursday (all organic) and Saturday, local farmers and chefs set up booths vending a far-flung range of delicacies, including olives, avocados, coffee beans and vegan Mexican food, along with baked goods, jams, plants and flowers. More than half the markets' produce is organically grown. Musicians often provide entertainment; food and social justice activists are usually in attendance as well.

Saturday 10 a.m-3 p.m., Tuesday 2-7 p.m., Thursday 3-7 p.m.

LOS GATOS

FARMER'S MARKET

Town Plaza Park, North Santa Cruz Avenue and Main Street, Los Gatos; www.losgatosca.gov

Purchase organic and non-organic produce, specialty foods and fresh flowers from local farmers at this market. There are usually plenty of foods to sample as you browse. The market takes place rain or shine.

April-December, Sunday 8 a.m.-noon; January-March, Sunday 9 a.m.-noon.

PALO ALTO

STANFORD SHOPPING CENTER

680 Stanford Shopping Center, Palo Alto, 650-617-8200; www.stanfordshop.com

One of the largest malls in Northern California, this open-air facility is home to more than 140 tenants, including top-tier department stores Bloomingdales and Nordstrom, and a variety of restaurants and specialty stores—including an upscale supermarket, an open-air farmers' market and several cafés and bakeries. In summer, come on Thursday evenings for a jazz concert series.

Monday-Friday 10 a.m.-8 p.m., Saturday 10 a.m.-7 p.m., Sunday 11 a.m.-6 p.m.

SAN JOSE

SAN JOSE FARMERS' MARKET

San Pedro Square, San Pedro St., San Jose, 408-279-1775; www.sjdowntown.com

From late May to December, head to San Pedro Square in downtown San Jose on Fridays to shop for local produce, fresh flowers and gourmet foods, and enjoy cooking demonstrations and musical performances. Among the special events is the twice-monthly Chef at the Market event, where a popular local chef prepares a dish for all to sample.

May-December, Friday 10 a.m.-2 p.m.

SAN JOSE FLEA MARKET

1590 Berryessa Road, San Jose, 408-453-1110; www.sjfm.com

Flying in the face of Silicon Valley's high-tech reputation, the San Jose Flea Market is a decidedly low-tech spectacle. The largest open-air market in the nation, it encompasses 120 acres and eight miles of retail-laden pathways. Founded in 1960 by a landfill operator who saw too may good items going to waste, the market now attracts more than 4 million visitors a year to its shops, carts, restaurants and other attractions. The quarter-mile long Produce Row overflows with fresh fruits and vegetables; there's also a carousel, arcade, two playgrounds and street musicians.

Wednesday-Sunday sunrise-sunset.

SANTANA ROW

3055 Olin Ave., San Jose, 408-551-4611; www.santanarow.com

Visit this upscale shopping center adjacent to the Hotel Valencia to take advantage of brand stores including Diesel and Gucci, as well as mall staples like Crate & Barrel and Borders Books and Music. There's also a fitness center, day spas, a movie theater, restaurants and an open-air café that regularly draw in the residents of Santana Row's lofts and townhomes.

Monday-Saturday 10 a.m.-9 p.m., Sunday 11 a.m.-7 p.m.

WEST SAN CARLOS STREET ANTIQUE ROW

West San Carlos Street and Bascom Avenue, San Jose, 408-947-8711;
www.sancarlosstreet.com

This 15-block stretch of West San Carlos Street has one of the highest concentrations of antique shops on the Pacific Coast. The selection runs the gamut from European crystal to African art to Western Americana. There are multidealer collectives among the shops, including **Laurelwood Antiques** *(1824 W. San Carlos St.)*, **Briarwood Antiques & Collectibles** *(1885 W. San Carlos St.)* and **Antiques Colony** *(1915 W. San Carlos St.)*. A number of resale shops are packed with vintage and almost new clothing and décor, and there are also a few standard thrift stores.

Hours vary.

NAPA VALLEY

It doesn't matter if you're a serious connoisseur or don't know the difference between a burgundy and a brut; both types of people populate the Napa Valley's tasting rooms to sniff, swirl and sip their way through this bucolic countryside before retiring to one of the top-notch restaurants at night for even more wine and mouthwatering cuisine. That's Napa—and from a purely decadent point of view, it simply can't be beat. With more than 200 wineries, Napa is one of the most famous wine regions in the world. You'll find all the major names in the business here—Mondavi, Krug, Beringer. There are the large estates that look like they were transported from Italy, but there are also the smaller, less grand wineries that many visitors love to seek out, and that throw open their doors to guests. On the other hand, a few places keep them tightly shut, sealing in their "cult" status. It's a large, varied wine country (and not just in terms of soil), with much to see and taste.

Several small towns actually make up what everyone simply refers to as "Napa." The Napa Valley is about 30 miles long and includes the towns (from north to south) of Calistoga, St. Helena, Rutherford, Oakville, Yountville and Napa. Each has its particular charm. Calistoga has spas and hideaway hotels; St. Helena is full of shops; Yountville is something of a culinary mecca, lined with exceptional restaurants. Add to this the magnificent beauty of the place, and you'll want to make trip after trip to this wine capital.

WHAT TO SEE

CALISTOGA

CA'TOGA GALLERIA D'ARTE

1206 Cedar St. (just off Lincoln Avenue), Calistoga, 707-942-3900; www.catoga.com

See the works of Italian muralist Carlo Marchiori, which include ceramics, tiles, paintings, sculptures and furniture in Neo-Classical and Baroque styles, at his beautiful estate, which is a replica of a Palladian-style home, a style seen in Veneto, Italy. There's also a nice selection of gift and design items.

Thursday-Monday.

CALISTOGA INN RESTAURANT AND BREWERY
1250 Lincoln Ave., Calistoga, 707-942-4101; www.calistogainn.com

Indulge your inner rebel and visit the first company to begin brewing beer commercially in Napa since Prohibition. With a full-time brewmaster, the facility creates award-winning beers and ales while limiting production to 450 barrels a year. Most of it is served on draft at the adjacent Calistoga Inn, where you'll find a restaurant, English-style pub and beer garden. On weekends, hit the pub for rhythm-and-blues bands and come back Wednesdays for open mic night. During the high season, live jazz guitar is played every night out on the patio.

Monday-Friday 11:30 a.m.-9:30 p.m., Saturday-Sunday 11:00 a.m.-10 p.m.

MADRIGAL VINEYARDS
3718 North St. Helena Highway, Calistoga, 707-942-6577;www.madrigalvineyards.com

Since the 1930's, the Madrigal family has harvested grapes in the Napa Valley, and in 1995 they put that experience to good use, opening Madrigal Vineyards in the historic Larkmead District. If you're a fan of petite sirah, this is the place to pick up a bottle. The bold fruit flavor and rich, smooth finish keeps those in the know coming back year after year. Tour guides are friendly and the small-vineyard atmosphere is casual and welcoming; an ideal stop for wine country novices.

Daily 10 a.m.-4 p.m., by appointment.

MOUNT ST. HELENA
Highway 29, Calistoga 707-942-4575; www.parks.ca.gov

Broke, ill and newly married, Scottish author Robert Louis Stevenson honey-mooned on the slopes of this extinct volcano in 1880. Bring a copy of *The Silverado Squatters*, Stevenson's travel memoir describing those two memorable months, and hike to the nearby Silverado Mine. The five-mile hike up Mount St. Helena is not easy, but is certainly worth the view from the top; on clear days, you might be able to see Mount Shasta, which is 192 miles away. The trail begins in Robert Louis Stevenson State Park and takes you through the forest at first, and then a steep uphill climb over rock, trees and bushes.

Daily sunrise-sunset.

OLD FAITHFUL GEYSER OF CALIFORNIA
1299 Tubbs Lane, Calistoga, 707-942-6463; www.oldfaithfulgeyser.com

It's safe to expect a show from Old Faithful, one of only three regularly erupting geysers in the world. Nearly every half-hour—for about three minutes each time—a towering plume ascends from the source, unless an earthquake disrupts the geyser's timing. An underground river boils up to 350 degrees Fahrenheit, causing vapor and steam to escape to heights of 60 to 100 feet.

Admission: adults $10, seniors $7, children 6-12 $3, children 5 and under free. Daily 9 a.m.-5 p.m., until 6 p.m. in summer months.

THE PETRIFIED FOREST
4100 Petrified Forest Road, Calistoga, 707-942-6667; www.petrifiedforest.org

Some three million years ago, a volcanic eruption turned a forest of giant redwoods into solid quartz and stone. Discovered in 1857, these preserved trees offer insight into geological formations and give visitors a glimpse of a

BEST ATTRACTIONS

WHAT ARE THE TOP THINGS TO DO IN THE NAPA VALLEY?

HIKE MOUNT ST. HELENA
The five-mile hike up Mount St. Helena is not easy, but is certainly worth the view from the top; on clear days, you might be able to see Mount Shasta, which is 192 miles away.

CHECK OUT THE OLD FAITHFUL GEYSER
Nearly every half-hour, a towering plume ascends from the source when an underground river boils up to 350 degrees Fahrenheit, causing vapor and steam to escape to heights of 60 to 100 feet.

GO WINE TASTING
You can't come to Wine Country without visiting the numerous wineries and vineyards. You'll find everything from large wineries with popular tasting rooms to small, by-appointment-only tasting facilities.

prehistoric world. You can also take a guided meadow walk to learn more about the volcanic activity, among oak, douglas fir, madrone and manzanita trees, wildflowers and views of Mount St. Helena. In 1880, Robert Louis Stevenson wrote about his visit here in his book *The Silverado Squatters*.

Admission: adults $8, seniors $6, children 12-17 $6, children 6-11 $3, children 5 and under free. Daily 9 a.m.-5 p.m., until 7 p.m. in summer months. Meadow walk tours: Sunday 11 a.m., weather permitting.

ROBERT LOUIS STEVENSON STATE PARK
Highway 29, Calistoga, 707-942-4575; www.parks.ca.gov
Commemorating the famous author who spent his 1880 honeymoon here, the park provides a rugged respite from the wine crowds. Little of the 3,600 acres are developed, but there is a good, five-mile trail up to the summit of Mount St. Helena, an extinct volcano and the highest peak in the Napa Valley at 4,343 feet. On the way up to the top, look for the marker identifying the site of the bunkhouse of the abandoned Silverado Mine, where Stevenson and his bride, Fanny Osbourne, slept.
Daily dawn-dusk.

SCHRAMSBERG VINEYARDS
1400 Schramsberg Road, Calistoga, 707-942-4558; www.schramsberg.com
Lauded as "America's first house of sparkling wine," Schramsberg is one of Napa's oldest vineyards and a mandatory stop for anyone who enjoys a glass

of bubbly. Visitors are immediately wooed by the elaborate gardens surrounding the 19th-century home of the winery's founder, Jacob Schram. But the real treat comes on the tour, as enthusiastic guides take you through caves hand-dug by Chinese laborers in the late 19th century, revealing a collection of nearly two million bottles. The tour fee includes a sampling of three sparkling wines and one still variety (opt for the cabernet sauvignon, if available). A food and wine tour was also recently added which offers a tasting of five small plates with sparkling wine or cabernet sauvignon.

Tours: 10 a.m., 11:30 a.m., 12:30 p.m., 1:30 p.m. and 2:30 p.m. Food and wine tour: Tuesday-Thursday noon. Reservations required. No children permitted.

STERLING VINEYARDS
1111 Dunaweal Lane, Calistoga, 707-942-3344, 800-726-6136; www.sterlingvineyards.com

Take the aerial tramway up to Sterling Vineyards for the view and stay for the wine. In a whitewashed building modeled after villages on the Greek island of Mykonos, these vineyards helped establish chardonnay and merlot grapes in California. Take a self-guided tour of the premises and watch the winemaking operations from elevated walkways, sample current releases in the main tasting room or check out the Reserve Tasting and Cellar Club rooms.

Monday-Friday 10:30 a.m.-5:00 p.m., Saturday-Sunday 10 a.m.-5 p.m.

ST. HELENA
BERINGER VINEYARDS
2000 Main St., St. Helena, 707-967-4412; www.beringer.com

Beringer has welcomed guests since 1934, making it the oldest continuously operating winery in the Napa Valley. The comprehensive tours include a walk through hand-dug, aging tunnels, as well as informative talks about how wine is made and aged—followed, of course, by wine tasting.

May 30-October 22, 10 a.m.-6 p.m.; October 23-May 29, daily 10 a.m.-5 p.m.

CHAPPELLET VINEYARD AND WINERY
1581 Sage Canyon Road, St. Helena, 707-963-7136; www.chappellet.com

The Chappellet family has been making wine on the steep, rocky slopes of Napa Valley's Pritchard Hill—one of the coolest spots in the Napa Valley—for more than 40 years. The winery produces extraordinary cabernet sauvignons, as well as chardonnay, chenin blanc, merlot, cabernet franc and a mountain cuvee Bordeaux blend. The wines are a real find, and the gorgeous setting and the warm hospitality you'll encounter at this winery make this tour a must. The diverse land (there are 34 individual vineyard blocks, each highlighting various soil types, elevations, exposures and grades), which rises from 800 to 1,800 feet above sea level, is some of the most prized in the Napa Valley. Tours allow you to amble through the vineyards and taste wine around a table inside the elegant facility. From May to October, sign up for the back road excursion, which includes a ride to the top of Pritchard Hill in a Pinzgauer to enjoy the stunning views.

Monday-Friday by reservation at 10:30 a.m., 1 p.m. and 3 p.m.; Saturday-Sunday by reservation at 11 a.m., 1 p.m. and 3 p.m. $25 per person. Back Road Excursion: Wednesday, Friday at 2 p.m., subject to weather. (Back Road Excursions are limited to 8 people due to the size of the Pinzgauer.) $40 per person.

CHARBAY WINERY & DISTILLERY
4001 Spring Mountain Road, St. Helena, 707-963-9327; www.charbay.com

Although wine is only a small percent of the focus here, the result is no less impressive. Infused flavored vodkas, from original and green tea to pomegranate and ruby red grapefruit, along with other spirits including whiskey, rum and pastis, keep this family-run property busy year-round. The worthwhile one-hour tour outlines the basics of distillation and gives you a chance to sample Charbay's prized Oakville Cabernet Sauvignon—unfortunately, the law prohibits tastings of their distilled spirits.

Daily 10 a.m.-4 p.m.

THE CULINARY INSTITUTE OF AMERICA AT GREYSTONE
2555 Main St., St. Helena, 707-967-2320, 800-333-9242; www.ciachef.edu

Serious chefs and enthusiastic foodies will want to make the pilgrimage to the West Coast outpost of the famed Culinary Institute of America. Housed in a beautiful old stone building, the institute specializes in professional development for chefs, but also offers one-hour cooking demonstrations (Saturday-Sunday 10:30 a.m. and 1:30 p.m.), tours and several restaurants, including the Wine Spectator Greystone Restaurant. Recently added classes include a 2-hour wine tasting and a 6-hour cooking class based on the CIA cookbook. You can also spend a week in culinary bootcamp. There's a new 16-seat flavor bar where you can taste everything from olive oils to chocolate.

Tickets for demos: $15. Tours of Greystone: $10. Tours: Saturday-Sunday 11:45 a.m., 2:45 p.m., 5 p.m. (tours can be added to demo reservations).

KELHAM VINEYARDS
360 Zinfandel Lane, St. Helena, 707-963-2000; www.kelhamvineyards.com

A true family affair, the Kelhams have been farming on their 60-acre vineyard for more than 35 years. Before producing its own label, the vineyard harvested its premium grapes for such esteemed vintners as Cakebread, Mondavi and Beaulieu. Unlike some of the larger estates in the area, Kelham's offers only formal wine tastings, a seated affair either in the tasting room or out on the veranda, where vineyard owner and host Susanna Kelham explains the intimate process behind each of the wines presented.

By appointment only.

KULETO ESTATE VINEYARD
2470 Sage Canyon Road, St. Helena, 707-302-2200; www.kuletoestate.com

Spanning 761 acres of wild hillside land on the eastern edge of Napa Valley, this family estate blends unique architecture—think Frank Lloyd Wright meets a Tuscan villa—with award-winning wines and expansive natural surroundings overlooking Lake Hennessey. Originally a designer and restaurateur, the vineyard's founder, Pat Kuleto, carried his love of food and wine directly to the soil, harvesting hillside-grown grapes for more than a decade and yielding wines full of richness and depth. The intimate tour includes four wines and complimentary food pairings ($35 per person). Afterward, relax on the rustic patio to savor your wine and the gorgeous setting. One sip of Kuleto's Tuscan-style sangiovese, and you'll be hardpressed to leave without a case.

Tours: Daily 10:30 a.m., 11:45 a.m., 1 p.m., 2:30 p.m., by appointment only.

LOUIS M. MARTINI WINERY
254 St. Helena Highway South, St. Helena, 707-968-3362; www.louismartini.com

One of the first to venture into the Carneros region now famous for its cabernet sauvignon, the Martini family helped put Napa Valley on the international wine map with its innovative grape growing and winemaking techniques. This third-generation, family-owned winery gives regular tours and tastings and its grounds include a fine reserve tasting room along with charming gardens and picnic areas.
Daily 10 a.m.-6 p.m.

MERRYVALE VINEYARDS
1000 Main St., St. Helena, 707-963-2225; www.merryvale.com

Specializing in wine education, this winery offers a variety of programs for both the experienced connoisseur and the novice. The popular Saturday and Sunday 10:30 a.m. Wine Component Tasting seminars include a tour of the historic winery with its spectacular cask room. With 2,000-gallon oak casks on display, the cask room is regarded as one of the most enchanting places to drink wine in Napa Valley. Merryvale produces distinct chardonnays as well as bordeaux-blend red wine.
Daily 10 a.m.-6:30 p.m.

NAPA SOAP COMPANY
651 Main St., St. Helena, 707-963-5010; www.napasoapcompany.com

Find all-natural soaps made from local Napa Valley ingredients like grapeseed oil, lavender, herbs, beeswax, honey and even a little cabernet. You can also see how soap is made at this charming shop located just south of downtown, which came to be after the owner planted too much lavender on her property and decided to use it to make soap to clean her brood of boys.
Daily 10 a.m.-5 p.m.

OLIVIER NAPA VALLEY
1375 Main St., St. Helena, 707-967-8777; www.oliviernapavalley.com

Pop into this storefront right on St. Helena's main drag and indulge in its vast selection of gourmet olive oils, sauces and other savory items. Whether you're in the market for one of nearly a dozen flavored oils or just curious to taste toasted shallot dark beer mustard (which, by the way, is delicious), Olivier's will have your taste buds buzzing within minutes of stepping inside.
Monday-Saturday 10 a.m.-6 p.m., Sunday 10 a.m.-5 p.m.

ST. CLEMENT VINEYARDS
2867 St. Helena Highway, St. Helena, 707-265-5000; www.stclement.com

Originally built in 1878 by a San Francisco manufacturer of fine mirror and glass, the Rosenbaum House is the focal point of St. Clement, offering peerless views from the front porch's café and an intimate tasting room inside. The tour elaborates upon the history of the Victorian mansion and the surrounding winery, though much of the fruit used to produce St. Clement's wine is purchased from other vineyards. Cabernet sauvignon, chardonnay, sauvignon blanc and merlot are made at this boutique winery, but the shining star is the Oroppas, a meritage-style blend of full-bodied excellence.
Daily 10 a.m.-5 p.m. Reservations recommended.

WOODHOUSE CHOCOLATE
1367 Main St., St. Helena, 800-966-3468, 707-963-8413; www.woodhousechocolate.com

This cozy, butter-yellow colored shop sells handcrafted chocolates, truffles and toffees. The business is a family affair, started by a couple that left the wine business for the upscale chocolate trade, an effort that has been a sweet success. *Daily 10:30 a.m.-5:30 p.m.*

V. SATTUI WINERY
1111 White Lane, St. Helena, 707-963-7774; www.vsattui.com

When you're ready to picnic, head to this family-owned, 125-year-old winery, which has one of the best gourmet food shops in the valley. While you can sample wines on the premises—the winery only sells directly to customers— it's better to stock a picnic basket with wine and something from the amazing assortment of cheeses, meats, breads, spreads and sweets for a picnic on its lovely grounds. *April-October, daily 9 a.m.-6 p.m.; November-March, daily 9 a.m.-5 p.m.*

RUTHERFORD
BEAULIEU VINEYARD
1960 St. Helena Highway South, Rutherford, 707-967-5233, 800-264-6918; www.bvwines.com

Founded more than 100 years ago by venerable winemaker Georges de Latour, this historic Vineyard contributed to the development of premium chardonnay and pinot noir, which lead to the official designation of Carneros as a separate and unique appellation. Tours cover the historic production facilities and offer a tasting based on your wine preference. Samples of reserve wines are available for a small fee in the reserve tasting room. *Daily 10 a.m.-5 p.m.*

PEJU PROVINCE WINERY
8466 St. Helena Highway, Rutherford, 800-446-7358; www.peju.com

Though many come for the wine, they often stay for the entertainment. This exquisite estate, replete with a unique castle-like copper-topped tower, a reflecting pool, fountains and beautifully landscaped gardens, appeals to all the senses with tastings, cooking classes, art exhibits and more. The wines aren't too shabby, either. In fact, Peju's Reserve 2004 Cabernet Sauvignon is one of the best in the region. *Daily 10 a.m.-6 p.m.*

ROUND POND OLIVE MILL
886 Rutherford Road, Rutherford, 888-302-2575; www.roundpond.com

Round Pond Olive Mill produces some of the valley's finest gourmet olive oils. You could easily spend an entire afternoon here. For the full experience, make reservations for the alfresco lunch, tour the olive mill and learn about the meticulous cold-press process behind Round Pond's signature oils: Italian varietal, Spanish varietal, blood orange and Meyer lemon. A guide will lead you through tastings of each paired with vinegars (also made here), fresh organic produce and gourmet bread. The afternoon is topped off with a family-style lunch of local cheeses, meats, fruits and olive oil cake for dessert. On the third Saturday of every month from noon to 4 p.m., purchase fresh olive oil straight from the spigot. They also make wine at the charming vineyard across the street.

Estate Tastings: $25. Daily 11 a.m.-4 p.m., by appointment. Guided tours and tastings: $35. Daily 11 a.m., 1 p.m., by appointment. Olive mill tour and tasting: $25. Daily 10 a.m., 12:30 p.m., 3:30 p.m.

RUBICON ESTATE

1991 St. Helena Highway, Rutherford, 707-968-1100; www.rubiconestate.com

If you take one winery tour while visiting Napa, make it Rubicon. The knowledgeable and engaging tour guides will fill you in on how Francis Ford Coppola came to own this winery, and how he brought it full circle. It's the kind of story that makes movie magic, but this vineyard has no Hollywood flash. While you can easily envision Coppola sitting at one of the outside tables puffing on a cigar, the vineyard, which looks like it was transported from Italy, is where the famous director quietly raised his family outside of the spotlight, and where he and his wife still reside. You may also be surprised by how good the wines are, particularly the Rutherford Edizione Pennino Zinfandel (the label has a picture of Italy and the Statue of Liberty, a homage to Francis' grandfather) and the Cask cabernet sauvignon, a tribute to the stylized cabernets of the previous owner.

Daily 10 a.m.-5 p.m.

STAGLIN FAMILY VINEYARD

1570 Bella Oaks Lane, Rutherford, 707-963-3994; www.staglinfamily.com

Located behind its more famous neighbor, Robert Mondavi Vineyards, Staglin Family is a true family-run, locally-loved vineyard. This by-appointment only winery produces some of the area's most highly regarded cabernet sauvignon in the valley. The tour ends in the underground wine caves, as you're invited to pull up a chair at the grand dining room table and taste the fruits of their labor—literally.

Monday-Friday 11 a.m.-3 p.m.; reservations required.

ST. SUPÉRY VINEYARDS AND WINERY

8440 St. Helena Highway, Rutherford, 707-963-4507; www.stsupery.com

St. Supery recently celebrated its 90th anniversary and tours featurning library tastings are available by appointment. You can also take a free self-guided tour or sign up for a one-hour guided tour, held daily at 1 p.m. and 3 p.m., as well as participate in public tastings. The center provides a hands-on lesson in grape-growing and winemaking, from planting through bottling. Those who are just learning about wine will appreciate the "SmellaVision" course, which enables you to deconstruct a wine's bouquet.

Daily 10 a.m.-5 p.m.

YOUNTVILLE
CLIFF LEDE VINEYARDS

1473 Yountville Cross Road, Yountville, 707-944-8642; www.cliffledevineyards.com

Claiming 60 acres of Napa Valley's Stags Leap District, the Cliff Lede Vineyards utilize state-of-the-art techniques, including gravity-flow and berry-by-berry sorting systems to produce some of the best cabernet sauvignon in the region, along with sauvignon blanc and claret varietals. Tours of the vineyard, which commence in the perfectly restored craftsmanstyle tasting room, are small and informative, but the real treat is relaxing on one of the cozy porch swings, which offers views of the Lede vineyards and beyond. Another great post-tasting option is to stroll through the property's art gallery.

Daily 10 a.m.-4 p.m.; private tours by appointment.

DOMAINE CHANDON
1 California Drive, Yountville, 707-944-2280; www.chandon.com

Founded in 1973 by the parent company of champagne maker Moët & Chandon, Domaine Chandon is one of America's leading sparkling wine producers. You'll feel the true romance of the place when you tour the winery and the beautifully landscaped premises. On the terrace, you can sip some bubbly and enjoy lunch outdoors, a fitting conclusion to a jaunt into wine country.

Daily 10 a.m.-6 p.m.

NAPA

ARTESA VINEYARD & WINERY
1345 Henry Road, Napa, 707-224-1668; www.artesawinery.com

A striking contrast to the restored historic vineyards so common to Napa Valley, the region's newest winery has sleek, modernist architecture and its own artist in residence. Built by the Codorniu family, Spain's largest makers of sparkling wine, Artesa (which means craftsman and suggests that something is handcrafted in the Catalan language) started with sparkling but has since expanded to quality still wines.

Daily 10 a.m.-5 p.m.

BOUCHAINE VINEYARDS
1075 Buchli Station Road, Napa, 800-654-9463; www.bouchaine.com

Boasting more than 100 acres, Bouchaine is best known for its pinot noir, a grape that thrives in the cool Carneros region. Renovated extensively in 1995, the winery received numerous local architectural and historic awards, due in part to its use of recycled materials. The end result is a fireplace-warmed tasting room, as well as a deck and terrace with hill views, which make for cozy wine tastings.

Daily 10:30 a.m.-4 p.m.

CALDWELL
169 Kreuzer Lane, Napa, 707-255-1294; www.caldwellvineyard.com

If you're looking for something more than your typical tour or public tasting, this is it. You can have lunch or dinner with charming owners John and Joy Caldwell inside their $90 million wine cave. Both will regale you with stories of smuggled vines, while a former Cyrus chef will tantalize your tastebuds with a multi-course meal with wine pairings.

By appointment.

DARIOUSH

4240 Silverado Trail, Napa, 707-257-2345; www.darioush.com

A visit to Darioush is more akin to a journey to ancient Persia than Napa Valley. From the 16 monumental freestanding columns greeting visitors as they enter to the richly textured travertine stone surrounding the entire compound and the amphitheater used for special events and performances, Darioush vineyard is an experience in itself. Proprietor Darioush Khaledi grew up in Iran's shiraz region, bringing his international expertise to California's famous wine country in 1997. The results are award-winning. The chardonnays, viogniers and cabernet sauvignons are all smooth and well balanced, and the signature shiraz is not to be missed. The large tasting bar resembles something of an extravagant hafla (an Arabic dance party)—it can get packed and quite lively.

Daily 10:30 a.m.-5 p.m.

DOMAINE CARNEROS

1240 Duhig Road, Napa, 800-716-2788; www.domainecarneros.com

Those looking to embrace the essence of France without flying across the Atlantic need go no further than Domaine Carneros. The property occupies prime real estate in the heart of Napa and its apex, the majestic Domaine Carneros chateau, was modeled afterhistoric 18th-century mansion near Champagne, France and owned by the Taittinger family. The winery specializes in sparkling wines including brut, brut rosé and blanc de blancs, and uses only locally grown grapes to gain the perfect delicate balance of flavors. In lieu of a traditional tasting, Domaine offers flights, as well as full glass or bottle table service in the main chateau or along the back terrace. Caviar and other savory hors d'oeuvres are also available, set to match the bottles of bubbly. Though not the cheapest option, it certainly costs a lot less than a flight to Paris.

Daily 11 a.m., 1 p.m. and 3 p.m.

KENZO ESTATE

3200 Monticello Road, Napa, 877-977-7704; www.kenzoestate.com

Kenzo Tsujimoto (who made a fortune making video games) spared no expense in building and planting this winery on 4,000 acres. He brought in acclaimed winemaker Heidi Barrett to craft the first vintages and also enlisted chef Thomas Keller to provide food to go along with the wine tastings. The winery and tasting room, which has a sleek residential feel, is worth a trip to see the stunning facilities. Right now the winery produces just four wines: a sauvignon blanc, a cabernet sauvignon, and two Bordeaux-style blends.

By appointment.

NAPA VALLEY OPERA HOUSE

1030 Main St., Napa, 707-226-7372; www.napavalleyoperahouse.org

The opera house was built in 1879 as one of the first "respectable" venues west of the Mississippi river. The building went dark in 1914 and was finally renovated and reopened to the public in 2002 after being restored to its former splendor. The show schedule includes everything from jazz and classical concerts to theater and dance productions.

OXBOW PUBLIC MARKET
610 First St., Napa, 707-226-6529; www.oxbowpublicmarket.com

After a day of vineyard hopping, you'll no doubt be exhausted—and hungry. If you're looking for more of a DIY dinner option, head to Oxbow Public Market, a one-stop artisanal food and wine shop located in Napa's up-and coming Oxbow District. Grab a cup of made-to-order coffee from San Francisco's own Ritual Coffee Roasters, pick up a bottle of local wine from Oxbow Wine Merchant, grab some fresh-baked bread at The Model Bakery and some house cured meats at The Fatted Calf. You'll also find an outpost of Gott's Roadside for burgers and garlic fries, while newly shucked oysters can be found at Hog Island Oyster Company (locals go on Tuesday when they're $1). For dessert, there's Kara's Cupcakes. Whatever you grab, you can be assured it'll be local, and tasty.

Monday-Friday 9 a.m.-7 p.m., Saturday-Sunday 9 a.m.-6 p.m. Hours may vary.

PATZ & HALL
851 Napa Valley Corporate Way, Napa, 707-265-7700; www.patzhall.com

Since 2006, Patz and Hall has taken the concept of wine tasting a step further, creating a comfortable offsite salon to enjoy its single-vineyard varietals. Boasting a living room-like atmosphere with artwork on the walls and plush seating arrangements, the Patz & Hall Tasting Salon affords passionate wine aficionados and curious newbies the opportunity to sample, converse and compare different wines in a laid-back and relaxing setting. The private tastings include pinot noir and chardonnay wines, and seasonal victuals to match.

Private tastings by appointment only (10:30 a.m., 1 p.m. and 3 p.m.). Salon experience: daily 10 a.m.-4 p.m.

REGUSCI WINERY
5584 Silverado Trail, Napa, 707-254-0403; www.regusciwinery.com

This fantastic winery goes way back. In fact, it's one of the few "ghost wineries," a term given to those wineries that were around before 1900. During the 1890s, many vineyards were wiped out because of a phylloxera infestation. However, a few were folded into more modern facilities, one of which was located on the Regusci ranch. In 1932, Gaetano Regusci bought the historic property, at first farming other crops, and it has been a family business ever since. Today, the family only farms grapes, having established the winery in 1996. The tasting room is a real find; you'll taste impressive cabernet sauvignon, as well as merlot, zinfandel and chardonnay.

SILVER OAK WINERY
915 Oakville Cross Road, Oakville, 707-942-7022; www.silveroak.com

Silver Oak is a favorite among wine enthusiasts who come back year after year to taste the newest cabernet sauvignon. There is now a new winery to visit (a welcome relief if you visited the temporary facility). The Tudor-style estate features a tasting room with a stone fireplace and oak tasting bar with steel barrel hoops, designed to resemble the winery's signature American oak barrels. Many gladly fork over upwards of $100 for a bottle of the dark and velvety cabernet. The family also owns Twomey Cellars (www.twocellars.com), which produces merlot, pinot noir and sauvignon blanc.

Monday-Saturday 9 a.m.-5 p.m.

WHERE TO STAY

CALISTOGA

★★★★CALISTOGA RANCH

580 Lommel Road, Calistoga, 707-254-2800, 800-942-4220;
www.calistogaranch.com

This 48-room resort offers a quiet retreat after a day spent exploring local vineyards. Each room is housed in a free-standing lodge, decorated using natural materials with fireplaces, plush beds topped with down duvets and private outdoor showers. The onsite restaurant has a hearty American menu created by chef Erik Villar that is paired with local wines. A chef is also available to prepare a private dinner in guest lodges. The spa features soaking pools and offers a full menu of luxurious treatments, such as wine body scrubs, while the fitness center, yoga deck and organized hikes will help you balance out all those calories you're blissfully consuming.

48 rooms. Restaurant. Fitness center. Spa. $351 and up

★★★SOLAGE CALISTOGA

755 Silverado Trail, Calistoga, 866-942-7442;
www.solagecalistoga.com

As if the sprawling, scenic vineyards of Napa Valley aren't relaxing enough, Solage Calistoga brings eco-friendly luxury to the region with a resort spanning 22 acres and boasting countless amenities, including complimentary cruiser bikes, daily movement classes, a mud bar and bathhouse, and geothermal spa pools. Modern, studio-style accommodations offer semi-private patios and flat-screen TVs, and the furnishings are all fashioned from reclaimed, natural products. Solage further embraces the green movement by implementing a recycling program and onsite composting. The restaurant, Solbar, uses locally grown produce from independent, organic farms.

89 rooms. Restaurant, bar. Fitness center. Spa. Pool. $351 and up

NAPA

★★★THE CARNEROS INN

4048 Sonoma Highway, Napa, 707-299-4900;
www.thecarnerosinn.com

Between Napa and Sonoma, and surrounded by vineyards, this inn was designed to resemble the countryside with barns and ranchers' cottages. The stylish, private cottages offer luxurious accommodations with an array of modern amenities—heated slate floors in the bathrooms, flat-screen TVs and gas fireplaces—and all have large patios (where you can dine alfresco) and indoor/outdoor showers. The restaurant, Farm, packs them in nightly for its fantastic food and wine list. Locals swear by the Boon Fly Café for breakfast—especially for the homemade doughnuts, widely considered the best hangover cure.

86 rooms. Restaurant, bar. Fitness center. Spa. Pool. $351 and up

RUTHERFORD
★★★AUBERGE DU SOLEIL
180 Rutherford Hill Road, Rutherford, 707-963-1211, 800-348-5406;
www.aubergedusoleil.com

This sun-drenched sanctuary is perched on a quiet, 33-acre hillside olive grove in Rutherford. What began in 1981 as a simple Provence-inspired restaurant is now a full-fledged sanctuary. Luxurious touches include Italian linens, plasma TVs, wet bars with stocked refrigerators (full-sized in suites), espresso machines, large soaking tubs, CD players with a choice of CDs, wine, daily fresh fruit and a personal welcome note. Be sure to visit the exclusive Auberge Spa featuring Meyer lemon olive oil massages, among other treats, and the indulgent private Melisse Suite. The accommodations portion of the resort was recently gated to ensure maximum privacy.

52 rooms. No children under 16. Restaurant, bar. Fitness center. Spa. Pool. Tennis. $351 and up

ST. HELENA
★★★THE INN AT SOUTHBRIDGE
1020 Main St., St. Helena, 707-967-9400, 800-520-6800; www.innatsouthbridge.com

Renowned architect William Turnbull Jr. had the small-town squares of Italy in mind when he designed this upscale, contemporary inn. Soft cream stucco buildings house spacious guest quarters with vaulted ceilings, fireplaces and French doors opening onto private balconies with views of the courtyard. Amenities include terrycloth bathrobes, down comforters and Gilchrist & Soames bathroom products. The scenic property also includes Merryvale Winery, Tra Vigne restaurant and Pizzeria Tra Vigne.

21 rooms. Complimentary breakfast. Restaurant, bar. Spa. $351 and up

★★★★MEADOWOOD NAPA VALLEY
900 Meadowood Lane, St. Helena, 707-963-3646, 800-458-8080; www.meadowood.com

Spanning 250 wine-country acres, Meadowood is large, but its staff is attentive—from the esteemed resident wine tutor to the guest services manager assigned to each arriving visitor. Enjoy a game of croquet, tennis or golf, or simply lounge by the pool. The suites, cottages and lodges blend classic country style and California sensibilities with their stone fireplaces, skylights, vaulted ceilings, private decks and luxurious bathrooms—not to mention plenty of modern amenities such as flat-screen TVs, DVD/CD players, coffee and tea pots and toasters. The Grill is available for casual dining under the shade of an umbrella, and the restaurant turns out eager-to-please gastronomic delights.

85 rooms. Restaurant, bar. Fitness center. Spa. Pool. $351 and up

YOUNTVILLE
★★★VILLAGIO INN & SPA
6481 Washington St., Yountville, 707-944-8877, 800-351-1133; www.villagio.com

An Italian-style retreat, this inn has rooms with fireplaces, sunken bathtubs, private patios or balconies and beds topped with luxury bedding. A champagne breakfast buffet is served each day, and tea, coffee and cookies are served every afternoon. The onsite spa has an expansive menu of treatments, from massages to wraps. Spa suites are filled with ways to pamper yourself before or after your treatment, including fireplaces, sunken soaking tubs, steam showers and flat-screen TVs.

112 rooms. Complimentary breakfast. Pool. Spa. $251-350

★★★YOUNTVILLE INN

6462 Washington St., Yountville, 707-944-5600, 888-366-8166; www.yountvilleinn.com

The high-ceilinged, wood-beamed rooms at this inn, which feature fireplaces and views of the surrounding gardens, are perfect to retreat to after a day of touring local wineries. Some rooms have French doors that open to private patios. Guests receive a pass that offers specials at local wineries, and can take part in the inn's own complimentary wine tasting.

51 rooms. Complimentary breakfast. Pool. $251-350

★★★VINTAGE INN

6541 Washington St., Yountville, 707-944-1112, 800-351-1133; www.vintageinn.com

Inspired by the country inns of France, this intimate property sits on three-and-a-half acres of beautifully lush surroundings in the heart of wine country. After a day of vineyard hopping, relax in bright, spacious rooms with private patios or balconies, wood-beamed ceilings and large fireplaces, or lounge by the heated outdoor pool. The daily champagne breakfast buffet is a local favorite and if you're still hungry, there's afternoon tea or coffee and cookies.

80 rooms. Complimentary breakfast. Pool. $251-350

RECOMMENDED

YOUNTVILLE

BARDESSONO

6526 Yount St., Yountville, 707-204-6000; www.bardessono.com

This newly built resort brings a contemporary, eco-minded bent to the lodging options in Napa Valley. Rooms are streamlined but luxurious, with fireplaces, down-duvet topped beds and massive bathrooms, which include large wardrobes and steam showers which open up to outdoor showers. Seperate bedrooms have fireplaces, daybeds and outdoor patios, and include thoughtful touches such as jars of fruit-infused water and lavender patches by the bed to lull you to sleep. Every material used in the rooms is selected with the environment in mind, from the organic linens to the cleaning products used in the suites. Besides a full-service spa and restaurant, the resort has a cabana-lined pool and complimentary bikes for exploring Yountville.

62 rooms. Restaurant, bar. Spa. Pool. $351 and up

WHERE TO EAT

CALISTOGA

★★★SOLBAR

Solage Resort and Spa, 755 Silverado Trail, Calistoga, 707-226-0850; www.solbarnv.com

Located within Solage Calistoga, Solbar is a casual restaurant and lounge with an eco-chic interior. Dine inside or alfresco on the terrace, and try fresh, locally sourced ingredients in dishes such as chilled sweet pea soup with mint creme fraiche and pickled mustard seeds, and cripsy halibut tacos with sweet and sour cabbage, cilantro and lime aioli. The signature cocktails incorporate fresh juices, local herbs and spices, as in the ginger strawberry mojito made with local strawberries and fresh ginger.

Contemporary American. Breakfast, lunch, dinner, Sunday brunch. Outdoor seating. Children's menu. Bar. $36-85

NAPA
★★★NAPA VALLEY WINE TRAIN
1275 McKinstry St., Napa, 707-253-2111, 800-427-4124;
www.winetrain.com

Ride the "Gourmet Express" for a well-crafted culinary and wine experience. This unusual tour will take you through the heart of the Napa Valley in meticulously restored Pullman dining cars (circa 1915) with luxurious interiors, or 1952 Vista Dome cars for an elevated scenic view. The onboard wine tasting bar includes more than 100 wines. Lunch or dinner is delivered with white linen service and features seasonal menus.

American. Lunch, dinner. Bar. Children's menu. Reservations recommended. $16-35

RUTHERFORD
★★★★AUBERGE DU SOLEIL RESTAURANT
180 Rutherford Hill Road, Rutherford, 707-963-1211, 800-348-5406;
www.aubergedusoleil.com

French-born San Francisco restaurateur Claude Rouas set out to create a Provence-like destination restaurant in northern California when he opened Auberge du Soleil in 1981. Diners liked it so much they demanded overnight accommodations—and received them four years later. The seasonal French-California menu features artisanal ingredients and products from local farms, spotlighted in dishes such as English pea risotto with wild shrimp and applewood smoked bacon, Delta asparagus soup with shitake mushrooms, and roasted lamb with gnocchi. Don't miss the local cheese selections for dessert. The six-course tasting menu is available with wines to match from the large, locally strong list. If you're touring the valley by car, consider a lunch stop where you can enjoy the views from the terrace.

American, French. Breakfast, lunch, dinner. Bar. Reservations required. Outdoor seating. $86 and up

ST. HELENA
★★★MARTINI HOUSE
1245 Spring St., St. Helena, 707-963-2233; www.martinihouse.com

The cuisine at this 1923 Craftsman-style bungalow is fresh and flavorful, but for many the extensive drink list is reason enough to show up. The restaurant has a 600-bottle wine list, many specialty cocktails and a large beer selection. The ambiance is no less impressive—renowned restaurant designer Pat Kuleto's eye for style incorporates Napa Valley's Native American history with deep burgundy leather booths and several fireplaces. (Be sure to visit his winery.) The earthy ingredients weaved throughout the menu complement the restaurant's casual upscale appeal and keep guests satisfied with dishes such as butter-basted Alaskan halibut with curry-toasted almond crust and golden raisins. The outdoor garden, surrounded by vine-covered arbors and an antique fountain, is an ideal spot for dining on a temperate evening.

American. Lunch (Friday-Sunday), dinner. Bar. Reservations recommended. Outdoor seating. $36-85

★★★★THE RESTAURANT AT MEADOWOOD

Meadowood Napa Valley, 900 Meadowood Lane, St. Helena, 707-967-1205; www.meadowood.com

Remaining true to Meadowood's natural, serene setting, The Restaurant concentrates on the purity of regional flavors, using several ingredients from the resort's onsite garden. The result is a menu replete with fresh, delectable choices, which may include organic strawberries and foie gras with aged Balsamic and garden arugula, and roasted turbot with artichoke, caperberry and preserved lemon. From the extensive list of 1,100 wines, sommelier Rom Toulon assists in pairing varietals to fully complement the essence of each dish. There are numerous prix fixe and à la carte options, but those in the know leave their evening in the hands of executive chef Christopher Kostow, whose nightly tasting menu epitomizes the casual elegance of California's wine country. A modern dining room with stone fireplaces, white wainscoting and rows of windows revealing the beautiful grounds adds to the magical experience.

American. Dinner. Closed Sunday. Bar. Children's menu. Jackets recommended. Reservations recommended. Outdoor seating. $86 and up

★★★★TERRA

1345 Railroad Ave., St. Helena, 707-963-8931; www.terrarestaurant.com

Chef and owner Hiro Sone has been wowing diners at Terra, his cozy, intimate Napa Valley restaurant, since 1988. Set one block off the main drag on Railroad Avenue in St. Helena, Terra is located in a charming, old stone building, rustically finished with vintage red-tiled floors, exposed stone walls and wood-beamed ceilings. The food is spectacular—a successful blend of flavors from Italy, France and Asia. Signature dishes change with the seasons and may include free range veal chop with forest mushrooms, grilled Hokkaido scallops, and chocolate truffle cake with espresso ice cream and fudge sauce. With gracious hospitality and warmth, the staff at Terra makes you feel like you're dining at home.

French, Italian. Dinner. Closed Tuesday and two weeks in early January. Reservations recommended. $36-85

YOUNTVILLE

★★★AD HOC

6476 Washington St., Yountville, 707- 944-2487; www.adhocrestaurant.com

An experiment gone fabulously right, Ad Hoc originated as a temporary venture for the legendary chef Thomas Keller and his crew. Planned as a place to serve a four-course family style meal five days a week, the place became so popular Keller decided to open Ad Hoc permanently. The atmosphere is adventurous and easy-going. There's only one menu per night, so you'll have to go with it, but you're bound to love whatever is being served. A meal might start with assorted charcuterie, followed by a Colorado rack of lamb with frisée and currants, and an almond and broccolini couscous. This could be followed by almond cake with chocolate ganache or chocolate chip cookies. The place gets booked weeks in advance for the famous fried chicken served every other Monday. Friendly servers will help you find just the right wine.

Contemporary American. Dinner, Sunday brunch. Closed Tuesday-Wednesday. Reservations recommended. Bar. $36-85

★★★BRIX

7377 St. Helena Highway, Yountville, 707-944-2749; www.brix.com

Healthful and flavorful cuisine is served against a backdrop of vineyards, landscaping and the Mayacamas Mountains, captured by a wall of windows and glass doors in the stylish, contemporary dining room. The rustic space also has a long bar and an extensive L-shaped exhibition kitchen with a wood-burning oven. While all of the California cuisine on the menu is well-prepared, it's the weekend brunch that draws the biggest crowds, when fans swarm in for the sourdough pancakes with pecans and powdered sugar. A wine and gift shop lies just past the entrance.

French, Italian. Lunch, dinner, brunch. Reservations recommended. Outdoor seating. Bar. $36-85

★★★BOUCHON

6534 Washington St., Yountville, 707-944-8037; www.bouchonbistro.com

If you can't get into The French Laundry, try Thomas Keller's more casual French bistro. Like most Napa Valley restaurants, the fare is seasonal, but Bouchon maintains a decidedly bistro flavor, right down to the pommes frites, chalkboard specials and newspaper rack by the nickel bar. You can't go wrong with any of the fresh seafood, and the comfort dishes such as steak frites and croque madame are especially enjoyable. Desserts include pot de crème and profiteroles with vanilla ice cream and chocolate sauce. Be sure to stop by the next-door Bouchon Bakery. The éclairs and macarons are spectacular.

French. Lunch, dinner, late-night. Bar. Reservations recommended. Outdoor seating. $36-85

★★★ÉTOILE

1 California Drive, Yountville, 800-242-6366; www.chandon.com

An acclaimed restaurant inside the Domaine Chandon winery, Étoile serves California cuisine with a French influence in a sophisticated, candlelit setting. Choose from the prix fixe menu or from the a la carte menu. Dishes include duck breast with salt roasted pears and potato gnocchi with wild mushrooms, spring onions, parsley root and black truffles. Pair your choice with a bottle from Domaine Chandon's own vineyards—the sparkling wines are particularly appealing.

American, French. Lunch, dinner. Closed Tuesday-Wednesday; January. Reservations recommended. Outdoor seating. Bar. $36-85

★★★★★THE FRENCH LAUNDRY

6640 Washington St., Yountville, 707-944-2380; www.frenchlaundry.com

At this former French steam laundry, chef Thomas Keller has raised the standard for fine dining in America. While the country locale—a circa-1900 rock and timber cottage—makes diners feel at home. Tables topped with limoges china, crystal stemware and floor-length linens, set the tone for the nine-course French or vegetarian tasting menus that change daily but always rely on seasonal produce and organic meats. Dishes are small and prompt contemplation on the perfect marriage of fresh, pristine ingredients on each plate. The affable staff keeps the experience casual and comfortable, yet refined and memorable. Reservations are taken two months in advance, so be prepared if you're hoping to snag a table at this perennially outstanding American classic. *French. Lunch (Friday-Sunday), dinner. Closed two weeks in January and one week in late July-early August. Reservations required. Jackets required for lunch and dinner. $86 and up*

★★★REDD

6480 Washington St., Yountville, 707-944-2222;
www.reddnapavalley.com

Locals love to love Redd, Napa's newest epicurean destination. This chic restaurant represents chef/owner Richard Reddington's view of wine country cuisine with influences from all over the map. The unadorned white-walled interior and wood doorframe speak to the simplicity of Reddington's cooking. But don't think you're getting bland basics here. You'll be won over by such dishes as Alaskan halibut with chickpea purée, sweet peppers, prosciutto and salt cod beignets, and organic chicken with faro, bacon and asparagus saltimbocca. Desserts such as the red wine tart with spring fruits and fontainebleu are the perfect complement to any of the varietals on the wine list. *Contemporary American. Lunch, dinner, Sunday brunch. Bar. Reservations recommended. Outdoor seating. $36-85*

RECOMMENDED

NAPA
UBUNTU

1140 Main St., Napa, 707-251-5656; www.ubuntunapa.com

Though you'll find no meat on the menu, the focus at Ubuntu is less on depravity than fresh, innovative cuisine from local community gardens. Named after the Zulu term for "humanity toward others," the space functions as both a vegetarian restaurant and a yoga studio. The open kitchen serves up succulent dishes such as onion fennel and fig leaf gazpacho, smoked pecans and Meyer lemon, and horseradish gnocchi with assorted roots. Most of the restaurant's food is grown on its own biodynamic farm (there's even a yoga studio onsite if you want to take a class before your meal), and the eclectic menu of items are sure to please even the most stubborn carnivore. Lest you forget you're in Napa Valley: Wine pairings are offered to complement the nightly garden menu. *Vegetarian. Dinner, Saturday-Sunday brunch. $16-35*

ST. HELENA
GOTT 'S ROADSIDE

933 Main St., St. Helena, 707-963-3486; www.gottsroadside.com

If you can't imagine a greasy patty melt and a smooth glass of pinot noir going together, you haven't been to Gott's (previously called Taylor's Automatic

Refresher). This old-school roadside burger shack, owned by winemaker Joel Gott, has developed a cult following with visitors and locals alike. And for good reason: The burgers are tasty and generous and the signature garlic fries, tossed in garlic butter and parsley are positively addicting (and make the often lengthy wait in line worth it). Try to avoid the lunch rush to guarantee a seat at one of the shaded picnic tables. The concept has been so successful there are now sister restaurants in Napa and San Francisco.

American. Lunch, dinner. Outdoor seating. $15 and under

YOUNTVILLE
BOTTEGA
6525 Washington St., Yountville 707-945-1050; www.botteganapavalley.com

At Bottega, which means "artist's workshop" in Italian, chef, author and television personality Michael Chiarello is back in the kitchen serving the dishes from across Italy that made him famous. In fact, don't be surprised to see the chef cooking in the open kitchen at this upscale farmhouse. Ingredients here are always artisanal, heritage or homemade. The antipasti menu incorporates organic proscuitto, house-cured salami and wood-grilled octopus. Pasta dishes include crispy potato gnocchi with English pea and tallegio fonduta and hand-cut whole egg linguine with manilla clams and sausage, while main dishes might feature wood-oven roasted whole fish with lemon, asparagus and romesco sauce.

Lunch, dinner. Bar. Reservations recommended. $86 and up

NAPA STYLE
6525 Washington St., Yountville, 707-945-1229; www.napastyle.com

Chef Michael Chiarello's wine country shop is a great place to pick up sandwiches before heading out on your day of wine tasting. A handful of tasty panini are available each day, including hot paninis with ragu of pork, and cold ones such as the caprese or pesto egg salad, as well as salads, soups and sides. You can also purchase several of the chef's specialty food items in the shop, including dips and sauces (try the cabernet sauce for your next barbecue), as well as a variety of kitchen and cooking items. Beautiful tableware, including vintage silverware, and home and garden items such as vintage milk bottles in authentic crates complete the offerings. Of course, the shop also sells the chef's cookbooks. A few tables are located outside on the gravel patio if you want to enjoy your casual lunch on the spot.

Deli: daily 11a.m.- 4 p.m. Store: Monday-Sunday 10 a.m.-6 p.m.

SPAS

CALISTOGA
★★★★THE SPA AT CALISTOGA RANCH
Calistoga Ranch, 580 Lommel Road, Calistoga, 707-254-2820; www.calistogaranch.com

The Spa at Calistoga Ranch was opened in 2004 by the group behind sister property Auberge du Soleil and features five treatment rooms, inspired by the native landscape and designed with organic elements such as copper, stone, wood and water. Three of the treatment rooms include large terraces with soaking tubs and showers, and all are tailor-made for treatments involving a bath: buttermilk baths, mud baths or thermal mineral pool soaks. The spa draws water from the local hot springs and uses Napa Valley ingredients, including honey, grapeseed and bay laurel, in many of the treatments. The mud wrap promises to boost immunity. Morning yoga takes place in the resort's wine cave.

★★★★THE SPA AT MEADOWOOD
Meadowood Napa Valley, 900 Meadowood Lane, St. Helena, 800-458- 8080; www.meadowood.com/wellness

Massages delivered fireside, a rejuvenating facial with organic ingredients, a relaxing yoga class. These are just some of the pampering, incredibly indulgent services available at this wine country spa. Signature treatments include the Meadowood Harvest Wrap, which begins with a hot towel compress that prepares your skin for a tea tree exfoliant and ends with your body swaddled in warm towels and blankets while you soak in the benefits of a hydrating body masque. If you've been walking around a lot of wineries, ask to add the 30-minute foot relief to a massage or facial. The treatment includes just enough of a pressure-point relieving massage to invigorate you for another day of wine tasting.

RUTHERFORD
★★★★THE AUBERGE SPA
Auberge Du Soleil, 180 Rutherford Hill Road, Rutherford, 707-963-1211; www.aubergedusoleil.com

The glorious Napa Valley surroundings have inspired this spa's philosophy, with vineyard, garden and valley themes dominating the treatment menu. Nutrient-rich grape seed and locally grown herbs and flowers are the foundation for the vineyard's massages, body treatments and facials. Try unique massage techniques, such as the Rhythmic Water Massage which takes place in water while your therapist guides you through stretches and massage. Seasonal treatments are also a highlight of a visit to this spa, where a couples mustard bath is featured in spring, a luscious peaches and cream body mask is available in summer, a harvest-inspired cleanse or body glaze in fall and a peppermint and eucalyptus body treatment in winter. You can schedule personal fitness classes from yoga to pilates. If you're spending the weekend with a significant other or just a group of friends, you can schedule treatments in the Melisse Suite, which can accommodate four people, featuring a fireplace, private tanning deck and heated pool.

NAPA
★★★★THE SPA AT THE CARNEROS INN
The Carneros Inn, 4048 Sonoma Highway, Napa, 707-299-4900; www.thecarnerosinn.com

Napa Valley's Carneros Inn takes the country farmhouse and turns it on its head, with clean lines and simple sophistication, and the sun-filled, mood-lifting spa perfectly complements the resort's laid-back attitude. The themed treatment menu draws from the harvests, farms, cellars, minerals and creeks of the Carneros Valley. Therapies include honeydew exfoliations, goat butter body wraps, grape seed and guava body scrubs, and apricot and chardonnay manicures. If you'd rather not leave your private cottage but desperately need a massage, the spa presents a menu of in-room treatments, including organic garden wraps and couples' massages.

SONOMA

The quieter sister to nearby Napa, Sonoma has plenty of top-notch wineries, luxurious inns and spas, and superlative dining, but without the crowds. The area includes the towns of Sonoma and Healdsburg, which are the most popular for touring wineries. The oldest town in the wine region, Sonoma was arranged around the eight-acre plaza like a traditional Mexican village because up until 1846, it was under Mexican rule. On June 14 of that year, a group of settlers rebelled in the so-called "Bear Flag Revolt," and for a brief 25 days, Sonoma was declared the capital of California. The U.S. government then annexed California, ending Sonoma's days as the seat of state government. Today, the history of the town is well preserved. City Hall, built in the heart of the plaza in the early 20th century, is still used, and the Franciscan mission **San Francisco Solano** *(114 E. Spain St., 707-938-9560; tours are typically given on the hour between 11 a.m. and 2 p.m. on weekends)*, dating back to 1823, is open to the public. In addition to the history, Sonoma's shops and restaurants are well worth the visit. Of course, there are the famed wineries.

In the center of some of Northern California's most esteemed winemaking appellations, including Alexander Valley, Dry Creek, Chalk Hill and Russian River Valley, is the thriving and charming wine town of Healdsburg, where palm trees and 100-year old redwoods shade manicured grounds and benches in the town square. The town of Healdsburg is centrally located with access to more than 70 world-class wineries, from the grandest European-style villas to the more rustic, yet no less well-crafted mom-and-pop shops. Just outside of town is one of the most beautiful drives in Northern California—Dry Creek Road—home to many of the area's wineries. Its windy turns provide a leisurely way to spend an afternoon as you hop from one tasting to the next.

WHAT TO SEE

HEALDSBURG
BELLA VINEYARDS AND WINE CAVES
9711 W. Dry Creek Road, Healdsburg, 866-572-3552;
www.bellawinery.com

It's the classic tale: Girl meets boy. Girl marries boy. Couple moves to wine country and learns how to make wine. Classic or not, few could pull it off like Scott and Lynn Adams, earning accolades for producing some of the best wine in the region. Bella harvests a varied crop of wines from its three distinct vineyards in the Dry Creek and Alexander valleys, including zinfandels and syrahs. While the wines are certainly top-notch, a big reason for Bella's appeal is its beautiful caves. Entering on the side of a hill underneath an arbor of vines, you'll be given a glimpse into the inner workings of the winery, as well as an underground taste or two.

Daily 11 a.m.-4:30 p.m.

LAMBERT BRIDGE WINERY

4085 W. Dry Creek Road, Healdsburg, 707-431-9600;
www.lambertbridge.com

The beauty of visiting Lambert Bridge Winery is best summed up in its mission statement: "Great wine served with great food shared by great friends." When you visit the family-run vineyard, located in the heart of the Dry Creek Valley, you will immediately recognize its commitment to this vision. The well-manicured grounds and gardens bursting with edible flowers and herbs offer teak tables and chairs for enjoying an impromptu alfresco picnic and a bottle of the Lambert Bridge 2006 Viognier. Or take your visit a bit further by joining chef Andrea Mugnaini in the stunning outdoor kitchen for a class on wood-fired cooking, before feasting on your creations with wines to match.

Daily 10:30 a.m.-4:30 p.m.

PRESTON OF DRY CREEK

9282 W. Dry Creek Road, Healdsburg, 707-433-3372; www.prestonvineyards.com

It's all about sustainability at this small, family-run winery in the Dry Creek Valley. Owned by Lou and Susan Preston for more than three decades, the wines are made from organically grown grapes, and the selection of fresh produce sold from an ad hoc stand on the front porch is also organic. Preston epitomizes down-home charm, with weather-worn farmhouses dotting the estate and a verdant yard with picnic tables and bocci courts for visitors to enjoy. Grab a loaf of house-made bread, some local cheese and a bottle of their crisp vin gris rosé and relax under a canopy of lemon trees.

Daily 11 a.m.-4:30 p.m.

QUIVIRA VINEYARDS

4900 W. Dry Creek Road, Healdsburg, 707-431-8333; www.quivirawine.com

Just down the road from Lambert Bridge Winery in the heart of the Dry Creek Valley, this innovative estate is committed to organic and biodynamic winemaking practices, transforming the once wood-and-cinder barn into a solar-paneled, high-tech edifice. Reds are the specialty here, with such smooth varietals as the 2006 Steelhead Zinfandel, a robust blend named after the wild trout that spawn in the onsite creek each year. On a hot day, the sauvignon blanc is a real treat, especially under the shade of Quivira's ancient fig trees.

Daily 11 a.m.-5 p.m.

SONOMA

BARTHOLOMEW PARK WINERY

1000 Vineyard Lane, Sonoma, 707-935-9511; www.bartpark.com

Grapes have been grown on this land since the 1830s, but Bartholomew Park has existed as a winery only since 1994. With winemaker Jim Bundschu (of the long-time Sonoma family behind nearby Gundlach Bundshcu winery's Rhinefarm) at the helm, expect to find limited-production single vineyard wines that range from soft, full merlots to crisp, refreshing whites. Pick up a

BEST ATTRACTIONS

WHAT ARE THE TOP THINGS TO DO IN SONOMA?

STROLL THROUGH HEALDSBURG

Check out some of the town's 70 world-class wineries and well-crafted mom-and-pop shops.

PACK A PICNIC

As you head from winery to winery, be sure to plan a picnic at one. Many of the wineries have scenic spots from which to take in the countryside.

picnic in town and plan on a hike through the winery's trails, which on a clear day deliver views across the valley to San Francisco. Afterward, buy a cold bottle of sauvignon blanc from the tasting room and take a seat at one of the picnic tables that overlook the vineyards for an unforgettable lunch.
Daily 11 a.m.-4:30 p.m.

BUENA VISTA CARNEROS HISTORIC TASTING ROOM

18000 Old Winery Road, Sonoma, 707-938-1266; www.buenavistacarneros.com
Founded in 1857, Buena Vista is California's oldest premium winery and a California historic landmark. The 1862 Press House stands as the estate's tasting room, and history buffs will particularly enjoy the tour, as it recounts Buena Vista's past and the life of Count Agoston Haraszthy, the man behind today's winemaking techniques. There are a number of different tasting options—from library vintages to seated food and wine pairings—so be sure to call ahead for details.
Daily 10 a.m.-5 p.m. Reservations recommended.

GLORIA FERRER CAVES & VINEYARDS

23555 Highway 121 (Arnold Drive), Sonoma, 707-996-7256; www.gloriaferrer.com
The first sparkling wine house to settle in the Sonoma Carneros region, Gloria Ferrer is an idyllic stop for a glass of brut rosé and a nibble on some of the delicious, addicting house-roasted spicy almonds. The daily tours include a peek at century-old winemaking equipment and a journey into the estate's cellar. Unlike other wineries in the area, Gloria Ferrer does not provide tasting samples; rather, they sell their wines by the full glass or bottle. Grab a flute, head out to the sun-drenched Vista Terrace and relax as you overlook the estate vineyards. For those who prefer still wines, Gloria Ferrer also offers a limited-release pinot noir rosé and a variety of more robust pinot noirs.
Daily 10 a.m.-5 p.m. Tour reservations recommended for parties of 10 or more.

RAVENSWOOD

18701 Gehricke Road, Sonoma, 707-933-2332; www.ravenswood-wine.com

This Sonoma winemaker's well-priced zinfandels may be ubiquitous (you can find the vintner's blends in most grocery stores across the U.S.), but they're some of the most robust, deliciously drinkable American reds around. Winemaker Joel Peterson's mantra is "no wimpy wines," and that philosophy shows in the full-bodied wines Ravenswood produces. A visit to the rustic tasting room gives you a chance to sample some of the winery's limited-production vineyard designate zinfandels, all of which are acclaimed for their rich taste (think big flavor with notes ranging from vanilla to cedar to raspberry, depending on the vineyard).

Daily 10 a.m.-4:30 p.m.

WHERE TO STAY

HEALDSBURG

★★★HOTEL HEALDSBURG

25 Matheson St., Healdsburg, 707-431-2800; www.hotelhealdsburg.com

The Hotel Healdsburg is a hip oenophile's dream. This striking, contemporary hotel right on the historic Town Plaza is a showpiece of minimalist design. The clean lines and uncluttered décor create a serene ambience throughout the public spaces, and the guest rooms and suites echo that sentiment. Windows look out over the plaza or toward the hotel's garden. All of wine country is easily explored from here, but the property is a culinary destination of its own, with noted chef Charlie Palmer's lauded Dry Creek Kitchen.

55 rooms. Complimentary breakfast. Restaurant, bar. Fitness center. Spa. Pool. Business center. $351 and up

★★★★LES MARS HOTEL

27 North St., Healdsburg, 707-433-4211; www.lesmarshotel.com

Imagine the thrill of staying with close friends while on vacation. Now take that thought and add a bucolic wine country setting, a classic chateau-style residence and peerless attention to detail. Located on a side street just off the main strip, the hotel boasts 16 rooms individually decorated with antiques and luxurious linens. The hand-carved walnut-panel library offers a tranquil respite after a day of wine tastings, and the delicious complimentary breakfast delivered to your room each morning will make you think twice about ever staying with friends again.

16 rooms. Complimentary breakfast. Pool. $351 and up

SONOMA

★★★THE FAIRMONT SONOMA MISSION INN & SPA

100 Boyes Blvd., Sonoma, 707-938-9000, 800-257-7544; www.fairmont.com/sonoma

A local favorite since the 1920s, this idyllic country retreat sits on Boyes Hot Springs—a sacred healing ground for Native Americans—and within the valley's famous vineyards. Many of the sophisticated yet country comfortable guest rooms have French doors that open to a private patio or balcony. Romantic suites hold fireplaces and four-poster beds. Hearty American fare has been served for more than 50 years at the Big 3 diner, while Santé earns praise for its imaginative cuisine. Relax by the pool or play a round of golf on the historic 1925 course. Inspired by the thermal mineral springs that flow underneath the inn, the spa is a destination unto itself, wowing city slickers with its comprehensive treatment menu.

226 rooms. Restaurant, bar. Fitness center. Spa. $351 and up

★★★MACARTHUR PLACE
29 E. MacArthur St., Sonoma, 800-722-1866; www.macarthurplace.com

A lush country estate just a few blocks from the town plaza, this magical inn sits among seven acres of fragrant, blooming gardens. The Victorian-style buildings house 64 guest rooms and suites, some with fireplaces and oversized bathrooms that deliver California country charm and comfort. A nightly wine and cheese reception whets the appetite, but save room for the juicy steaks and succulent seafood at Saddles, the hotel's steakhouse. Even in this tranquil setting, the Garden Spa stands out for its sunlit space and local flower-, plant- and herb-based treatments.

64 rooms. Complimentary breakfast. Restaurant. $251-350

RECOMMENDED

EL DORADO HOTEL
405 First St. West, Sonoma, 707-996-3220; www.eldoradosonoma.com

Bringing a sleek, modern alternative to the historic Sonoma Plaza, the El Dorado offers stylish, contemporary rooms with private balconies and views of the town square or lush garden courtyard. The outdoor pool encourages afternoon lounging, and guests don't have to stray far for a world-class meal with El Dorado Kitchen positioned right off the lobby.

27 rooms. Restaurant, bar. Pool. $151-250

WHERE TO EAT

HEALDSBURG
★★★★CYRUS
29 North St., Healdsburg, 707-433-3311; www.cyrusrestaurant.com

Where better to indulge in life's luxuries than this elegant wine country eatery located off the lobby of the grand Les Mars Hotel? Leather banquettes, a cloister ceiling and a plethora of freshly cut flowers are just some of the intimate touches that make an evening at Cyrus a sybaritic affair. Start off with one of the restaurant's famous house-made specialty cocktails or enjoy a glass of champagne and a bite of caviar from their champagne and caviar cart rolled to you tableside. The prix fixe menu of three-, four- or five-courses changes daily, but often includes such dishes as roasted porcini risotto and rabbit ballotine, and a terrine of foie gras with rhubarb and sassafras. The wine list of more than 600-bottles offers a perfect accompaniment to any dish.

Continental. Dinner. Bar. Reservations recommended. $86 and up

★★★DRY CREEK KITCHEN

317 Healdsburg Ave., Healdsburg, 707-431-0330

Housed in the modern Hotel Healdsburg, the Dry Creek Kitchen suits many tastes. Sit outside in the morning with your latte and watch the town wake up, or settle inside and enjoy an exercise in rustic comfort, with down-home dishes and a waitstaff that's all smiles. Be sure to remember a bottle of local wine too, as the restaurant does not charge a corkage fee for up to two bottles of local vino.

American. Dinner. Bar. Reservations recommended. Outdoor seating. $36-85

SONOMA

★★★CARNEROS BISTRO & WINE BAR

1325 Broadway, Sonoma, 707-931-2042; www.carnerosbistro.com

About six blocks south of the Sonoma plaza, Carneros is adjacent to the lodge at Sonoma, sharing the circular drive. An extensive wine list, wine bar and wine education classes are offered along with an innovative menu of international fare. An open kitchen runs the length of the dining room. Check for special events and live entertainment and keep an eye out for celebrity bartenders.

International. Breakfast, lunch, dinner, brunch. Bar. Children's menu. Reservations recommended. Outdoor seating. $36-85

RECOMMENDED

HEALDSBURG

SCOPA

109A Plaza St., Healdsburg, 707-433-5282; www.scopahealdsburg.com

For those who have spent half their lives longing for an Italian grandmother, one trip to Scopa and you'll have found the only Nonna you'll need. A newcomer to the gourmet playground that is wine country, this sliver of an Italian bistro has an intimate white marble bar and unassuming interior. The food, however, is simple and delicious. Chef and owner Ari Rosen churns out housemade gnocchi with a Napolitano meat ragu and a spectacular moscardini of sautéed baby octopus with Yukon potatoes and caper berries. The wine list is thorough and surprisingly reasonable—by wine country standards—and if you can't find anything to your liking, bring your own bottle along (there's a $20 corkage fee).

Italian. Dinner. Closed Monday. $36-85

SONOMA

DELLA SANTINA'S

133 E. Napa St., Sonoma, 707-935-0576; www.dellasantinas.com

This family-run, old school Italian restaurant is just off Sonoma's main square and displays a palace-like stone exterior that you'd expect to find among the hills of Tuscany. The rosticceria turns out perfectly tender meats, and one bite of Della Santina's signature tiramisu from the pasticceria and you'll be ordering a second helping for a midnight snack. Highlights include the pappardelle alla lepre (wide noodles with rabbit meat sauce) and the daily gnocchi special. In warm weather, vie for a table on the patio.

Italian. Lunch, dinner. Outdoor seating. $16-35

EL DORADO KITCHEN

405 First St. West, Sonoma, 707-996-3030; www.eldoradosonoma.com

Both sophisticated and simple, dramatic and relaxing, this bustling eatery shows off the understated brilliance of chef Justin Everett's contemporary Californian cuisine, amidst an open kitchen, a long communal dining table and an intimate stone courtyard for dining under the Sonoma sky. Seasonal freshness is the focus and dishes such as free range Petaluma chicken breast with quinoa and squash blossom pesto, and herb-basted halibut with shiitake mushrooms, asparagus and house-cured pancetta, are paired with thoughtful selections from local artisan vintners, including more than 20 wines by the glass. If it's more of an afternoon sugar rush that you're after, the neighboring El Dorado Kitchenette has pastries galore, as well as gourmet sandwiches, salads and housemade ice cream.

American. Lunch, dinner, Sunday brunch. Bar. Reservations recommended. Outdoor seating. $36-85

THE GIRL AND THE FIG

110 W. Spain St., Sonoma, 707-938-3634; www.thegirlandthefig.com

Prepare yourself for fresh, rustic, French-influenced cooking at this simple, rustic restaurant on Sonoma's town square. The waitstaff can range from affable to absent, but once you dig into dishes such as fig and arugula salad with fresh balsamic dressing, or skillet steak with asparagus and truffle mac 'n' cheese, you'll forget about the service. A wine list heavy with local syrahs provides the perfect complement to the California cuisine offered on the constantly changing menu. The outdoor patio is a divine spot to indulge in weekend brunch or a romantic dinner.

American. Lunch, dinner, Sunday brunch. Bar. Reservations recommended. Outdoor seating. $16-35

HARMONY LOUNGE AT THE LEDSON HOTEL

480 First St. East, Sonoma, 707-996-9779; www.ledsonhotel.com

Enjoy a light meal of small plates with wine pairings at this grand antique hotel on the plaza. Try the beef carpaccio and duck confit and save room for the pear cabernet tart. Check for live entertainment.

American. Lunch, dinner. Bar. $15 and under

WHERE TO SHOP

HEALDSBURG

14FEET.

325 Center St., Healdsburg, 707-433-3391; www.14feet.net

The term vintage is thrown around a lot in Healdsburg, but the folks at 14feet. aren't talking about the grape variety. This storefront, specializing in one-of-a-kind industrial and mid-century pieces, is choc-a-block full of vintage tables, chairs, light fixtures, antique textiles and even an oversized ceramic peanut bank from the 70s. You never know what you'll find, but there's little chance you'll go home empty-handed.

Monday-Saturday 10 a.m-6 p.m., Sunday 11 a.m.-5 p.m.

LIME STONE
315 Healdsburg Ave., Healdsburg, 707-433-3080; www.limestonehealdsburg.com
This colorful corner shop housed in the Hotel Healdsburg is owned by Charlie
and Lisa Palmer of nearby Dry Creek Kitchen, and reigns as Healdsburg's go-to
for chic home accents. Take home a wine barrel chandelier, ox-cart table, classic
glass candlesticks or petite porcelain pear vases to remind you of your wine
country vacation.
Hours vary.

MYRA HOEFER DESIGN
309 Healdsburg Ave., Healdsburg, 707-433-2166; www.myrahoeferdesign.com
The store's namesake is as colorful a personality as you'll find in Sonoma. Her
impeccable and eccentric Parisian chic taste is evident in the limited, but well-
edited selection of antique furnishings, books and knick-knacks.
Monday-Friday noon-4 p.m., Saturday-Sunday noon-5 p.m.

CENTRAL COAST

Artists, celebrities and everyone in between are all drawn to California's Central
Coast. The region offers a good mix of urban and rural. Dominated by the Santa
Lucia Mountains, the sparsely developed Big Sur region gives nature room to
breathe. Drivers need travel only 30 miles south of Monterey on Highway 1,
considered an American National Scenic Byway, to see the beautiful rocky Big
Sur bluffs, redwood forests, canyons, waterfalls, secluded beaches and sheer
mountains—and gain access to several state parks south of Carmel. A great time
to visit Big Sur is in the fall, when humpback and blue whales migrate from Alaska
to Mexico and California condors fly above. On the southern part of Big Sur,
elephant seals, protected by the Marine Mammal Protection Act, congregate to
mate in the winter months.

From Carmel to Santa Cruz, this area offers sandy beaches, charming towns
and one of the best marine environments—Monterey Bay. What's known simply
as "Carmel" is divided into the town (officially called Carmel-by-the-Sea) and
Carmel Valley Village, about 13 miles inland. The former, whose famous mayor
was Clint Eastwood, almost looks like a movie set. It's that perfect—some say too
perfect. You'll find luxurious accommodations, plenty of restaurants, tidy shops
and art galleries. The valley is more dusty and sleepy—and full of wonderful
tasting rooms. Since the wineries in this area are very spread out, their tasting
rooms are clustered here, all pretty much within walking distance of each other.

Named in 1602 by a Spanish explorer for the Count of Monterey, this city
hid from European eyes for another 168 years, when it was rediscovered by
Fray Crespi, Fray Junipero Serra and Gaspar de Portola. The three founded the
Presidio and the Mission San Carlos Borromeo de Rio Carmelo. Since then,
Monterey has retained its calm harbor, white-sand beach, Monterey cypress,
pine and red-roofed white stucco houses. A mélange of Mexican, New England,
sea, mission and ranch makes Monterey uniquely Californian in its culture

and history—the first state constitution was written here. Once a whaling and sardine center—inspiring the novels *Cannery Row* and *Sweet Thursday* by John Steinbeck—overfishing depleted the bay of sardines and emptied the canneries. The row is now dominated by an aquarium, restaurants and art galleries, while Fisherman's Wharf is the launch point for fishing and sightseeing trips and home to the bay's famous sea otters.

The small town of Pebble Beach is known for its scenic beauty, the palatial houses of its residences and, most of all, its golf courses, where the annual National Pro-Amateur Golf Championship and other prestigious tournaments are held. It's also known for the scenery along 17-Mile Drive from Carmel to Monterey.

WHAT TO SEE

BIG SUR
BIXBY BRIDGE
www.beachcalifornia.com

A registered historic landmark, the Bixby Bridge, completed in 1932, is one of the highest single-arch bridges in the world and straddles a large canyon along the Big Sur coastline. This two-lane bridge reflects the time period in which it was built, with an Art Deco style. All-weather photographers come to capture this engineering marvel, whether clouds partially obscure the bridge's vast body or sunlight makes its white structural supports gleam.

JULIA PFEIFFER BURNS STATE PARK
Big Sur Station 1, Big Sur, 831-667-2315; www.parks.ca.gov

Stretching from the Big Sur coastline into nearby 3,000-foot ridges, the park holds a variety of trees—redwood, tan oak, madrone and chaparral—and an 80-foot waterfall that drops from granite cliffs into the ocean from the Overlook Trail. While at Overlook Trail, be sure to keep watch for whales that come close to the shore. Hike the backcountry via several trails, or check out the 1,680-acre underwater reserve (between Partington Point and McWay Creek), which protects a spectacular assortment of marine life, to look for seals, sea lions and sea otters in the cove. Experienced scuba divers can explore with special-use permits at Partington Cove.

POINT SUR STATE HISTORIC PARK
Big Sur Station 1, 831-625-4419; www.parks.ca.gov

Poised 361 feet above the surf on a large volcanic rock, the park is home to the Point Sur Lightstation, which is visible from the highway, and an active U.S. Coast Guard light station. The lightstation is only open to the public during docent-led tours (which are three-hour-long walking tours). From 1889 to 1974, lighthouse keepers and their families lived at the site when the lightstation was automated. There is even a moonlight tour, which tells tales of the "ghosts" of the lightkeepers from the past.
Admission: adults $10, children 6-17 $5, children 5 and under free.

CARMEL

ANTIQUE AND ART GALLERIES

San Carlos Street and Fifth Avenue, Carmel, 831-624-2522; www.carmelcalifornia.org

With more than 90 galleries displaying a wide variety of art and antiques, you can get a glimpse into what life is like as an artist in this beach community. Galleries showcase many different types of art from original oil paintings, figurative sculpture, contemporary artwork, emerging artists, expressionist art, etchings and much more.

CARMEL CITY BEACH AND OCEAN STREET BEACH

Ocean Avenue, 831-624-4909; www.carmel.com

Carmel City Beach and Ocean Street Beach, located at the foot of Ocean Avenue, are easily accessible, have white sands and surfer-friendly waters. Carmel City beach holds a sand castle competition annually. Dogs can run freely on the beach and bonfires are permitted south of 10th Avenue. This is a great beach to gather friends for an afternoon picnic or a late-night bonfire. Carmel beaches are the most photographed beaches in the region and are often an inspiration for many of the artists who live here.

Daily 6 a.m.-10 p.m.

CARMEL RIVER STATE BEACH

Carmelo Street and Scenic Road, 831-649-2836; www.parks.ca.gov

At Carmel River State Beach, south of Carmel on Scenic Road, find calm waters, tide pools and an adjacent bird sanctuary in a lagoon. This state beach is a great place for hiking, kayaking, bird-watching and sunbathing. Monastery Beach, which is also part of the park, is usually frequented by scuba divers.

EARTHBOUND FARMS

7250 Carmel Valley Road, Carmel, 831-625-6219; www.ebfarm.com

A major player in the produce field—its products are in 75 percent of all super-markets—Earthbound Farms started in 1984, producing herbs and a variety of organic greens for restaurants in the area. Its pre-washed salads put it on the map and the rest is history. The 30 acres in Carmel are devoted to research and development, the fruits of which are sold at the farm stand right up front. You'll find pink lemons, golden raspberries, multi-colored beets (prepared in a delicious salad) and, of course, more than 60 varieties of lettuce. Also sold are foamy lattes, warm panini sandwiches, freshly baked breads, sweet treats and more.

Monday-Saturday 8 a.m.-6:30 p.m., Sunday 9 a.m.-6 p.m.

POINT LOBOS STATE RESERVE

Highway 1, Carmel, 831-624-4909; www.ptlobos.org

With its natural grove of Monterey cypresses, hundreds of plant, bird and animal species, you'll understand why this state reserve has often been called "the crown jewel of the State Park System." From Point Lobos, you can see many marine mammals in their natural habitat, such as sea lions, different types of seals, sea otters, whales and dolphins. On land, you will probably see gray foxes, coyotes, bobcats and deer. Occasionally, but not often, mountain lions and badgers will come through the reserve looking for food. There is a picnic area, naturalist programs and scuba diving is permitted with proof of certification. Dogs are not allowed in the reserve.

Admission: $10 per car. Daily 8 a.m.-sunset.

RANCHO CAÑADA GOLF CLUB
4860 Carmel Valley Road, Carmel, 831-624-0111, 800-536-9459; www.ranchocanada.com

If golf is your game, and you're up for a challenge, then put your skills to the test at the acclaimed Rancho Cañada Golf Club in the heart of Monterey Peninsula at the entrance of Carmel Valley. There are two 18-hole championship courses: the East Course, with the Carmel River crossing the course five times, and the West Course, which has both broad and narrow fairways with the Carmel River intersecting three times. The Santa Lucia Mountains serve as a backdrop. There is a driving range, a golf shop, dining in the Golfers' Grill and a full bar.

SAN CARLOS BORROMÉO DE CARMELO MISSION
3080 Rio Road, Carmel, 831-624-1271; www.carmelmission.org

Founded in 1771 by Father Junipero Serra, the Spanish Franciscan priest and explorer, this is the oldest church in Carmel and headquarters for the California missions. The Convento Museum is dedicated to Father Serra, who lived and worked there. The Mora Chapel Gallery holds a life-size memorial cenotaph, which is also dedicated to Father Serra. You can tour the Basilica, which is surrounded by gardens and fountains.

Admission: adults $5, seniors $4, children 5-17 $1. Monday-Saturday 9:30a.m.-5p.m., Sunday 10:30 a.m.-5 p.m.

GILROY
FORTINO WINERY
4525 Hecker Pass Highway, Gilroy, 408-842-3305; www.fortinowinery.com

This small family-run winery is located in the Santa Clara Valley and offers tours, free wine tasting and a picnic area. The winery produces chardonnay, burgundy reserve, carignan, maribella, cabernet sauvignon, sangiovese, two sparkling wines and fruit wines.

Tuesday-Saturday 10 a.m.-5 p.m., Sunday 11 a.m.-5 p.m.

MONTEREY
CANNERY ROW
Cannery Row, Monterey, 831-649-6690; www.canneryrow.com

Immortalized in John Steinbeck's 1945 novel of the same name, Cannery Row grew up around the Asian and American companies that established canning and fishing operations in the area at the turn of the 20th century. The World War I boom turned the city into the Sardine Capital of the World, at least until the Monterey Bay sardine population collapsed due to overfishing. The Cannery Row described by Steinbeck followed in its wake, a haven for bums, prostitutes and eccentrics. Locals pushed to revitalize the decaying strip in the 1950s, an initiative that culminated in 1984 when the Monterey Bay Aquarium

BEST ATTRACTIONS

WHAT ARE SOME OF THE BEST PLACES FOR OUTDOOR FUN IN THE CENTRAL COAST?

TAKE IN VIEWS AT JULIA PFEIFFER BURNS STATE PARK
Big Sur is known for its untouched beauty. See it at this park, which is full of trees, cliffs and an 80-foot waterfall. You can also see whales from the Overlook Trail.

EXPLORE AT CARMEL CITY BEACH AND OCEAN STREET BEACH
Carmel beaches are the most photographed in the region. Come see the picture-perfect sandy shores and surfer-friendly waters at these popular beaches.

VISIT POINT LOBOS STATE RESERVE
This is one of the best parks in the state. You can see seals, sea otters, whales and dolphins in the water and gray foxes, coyotes, raccoons and deer on land.

COAST ALONG THE 17-MILE DRIVE
The 17-mile trek from Carmel to Monterey is hailed as one of the most scenic coastal drives in the world. You'll go past Pebble Beach and a number of other lovely spots.

was opened in a former cannery. Today, Cannery Row is a parade of waterfront hotels, nearly 100 shops and a dizzying array of seafood restaurants and other eateries.

CASA SOBERANES
336 Pacific St., Monterey, 831-649-7118; www.parks.ca.gov

This adobe house was built in 1842 and contains displays of Monterey history from 1840 to 1970. This Mexican Colonial building is an excellent example of adobe construction. The walls are 38 inches thick and it is filled with antique furniture, a collection of local artwork and silver. Part of the Monterey State Historic Park, this house can only be toured with a State Park guide.

Admission: Free. Guided Tours: Friday-Wednesday 11:30 a.m. and 3 p.m.

COLTON HALL MUSEUM
City Hall, Pacific and Madison streets, Monterey, 831-646-5648; www.monterey.org/museum

Built as a town hall and public school in 1849 by the Reverend Walter Colton, who served as the Chief Magistrate of the Monterey District during the

American occupation of California from 1846 to 1849, the architecture of this building is Classic Revival design of stone and adobe mortar. The first constitution of California (in Spanish and English) was written here. The Old Monterey Jail was added to the building in 1854, at which time Colton Hall served as the Monterey County Courthouse.

Admission: Free. Daily 10 a.m.-4 p.m.

CUSTOM HOUSE

20 Custom House Plaza, Monterey, 831-649-7118; www.parks.ca.gov

The oldest government building in California was a busy trading center in the 1800s. It used to be Mexico's primary port of entry on the coast of California. The building houses exhibits recreating what it looked like in the 1840s. Commodore John Drake Sloat raised the American flag over this adobe building in 1846, bringing 600,000 square miles into the Union.

Daily 10 a.m.-4 p.m.

MONTEREY BAY AQUARIUM

886 Cannery Row, Monterey, 831-648-4800; www.mbayaq.org

The preeminent aquarium in the United States, this space attracts nearly 2 million visitors each year. Located in a former Hovden Cannery, which canned squid and sardines until the early 1970s, the facility is now home to 35,000 plants and animals representing some 550 species, with a focus on local sea life. Impressive exhibits include a three-story kelp forest, Outer Bay (a million-gallon indoor ocean with sharks, barracuda, jellyfish, tuna and sea turtles) and a walk-through shorebird aviary. Kids can let loose in Splash Zone, an educational play area with tunnels, clam-shaped chairs, petting pools with bat rays and starfish and a penguin habitat.

Admission: adults $29.95, students and seniors $27.95, children 3-12 $17.95, children under 3 free. Daily 10 a.m.-6 p.m.; May 26-September 1, Daily 9:30 a.m.-6 p.m.; July-September, Saturday-Sunday 9:30 a.m.-8 p.m.

MONTEREY MUSEUM OF ART PACIFIC STREET

559 Pacific St., Monterey, 831-372-5477; www.montereyart.org

The Monterey Museum of Art focuses on American art and displays early Californian paintings, photography, contemporary art, and American and Asian art. There are also changing exhibitions of major American artists. Docent-guided tours are available; see website for details.

Admission: adults $5, students and military $2.50, children 12 and under free. Wednesday-Saturday 11 a.m.-5 p.m., Sunday 1-4 p.m.

OLD FISHERMAN'S WHARF

39 Fisherman's Wharf, Monterey; www.montereywharf.com

The fisherman's wharf is filled with restaurants where you can try fresh seafood. It's also packed with tourist shops, galleries, tackle and bait stores, as well as a theater that has been in operation since 1976. And it's a tour boat departure point for whale watching cruises, sailing and fishing. You can also see plenty of pelicans, sea otters and seals hanging out by the pier and in the water.

PATH OF HISTORY TOUR
20 Custom House Plaza, 831-649-7118; www.parks.ca.gov

This self-guided tour is a two-mile look at Old Monterey including adobes, gardens and other sites of interest. There are yellow tiles in the sidewalk that identify distinguished buildings—several of which are open for public viewing—and explain their history and architecture. The tour includes the Cooper-Molera House, the Custom House, Larkin House and Casa Soberanes, among others. Obtain a map at the Monterey Peninsula Visitor and Convention Bureau on Camino El Estero and Franklin streets.

PRESIDIO OF MONTEREY
360 Patton Ave., Monterey, 831-242-5104; www.monterey.army.mil

This presidio was developed in 1902 as a cantonment for troops returning from the Philippine Insurrection. It is the site of a monument to John Drake Sloat, commander of the American troops that captured Monterey. It is also the home of the Defense Language Institute. There are 12 historic sites and monuments on Presidio Hill to view.

ROBERT LOUIS STEVENSON HOUSE
530 Houston St., Monterey, 831-649-7118; www.parks.ca.gov

This state historic monument has a large collection of Robert Louis Stevenson memorabilia as well as beautiful gardens. Stevenson lived here for four months while visiting his future wife. At that time, the house was a boarding house known as the French Hotel. Part of the Monterey State Historic Park, this house can only be toured with a State Park guide.

Tours: Friday-Wednesday 2 p.m.

ROYAL PRESIDIO CHAPEL
500 Church St., Monterey, 831-373-2628; www.sancarloscathedral.net

Founded in 1770 by Father Junipero Serra, this chapel has been in continuous use since 1795, and is the only presidio chapel remaining in California. This National Historic Landmark has a uniquely ornate façade and has a Spanish Colonial style.

Daily.

PEBBLE BEACH
17-MILE DRIVE
Pebble Beach; www.pebblebeach.com

Stretching from Carmel to Monterey, along the Pacific and through the Del Monte Forest, this toll road is one of the most scenic coastal drives in the world. The winding road will take you past the Lodge at Pebble Beach; the ocean coast; the Spyglass Hill Golf Course; The Inn and Links at Spanish Bay; the trademark of Pebble Beach, the Lone Cypress tree; and through an exclusive neighborhood and many other points of interest. Stop for lunch along the way at the Seal Rock picnic area or visit one of the points on the ocean to watch for sea otters, seals and sea lions.

PEBBLE BEACH GOLF LINKS

1700 Seventeen Mile Drive, Pebble Beach, 831-644-7960; www.pebblebeach.com

Although it's quite a drive from San Francisco, an opportunity to play on one of the nation's most exclusive courses is irresistible. To get a tee time, call well in advance (at least a month) and be prepared to spend more than $400 per person. The course goes over the Pacific Ocean at times, and the sound and sight of waves lapping at the edges of the course is exhilarating.

WHERE TO STAY

BIG SUR

★★★★POST RANCH INN

Highway 1, Big Sur, 831-667-2200, 800-527-2200; www.postranchinn.com

Perched on a cliff overlooking Big Sur's rugged coastline, the inn is an ideal romantic getaway. Designed to blend with the Santa Lucia Mountains, the buildings resemble sophisticated modern tree houses. Each of the 40 guest rooms has an ocean or mountain view, king-size bed, wood-burning fireplace, indoor spa tub, private deck and digital music system. The wet bar and minibar are filled with complimentary snacks, juices and half-bottles of red and white wine. What you won't find: TVs or alarm clocks. Wake up when you want to and head to the Post Ranch Spa for a massage or body treatment. Take a private yoga class or a guided hike through the Santa Lucia and Ventana Mountains. End your evening at the Sierra Mar restaurant, which serves a superb prix fixe menu and has an extensive wine list.

40 rooms. Restaurant, bar. Complimentary breakfast. Fitness center. Pool. Spa. No children allowed. $351 and up

★★★VENTANA INN & SPA

48123 Highway 1, Big Sur, 831-667-2331, 800-628-6500; www.ventanainn.com

This stylish resort speaks to nature lovers who have a soft spot for luxury. From its perch 1,200 feet above the coastline on the Santa Lucia Mountains, the property sprawls across 243 acres of towering redwoods, wildflower-filled meadows and rolling hills. Each guest room is complete with a private balcony or patio with mountain or ocean views. After swimming, hiking or a guided Big Sur tour, indulge in a treatment at the Allegria Spa or dine at the Restaurant at Ventana, where the inventive cuisine competes with the panoramic view.

60 rooms. Restaurant, bar. Complimentary breakfast. Business center. Fitness center. Pool. Spa. No children allowed. $351 and up

CARMEL

★★★CYPRESS INN

Lincoln Lane and Seventh Street, Carmel, 831-624-3871, 800-443-7443; www.cypress-inn.com

Built in 1929, this landmark Mediterranean-style hotel is steps away from the town center's boutiques, art galleries and great restaurants. A courtyard off the main lobby welcomes dogs and cats, and the inn also offers pet-sitting services. (Hollywood actress and animal advocate Doris Day is a co-owner.) The sophisticated rooms include bathrobes, pet blankets, fresh flowers, fruit

bowls and sherry decanters. Some deluxe rooms come with a jet tub, a fireplace and a private entrance. The two-story tower suite offers an ocean view with a living area and sleeper sofa on the first floor. Terry's Lounge serves afternoon tea, lunch, tapas and dinner along with a long list of specialty cocktails and wines.
44 rooms. Restaurant, bar. Complimentary breakfast. Fitness center. Pets accepted. $151-250

★★★HIGHLANDS INN, A HYATT HOTEL
120 Highlands Drive, Carmel, 831-620-1234; www.highlandsinn.hyatt.com

Open since 1917, this sophisticated rendering of a mountain lodge is well suited to its rustic setting. The hotel's décor incorporates an abundance of wood and stone, and the rooms and suites are outfitted in contemporary, earth-tone furnishings. This inn features two restaurants and one lounge. California Market has a casual setting, with optional alfresco dining, and is open for breakfast, lunch and dinner. A more upscale option, Pacific's Edge features glass walls that allow views of the ocean and a wine list featuring over 1,400 labels. The Sunset Lounge delivers views of Point Lobos State Reserve, cocktails and live jazz music on Friday and Saturday nights. Take a complimentary mountain bike out for a ride through Carmel.
48 rooms. Restaurant, bar. Fitness center. Pool. $351 and up

★★★LA PLAYA HOTEL
Camino Real and Eighth Avenue, Carmel, 831-624-6476, 800-582-8900; www.laplayahotel.com

This renovated Mediterranean-style villa has rooms with tropical décor and ocean, garden or village views. There are five cottages with private gardens, and the hotel's location is only one block from the beach. Dine alfresco on the Terrace Grill's charming heated terrace, which overlooks the garden. Get a massage, facial, or reflexology treatment in the garden or in your room.
80 rooms. Restaurant, bar. Business center. Pool. Spa. $151-250

★★★MISSION RANCH
26270 Dolores St., Carmel, 831-624-6436, 800-538-8221; www.missionranchcarmel.com

Former Carmel mayor Clint Eastwood bought this 1850s farmhouse and saved it from demolition in the 1980s. Since then, it has been restored, expanded and filled with antiques and custom-designed rustic pieces. Surrounded by cypress and eucalyptus trees along with new gardens, the Bunkhouse is the oldest building on the ranch. The cozy guest rooms have quilted beds and patios from which to enjoy tranquil sunsets. There are six championship tennis courts on property along with a fitness center. Mission Ranch's restaurant serves dinner nightly and a Sunday jazz and champagne brunch. The Piano Bar is a fun place to frequent any night of the week.

31 rooms. Restaurant, bar. Complimentary breakfast. Fitness center. Tennis. $151-250

CARMEL VALLEY
★★★★BERNARDUS LODGE
415 Carmel Valley Road, Carmel Valley, 831-658-3400, 888-648-9463; www.bernardus.com

Long considered one of the finest winemaking estates in California, the Lodge has a scenic Central Valley location and impressive views of the surrounding mountains and countryside. The warm and spacious guest rooms include feather beds, fireplaces and oversized bathtubs for two. Check in is done in your room, where a complimentary bottle of Bernardus wine awaits. The spa offers a wide variety of treatments, while the Lodge's restaurant, Marinus, is an epicurean's delight.

57 rooms. Restaurant, bar. Business center. Fitness center. Pool. Spa. Tennis. $351 and up

★★★CARMEL VALLEY RANCH
1 Old Ranch Road, Carmel Valley, 831-625-9500, 866-282-4745; www.carmelvalleyranch.com

John Pritzker recently purchased this resort set on 400 rolling acres in the secluded Carmel Valley countryside and made several updates. All of the guest rooms and suites were upgraded, a lovely new spa was tucked into the resort, and two new pools with outdoor dining and natural fire pits were added. The 18-hole Pete Dye designed golf course was also spruced up, and the fitness facility was expanded to include a kids' playground, basketball court, bocce court and tennis courts.

144 rooms. Restaurant, bar. Fitness center. Pool. Spa. Golf. Tennis. $151-250

GILROY
★★★★CORDEVALLE, A ROSEWOOD RESORT
1 Cordevalle Club Drive, San Martin, 408-695-4500, 888-767-3966; www.cordevalle.com

CordeValle sprawls over 1,700 acres in the foothills between San Jose and Monterey, attracting small business groups as well as golfers and those looking for a romantic weekend. The spacious, high-ceilinged modern bungalows overlook a rolling 18-hole Robert Trent Jones, Jr. golf course. Rooms feature goose-down comforters, original artwork, flat-screen TVs and a fireplace. The Villa Suites are 1,100 square feet and offer the same amenities as the bungalows but also have a bathroom with steam shower and jetted tub and an enclosed patio with another outdoor shower and private whirlpool. Each treatment room in the resort's spa, Sense, has a private garden. Treatments include massages, body wraps, body scrubs and facials. Guests also get access to the spa's whirlpool, and steam room, outdoor heated pool, fitness center, tennis courts, outdoor yoga deck and hiking trails. The onsite vineyard produces the wine and cheese placed in guest rooms as a welcome gift.

45 rooms. Restaurant, bar. Fitness center. Pool. Spa. Golf. $351 and up

MONTEREY

★★★HILTON GARDEN INN MONTEREY

1000 Aguajito Road, Monterey, 831-373-6141, 800-234-5697; www.hiltongardeninn.com

Located a half-mile from the Monterey beaches, this hotel is set on a beautiful garden landscape among Monterey pine and oak trees. Guest rooms feature comfortable beds, complimentary Internet access, microwaves, refrigerators and private patios or balconies. The Pacific Grille features fresh California cuisine for breakfast and dinner. Unwind in the outdoor pool and whirlpool or sunbathe on the large outdoor patio.

204 rooms. Restaurant, bar. Business center. Fitness center. Pool. $151-250

★★★HOTEL PACIFIC

300 Pacific St., Monterey, 831-373-5700, 800-554-5542; www.hotelpacific.com

Just a block from Fisherman's Wharf in downtown Monterey, this Southwest-style boutique hotel has patios with potted plants, fountains and colorful umbrellas. The lobby features hand-tiled floors, original artwork and photos by Helmut Horn. Guest rooms are divided into living and sleeping spaces and include fireplaces, colorful goose-down featherbeds, hardwood floors, original artwork, tree trunk nightstands and private balconies or patios. A complimentary continental breakfast and afternoon snacks are served daily. Baths feature Aveda products and separate tubs and showers.

105 rooms. Complimentary breakfast. $251-350

★★★HYATT REGENCY MONTEREY

1 Old Golf Course Road, Monterey, 831-372-1234, 800-233-1234;
www.hyattregencymonterey.com

Located about a mile from downtown Monterey, this large, rustic resort on 23 acres of pine and cypress trees is adjacent to the Del Monte Golf Course. Rooms are decorated in natural earth tones and feature pillow-top mattresses, flat-screen TVs and iPod docks. Enjoy Tuscan cuisine with fresh ingredients at TusCA Ristorante. The resort's activities include two swimming pools, tennis, golf and bicycle rentals, and a full-service spa.

550 rooms. Restaurant, bar. Pool. Spa. Pets accepted. Golf. $251-350

★★★★MONTEREY PLAZA HOTEL & SPA

400 Cannery Row, Monterey, 831-646-1700, 800-334-3999; www.montereyplazahotel.com

Guest rooms at this luxuriously appointed, European-style hotel give guests the impression of being on a ship with an ocean-view balcony. Two restaurants provide culinary diversions, and golf, surf shops, kayak rentals and the Monterey Bay Recreation Trail are all nearby. The landscaped pool deck is right on the water and is the place to be at this coastal retreat.

290 rooms. Restaurant, bar. Business center. Fitness center. Pool. Spa. Beach. $251-350

★★★PORTOLA PLAZA HOTEL

2 Portola Plaza, Monterey, 831-649-4511, 866-711-1534; www.portolaplazahotel.com

This hotel is a short walk from Fisherman's Wharf, Pebble Beach and many shops and galleries. Rooms are furnished with pillow-top beds and artwork by local artists, and many have beautiful views of the bay. A host of outdoor activities are available, including golf, bicycling and kayaking. Dine alfresco at Jacks, which serves hearty cuisine and has an extensive wine list, or enjoy a beer and pub grub at Peter B's brewpub.

379 rooms. Restaurant, bar. Business center. Fitness center. Pool. Spa. $251-350

★★★SPINDRIFT INN

652 Cannery Row, Monterey, 831-646-8900, 800-841-1879; www.spindriftinn.com

At high tide, guests of this intimate, European-style inn can stand directly above the ocean to see the waves crashing in onto McAbee beach. Rooms have window seats, wood-burning fireplaces, flat-screen TVs, marble vanities and canopy beds; some offer views of the ocean. The onsite restaurant, Paradiso Trattoria, specializes in fresh seafood and has an oyster bar. Complimentary breakfast is delivered on a silver tray to your room, and a wine and cheese reception featuring wine from the local Ventana Vineyard takes place each evening.

45 rooms. Complimentary breakfast. Beach. $251-350

PEBBLE BEACH

★★★★CASA PALMERO AT PEBBLE BEACH

1518 Cypress Drive, Pebble Beach, 831-622-6650, 800-654-9300; www.pebblebeach.com

This grand Mediterranean-style estate overlooks the first and second fairways of Pebble Beach Golf Links and provides a pampering get-away. The guest rooms echo the resort's sophistication with their overstuffed furniture and neutral tones. In each room, you'll find a wood-burning fireplace, fresh flowers, a luxurious robe and slippers and oversized soaking tubs. The Spa Rooms are on the ground floor and feature a private patio with a whirlpool. If you're looking for more space, book a Palmero Suite with a living room and fireplace, wet bar, oversized bath, four-poster bed and an outdoor courtyard with a whirlpool. Enjoy the serene pool area or take advantage of the larger Pebble Beach complex's many restaurants, shops, private tennis club, yoga classes, spa and, of course, world-renowned golf. Guests also enjoy a breakfast basket and complimentary refreshments at the bar and lounge every evening.

24 rooms. Complimentary breakfast. Bar. Fitness center. Pool. Spa. Golf. Tennis. $351 and up

★★★★THE INN AT SPANISH BAY

2700 Seventeen Mile Drive, Pebble Beach, 831-647-7500, 800-654-9300; www.pebblebeach.com

Direct access to the revered links at Pebble Beach makes this inn popular with golfers, while the splendid natural setting overlooking the Pacific Ocean and Spanish Bay has universal appeal. Views of the Del Monte Forest, famed golf course and ocean are striking, especially when enjoyed from the privacy of a guest room or suite. With nine different types of guest rooms to choose from, you can decide whether you want a view of the Del Monte Forest, the ocean, the golf course, or the courtyard. Some rooms come with fireplaces, outdoor patios or balconies, deep soaking whirlpool tubs, sitting and dining areas, and even a grand piano, if you choose. A gallery of shops showcases fine sportswear and resort apparel along with tennis and golf equipment. From an expertly staffed tennis and fitness facility to the outdoor pool, the amenities are top notch. Four distinctive dining establishments tease taste buds with an array of offerings.

269 rooms. Restaurant, bar. Business center. Fitness center. Pool. Spa. Golf. Tennis. $351 and up

★★★★THE LODGE AT PEBBLE BEACH

1700 Seventeen Mile Drive, Pebble Beach, 831-647-7500, 800-654-9300; www.pebblebeach.com

Distinguished by its impressive architecture and spectacular oceanside setting, the Lodge at Pebble Beach is the jewel in the crown of the world-class Pebble Beach resort. The traditionally styled rooms are spacious, and most include a wood-burning fireplace and patio or balcony with views of flowering gardens or oceanside fairways. Spa rooms have a private garden with outdoor whirl-pools. For a panoramic view of the ocean, book an Ocean View room, which also has a view of the 18th hole/fairway and Stillwater Cove and a patio or balcony. Unwind by the pool or play tennis in the resort's state-of-the-art tennis facility. The four restaurants also offer a variety of elegant settings, and run the gamut from casual American fare and succulent seafood to updated, lightened versions of French classics. The Lodge's spa celebrates the diversity of natural resources indigenous to the Monterey Peninsula in its treatments and therapies.

161 rooms. Restaurant, bar. Fitness center. Spa. Golf. Tennis. $351 and up

RECOMMENDED

MONTEREY

THE CLEMENT MONTEREY

750 Cannery Row, Monterey, 831-375-4500; www.ichotelsgroup.com

This newer Intercontinental hotel offers stylish accommodations in the heart of Monterey. Guest rooms have marble bathrooms with soaking tubs, plasma TVs, media centers and iPod docs. Spacious suites have ocean views and balconies. The hotel offers a state-of-the-art fitness center, as well as a spa. Stop in the C Bar for a glass of bubbly and some appetizers.

208 rooms. Bar. Business center. Fitness center. Pool. Spa. $251-350

MONTEREY BAY INN

242 Cannery Row, Monterey, 831-373-6242, 800-424-6242; www.montereybayinn.com

Although its exterior is industrial looking, this inn has an excellent location overlooking the bay and Fisherman's Wharf, and the rooms are modern, comfortable, clean and well maintained. Rooms have balconies equipped with binoculars, CD players and local photography books. Get pampered at the Serenity Salon and Spa; enjoy a rooftop hot tub with views of the bay and ocean; and wander down to the accessible beach for scuba diving, sunbathing, swimming or just taking photos of the beautiful scenery.

49 rooms. Complimentary breakfast. Spa. Beach. $251-350

WHERE TO EAT

BIG SUR

★★★THE RESTAURANT AT VENTANA

Ventana Inn, 48123 Highway 1, Big Sur, 831-667-4242; www.ventanainn.com

This restaurant at the Ventana Inn shows off nature's bounty from its wide, rustic, outdoor patio with sturdy redwood tables shaded by market umbrellas. If you can't sit outside, the dining room is warm and cozy, with tall windows, a large stone fireplace, wood-beamed ceilings and a bird's-eye view of the exhibition kitchen, where you'll watch as plates of Mediterranean fare are prepared from California's finest ingredients.

Mediterranean. Lunch, dinner. Bar. Reservations recommended. Outdoor seating. $36-85

★★★★SIERRA MAR

Highway 1, Big Sur, 831-667-2800; www.postranchinn.com

This acclaimed restaurant, located in the Post Ranch Inn, blends comfort with elegance in natural surroundings—cliffs, mountains and the ocean below. Executive chef Craig von Foerster's menu focuses on California cuisine with French and Mediterranean influences. His four-course, prix fixe menu changes daily and utilizes seasonal organic products. You might find butter poached Maine lobster as a course, saffron seafood soup with gulf prawns and wild salmon, artichoke ravioli or roast rabbit. Desserts are equally appealing with options such as baked Valrhona milk chocolate crêpes with hazelnut brown butter sauce, a hazelnut lace cookie and bittersweet Valrhona chocolate sorbet. The restaurant has one of the most extensive wine cellars in North America with well-known wine producers and hard-to-find bottles from boutique vineyards. They also offer all guests a complimentary breakfast buffet.

American. Lunch, dinner. Reservations recommended. Outdoor seating. Bar. $86 and up

CARMEL

★★★ANTON AND MICHEL

Mission Street between Ocean and Seventh avenues, Carmel, 831-624-2406; www.antonandmichel.com

Though this long-standing restaurant's interior is ready for an update, the reliable French-inspired dishes are still as flavorful and satisfying as ever. Entrées include filet mignon, fresh-farmed abalone, rack of lamb and Châteaubriand carved tableside in the classic European tradition. Finales include flambé desserts, also prepared tableside. Choose a wine from a list that features more than 800 selections.

French. Lunch, dinner. Reservations recommended. Outdoor seating. Bar. $16-35

★★★CASANOVA

Fifth and Mission Streets, Carmel, 831-625-0501; www.casanovarestaurant.com

One of the first restaurants in Carmel to offer a European bistro experience, Casanova has been open since 1977. All four dining rooms (one of which includes Vincent van Gogh's table from Auberge Ravoux) feature a unique charm. The cuisine is influenced by the flavors of France and Italy and includes dishes such as pan-roasted wild salmon with dijon mustard-citrus olive oil sauce, and pasta with roasted tomato coulis and goat cheese pesto sauce. The hand-dug wine cellar lies 14 feet beneath the restaurant and holds the more than 30,000 bottles.

French, Italian. Lunch, dinner. Reservations recommended. Outdoor seating. Children's menu. $36-85

★★★THE FRENCH POODLE
Junipero and Fifth avenues, Carmel, 831-624-8643

This restaurant is an intimate hideaway known for artfully presented fare prepared French style. Sample truffles, foie gras with truffle dressing, filet mignon and fresh local abalone. For dessert, try the French flan or the flourless chocolate cake.

French. Dinner. Closed Sunday. Reservations recommended. $36-85

★★★FRESH CREAM RESTAURANT
Dolores Street and 8th Avenue, Carmel, 831-250-7943;
www.freshcream.com

Lauded by local and national foodies, Fresh Cream serves California-French fare. Try an appetizer such as foie gras pate, capers and onion with brioche toast; lobster ravioli with lobster butter and black and gold caviar; or Dungeness crab cakes. Entrées include grilled filet mignon with roasted portabellos and truffle madeira sauce; pan-seared ahi tuna; and broiled lobster tail and grilled prawns with white corn bisque and brioche toast. The wine list features wines from California and France.

French. Dinner. Reservations recommended. Bar. $36-85

★★★PACIFIC'S EDGE RESTAURANT
HIghlands Inn, 120 Highlands Drive, Carmel, 831-622-5445; www.pacificsedge.com

Enjoy the Pacific view, an extensive selection of mostly American wines and the local catch—Monterey spot prawns, for instance—which is usually richly accented with fresh herbs and plated with seasonal ingredients. The restaurant is located in the Highlands Inn.

American. Dinner. Reservations recommended. Bar. $36-85

CARMEL VALLEY
★★★★MARINUS
Bernardus Lodge, 415 Carmel Valley Road, Carmel Valley, 831-658-3595; www.bernardus.com

This warm, country inn-style restaurant located inside Bernardus Lodge features exposed-beam ceilings, vintage tapestries and a 12-foot-wide limestone fireplace. Dishes are prepared using organic and fresh ingredients—in fact, neighbors often stop by with extra tomatoes or fishermen come in with their catch of the day. Chef Cal Stamenov then turns the goods into fresh salads and main courses such as salmon with English peas, braised leek and beurre blanc. The huge wine cellar, which stocks more than 1,800 selections, is impressive, even in wine country. Try the tasting menu, which gives you the option of choosing between a four-, five-, six- or eight-course menu.

American. Dinner. Closed Monday-Tuesday. Reservations recommended. $86 and up

MONTEREY

★★★CIBO RISTORANTE ITALIANO

301 Alvarado St., Monterey, 831-649-8151; www.cibo.com

This sleek, downtown restaurant specializes in innovative interpretations of classic Sicilian cooking. You'll find favorites like gnocchi, ravioli, pasta with bolognese sauce, veal cannelloni, risotto, pizzas, seafood, filets, swordfish, pork chops, Italian sausage, lamb chops and more. Start with fried calamari or fresh oysters and then try the Pizza Cibo with thinly sliced green apple, leeks, prosciutto and mozzarella. A large wine list features vintages from Italy and California along with Cibo's own private labeled chardonnay and cabernet sauvignon. You can also hear an eclectic mix of jazz six days a week at this live music hot spot.

Italian. Dinner. Children's menu. Bar. $36-85

★★★THE DUCK CLUB

Monterey Plaza Hotel, 400 Cannery Row, Monterey, 831-646-1706; www.montereyplazahotel.com

This elegant restaurant tucked away in the Monterey Plaza Hotel features a seasonal menu and wood-roasted dishes prepared in an exhibition-style kitchen from executive chef James Waller. As the name suggests, duck is a specialty; try the Steinbeck's Duck dish with roasted potatoes and caramelized orange sauce. The menu also features fresh local produce and sustainable seafood.

American. Breakfast, dinner. Reservations recommended. Children's menu. Bar. $86 and up

★★★JOHN PISTO'S WHALING STATION

763 Wave St., Monterey, 831-373-3778; www.whalingstationmonterey.com

Located just two blocks from Cannery Row and Monterey Bay, John Pisto's serves generous portions in a handsome setting, which includes a horseshoe-shaped bar, copper walls, alabaster lamps, beveled glass windows and large French posters. Pick your lobster out of the tank or opt for a tasty sirloin, filet mignon or prime rib. Chef and restaurateur John Pisto, who owns four restaurants, also hosts a TV cooking show, *Monterey's Cookin' Pisto Style,* but you still might be able to catch him working in the kitchen.

American, steak. Dinner. Children's menu. Bar. $36-85

WHICH WINE COUNTRY RESTAURANTS HAVE THE BEST WINE OFFERINGS?

Casanova:
Be sure to drink up at Casanova, one of Carmel's first European-type bistros. The restaurant's hand-dug wine cellar contains a staggering 30,000 bottles.

Marinus:
Located on a winery, Marinus can't help but offer a great selection of wine. Try the Marinus Estate Bordeaux-style red, the winery's specialty.

Sierra Mar:
Sierra Mar has one of the most comprehensive wine cellars in North America, with both well-known producers and hard-to-find selections represented on the list.

★★★MONTRIO BISTRO

414 Calle Principal, Monterey, 831-648-8880; www.montrio.com

Housed in an old brick firehouse, this bistro's downtown Monterey dining room has soft sculptures suspended from the ceiling to muffle sound and track lighting made from fine metalwork twisted into the shape of grapevines. House specialties include crab cakes with spicy remoulade, rotisserie chicken over roasted garlic whipped potatoes and oven-roasted portobello mushrooms. For dessert, try the decadent flourless chocolate cake with port swirl ice cream.

American, Mediterranean. Dinner. Children's menu. Bar. $16-35

★★★SARDINE FACTORY

701 Wave St., Monterey, 831-373-3775; www.sardinefactory.com

Known as the flagship of Cannery Row, this restaurant serves New American cuisine in several elegant dining rooms, including the Captain's Room and the Conservatory, a glassed-in space. Start out with a cocktail in the lounge where a pianist plays Tuesday through Saturday, before heading to dinner. The menu consists of fresh fish, shellfish, meat and locally grown produce including dishes such as prawns with black truffle risotto and lemon caper sauce.

Seafood. Dinner. Reservations recommended. Children's menu. Bar. $36-85

★★★STOKES RESTAURANT & BAR

500 Hartnell St., Monterey, 831-373-1110; www.stokesrestaurant.com

Housed in a historic pink adobe building dating to 1833, this downtown restaurant has several dining rooms and a mix of contemporary and early California décor, including Mexican tile and chairs, and a wood-burning oven. The dining rooms feature large tables, wooden booths and banquettes with stencil designs and colorful paintings on the wall. The Mediterranean-inspired cuisine is made with regional produce, meats, fish and cheeses. Enjoy the housemade organic sourdough bread that's baked fresh daily. Try the pork shoulder with broccoli rabe, crispy polenta and star anise jus; or vegetarian crêpes with spinach béchamel, spring vegetables and aged Gruyère.

American, Mediterranean. Dinner. Bar. $16-35

★★★TARPY'S ROADHOUSE

2999 Monterey Salinas Highway, Monterey, 831-647-1444; www.tarpys.com

From a historic 1917 hacienda on Salinas Highway, Tarpy's serves innovative American country fare—steaks, wild game and seafood. Dishes include grilled rib-eye with herb au jus and horseradish sour cream on mashed potatoes; meatloaf with marsala-mushroom gravy on roasted garlic whipped potatoes; and grilled tiger shrimp on rice pilaf with citrus salsa and lemon beurre blanc.

American. Lunch, dinner, Sunday brunch. Outdoor seating. Children's menu. Bar. $36-85

PEBBLE BEACH

★★★CLUB XIX

The Lodge at Pebble Beach, 1700 Seventeen Mile Drive, Pebble Beach, 831-625-8519; www.pebblebeach.com

Located in the Lodge at Pebble Beach on the lower level of the main building, just off the famous 18th green of the championship Pebble Beach Golf Links, this restaurant has beautiful views of Carmel Bay. Enjoy seasonal fare prepared in a contemporary French style in the intimate inside dining room or outdoors on the patio, which has two fireplaces. During the day, you'll find a more Parisian café-like atmosphere with lighter fare. In the evening, a more elegant and romantic setting is set with a chef's tasting menu or à la carte choices featuring items such as foie gras, seared salmon and veal chop.

American, French. Dinner. Outdoor seating. Bar. $86 and up

RECOMMENDED

BIG SUR
NEPENTHE
48510 Highway 1, Big Sur, 831-667-2345;
www.nepenthebigsur.com
Located in the Santa Lucia Mountains, this restaurant has been a welcoming spot for artists, poets and travelers for 60 years. Comfort food favorites fill the menu, including naturally raised rib-eye steak, vegetarian lasagna and roast chicken with sage stuffing.

American. Lunch, dinner. Outdoor seating. Children's menu. Bar. $16-35

SPAS

BIG SUR
★★★★POST RANCH SPA
Post Ranch Inn, Highway 1, Big Sur, 831-667-2200, 800-527-2200;
www.postranchinn.com
This spa focuses on nature-based therapies, such as the wildflower facial with organic plants and Big Sur flowers, or the skin-renewing Hungarian herbal body wrap, which blends organic herbs (including sage, ivy, cinnamon and paprika) with a Hungarian thermal mud body masque. Several treatments also draw from Native American rituals, including the Big Sur jade stone therapy, which uses jade collected from nearby beaches and basalt river rocks with massage to relieve sore muscles, and cooled marble to release inflammation. Massages are offered on your private deck or in your room, and the spa also offers private guided hikes, meditation sessions, yoga and couples massage instruction. You can work out in the fitness room, and then relax by one of the two pools.

CARMEL VALLEY
★★★★THE SPA AT BERNARDUS LODGE
Bernardus Lodge, 415 Carmel Valley Road, Carmel Valley, 831-658-3400, 888-648-9463;
www.bernardus.com
This wine country spa has seven treatment rooms, an open-air "warming pool," steam and sauna rooms, and a fountain-filled meditation garden. Indigenous herbs, flowers, essential oils and healing waters are incorporated into the spa's treatments. Book the Vineyard Romance treatment, which includes a body exfoliation, lavender-grapeseed bath, warm grape seed oil massage and a tea service of grape seed herbal tea. Or try the Chardonnay Facial, an 80-minute, hydrating treatment that incorporates chardonnay grape seeds, which are

loaded with antioxidants. The spa's signature treatment, the Carmel Valley Escape, includes a massage, facial, spa lunch and manicure and pedicure.

GILROY
★★★★SENSE, A ROSEWOOD SPA
CordeValle, A Rosewood Resort, 1 Cordevalle Club Drive, San Martin, 408-695-4500, 888-767-3966; www.cordevalle.com

This top-notch facility treats its guests to luxurious amenities, elegant interiors and a full-service spa menu. Classic contemporary is the reigning style at this spa, where earth tones and sandstone fireplaces create a serene atmosphere. The services blend European traditions with modern philosophies, and most of the treatments use locally grown herbs, flowers and even grapes from the hillsides just outside the window. Several treatments have been created specifically with golfers' needs in mind. The restful pace found here is perhaps best enjoyed from the private gardens accompanying each treatment room.

PEBBLE BEACH
★★★★THE SPA AT PEBBLE BEACH
1700 Seventeen Mile Drive, Pebble Beach, 831-649-7615, 888-565-7615; www.pebblebeach.com

Blending California's Spanish-colonial heritage with Pebble Beach's gloriously rugged natural setting, the Spa at Pebble Beach is a perfect blend of exotic elegance, with its terra-cotta-hued exterior and in-room fireplaces. Water rituals revive, replenish and restore, and body treatments nourish the skin with grape seed and sea salt scrubs. The spa's signature treatments are worth noting, including the Palmero, which uses a papaya-pineapple enzyme scrub, then a hydrating wrap, a scalp massage with warm coconut oil and a coconut moisturizer. After a long day on the golf course, try the Par-Four Massage, with two therapists performing a massage at the same time. The spa features other holistic healing methods including acupuncture, energy balancing and shiatsu, reiki, reflexology, and Thai massages. With a full salon, the spa also offers facials, waxing, haircuts and coloring, manicures and pedicures.

WHERE TO SHOP

CARMEL
THE BARNYARD SHOPPING VILLAGE
3618 The Barnyard, Carmel, 831-624-8886; www.thebarnyard.com

Nearly an acre of terraced flower gardens surround rustic, old-style California barns that house shops, galleries and restaurants. The boutiques include apparel, jewelry, gifts and a florist. There are also salons, galleries and a variety of restaurants.

Monday-Saturday 10 a.m.-6 p.m., Sunday 11 a.m.-5 p.m.

GILROY
GILROY PREMIUM OUTLETS
681 Leavesley Road, Gilroy, 408-842-3729; www.premiumoutlets.com

Shopoholics flock to the nearly 150 outlet stores which include J. Crew, BCBG

Max Azria, American Apparel, Gap, Hugo Boss, Kenneth Cole, Jones New York, DKNY Jeans, Calvin Klein and Puma among many others.
Monday-Saturday 10 a.m.-9 p.m., Sunday 10 a.m.-6 p.m.

SACRAMENTO

From its humble origins, Sacramento has always been a fortune seeker's city. Captain John A. Sutter first built a small business empire here in New Helvetia, a colony for his Swiss compatriots, only to see his workers desert him and his dream collapse with the discovery of gold at Coloma in 1848. Sutter's son, however, took advantage of the situation when he laid out Sacramento City on family-deeded land near the boat line terminus. At the entrance to Gold Rush country, the city's population rocketed to 10,000 within seven months and became California's capital in 1854. The city remains the political base for the state, but has expanded its offerings to museums, restaurants, parks and a host of other family-friendly options.

WHAT TO SEE

CALIFORNIA INDIAN HERITAGE CENTER
2618 K St., Sacramento, 916-324-8112; www.cihc.parks.ca.gov
Native Americans of California are recognized and honored at this heritage center, which preserves their traditions and culture and tells the stories of their past. Everything is restored to the natural state in which California Native Americans would have used the land for living, ceremonial purposes and traditional gatherings. Displays, exhibits and galleries include dugout canoes, weapons, pottery and basketry.
Daily 10 a.m.-5 p.m.

THE CALIFORNIA MUSEUM
1020 O St., Sacramento, 916-653-7524; www.californiamuseum.org
This museum pays tribute to the great state of California, providing exhibits on state history with an emphasis on the state's inspirational people, places and events. Governor Schwarzenegger and First Lady Maria Shriver act as honorary co-chairs to the museum. Shriver established an exhibit focusing on the contributions of women in California called "California's Remarkable Women," and the permanent exhibit, California Hall of Fame, which honors those people who have left a mark on California.
Admission: adults $8.50, students and seniors $7, children 6-13 $6, children 5 and under free.
Monday-Saturday 10 a.m.-5 p.m., Sunday noon-5 p.m.

CALIFORNIA STATE CAPITOL MUSEUM
10th and L streets, Sacramento, 916-324-0333; www.capitolmuseum.ca.gov
A working museum and a fixture in California's state park system, this lavish Roman-inspired 1874 structure is surrounded by 40 lush acres with international

flora, including California natives such as redwoods and fan palms. The building's domed rotunda straddles the two houses of the Legislature, with many of the meticulously restored rooms—including the former governor's office, decorated to match its 1906 appearance—accessible to the public. In-depth guided tours cover the lawmaking process and California's often-turbulent political history.

Admission: Free. Daily 9 a.m.-5 p.m. Tours: Daily 9 a.m.-4 p.m. (every hour).

DISCOVERY MUSEUM SCIENCE & SPACE CENTER

3615 Auburn Blvd., Sacramento, 916-575-3941; www.thediscovery.org

A modern touch in Old Sacramento, this nonprofit center organizes engaging exhibits on history, science, space and technology to all ages. Artifacts from the city's history are enshrined in a replica of the 1854 City Hall, but the broader historical focus is on the California Gold Rush, depicted through a re-created mineshaft and other displays. There is a planetarium to learn about the night sky and 20-minute star shows. The Challenger Learning Center, also located here, explores space travel.

Admission: adults $5, seniors and children 13-17 $4, children 4-12 $3, children 3 and under free. September-June, Tuesday-Friday noon-4:30 p.m., Saturday-Sunday 10 a.m.-4:30 a.m.; July-August, Daily 10 a.m.-5 p.m.

FAIRYTALE TOWN

3901 Land Park Drive, Sacramento, 916-808-7462; www.fairytaletown.org

A city-owned, nonprofit kids' park that opened in 1959, Fairytale Town livens up classic children's stories and rhymes with 25 fantastic play sets. Don't expect big-budget, Disney-style rides, but rather a fun, low-tech experience that allows kids to climb up (and tumble down) Jack and Jill's hill, jump Jack-be-Nimble's candlestick and play on the Beanstalk Giant's foot in the span of an afternoon. Adjacent to the Sacramento Zoo, the town also has a puppet theater, snack bars and petting zoo. Unless accompanied by a child, adults are not permitted.

Admission: adults and children 3-12 $4 ($4.50 Saturday-Sunday), children 2 and under free. November-February, Thursday-Sunday 10 a.m.-4 p.m.; March-October, Daily 9 a.m.-4 p.m.

GOVERNOR'S MANSION STATE HISTORIC SITE

1526 H St., Sacramento, 916-323-3047; www.parks.ca.gov

Built by a hardware tycoon in 1877, this majestic Second Empire-Italianate mansion in downtown Sacramento served as California's executive mansion from 1903 to 1967, which was the end of Ronald Reagan's term as state governor. The lavish house is now a historic museum, offering guided tours on the hour (which is the only way to catch a glimpse of the inside of this mansion).

Admission: adults $4, children 6-17 $2, children 5 and under free. Daily 10 a.m.-5 p.m.

OLD SACRAMENTO

1004 Second St., Sacramento, www.oldsacramento.com

A slum by the 1960s, this area of Sacramento revived itself by looking back on its early days. Locals set out to simultaneously preserve and revitalize the

BEST ATTRACTIONS

WHAT ARE THE TOP THINGS TO DO IN SACRAMENTO?

VISIT THE CALIFORNIA INDIAN HERITAGE CENTER

Learn about the state's first inhabitants at this museum. It honors Native American culture with exhibits of dugout canoes, weapons, pottery and basketry.

FIND OUT ABOUT THE STATE'S HISTORY AT THE CALIFORNIA MUSEUM

The museum focuses on the people, places and events that shaped the state. Don't miss the "California's Remarkable Women" display to see the mark that ladies left.

WALK THROUGH OLD SACRAMENTO

This National Landmark, a revitalized district, offers a slew of nice shops, restaurants, nightclubs and museums.

TOUR THE SIERRA NEVADA BREWING COMPANY

Beer lovers will want to tour this microbrewery and see how it uses European methods to make its refreshing suds, like its famous Pale Ale.

district, and it soon became a National Landmark and a State Historic Park full of shops, eateries, nightclubs and museums, many of them housed in historic buildings. The area now known as Old Sacramento is the setting for numerous special events, including the renowned Jazz Jubilee music festival and Gold Rush Days, where the entire district dresses up 1850s style.

SACRAMENTO ZOO

3930 W. Land Park Drive, Sacramento, 916-808-5888; www.saczoo.com

Opened in 1927, this zoo features expanses that re-create natural habitats and fully realized ecosystems. Among the dozens of endangered animals are orang-utans, chimpanzees, tigers and cheetahs. Of special note is the Claire Mower Red Panda Forest, a mixed-species environment with a breeding pair of endangered red pandas living alongside Asian birds, fish and reptiles.

Admission: adults $9, seniors $8.25, children 3-12 $6.50, children under 3 free. February-October, Daily 9 a.m.-4 p.m.; November-January, Daily 10 a.m.-4 p.m.

SIERRA NEVADA BREWING COMPANY

1075 E. 20th St., Chico, 530-896-2198; www.sierranevada.com

One of the largest and best-known microbreweries in the United States (to the point where the micro prefix almost no longer applies), the Sierra Nevada Brewing Company's headquarters in Chico is a must-visit for beer aficionados. A free tour takes visitors from the brew house through the bottling plant, showcasing the brewery's European methods, which utilize only four ingredients: water, hops, yeast and barley malts. While the tour does not include complimentary samples, there is a retail store and a taproom/restaurant. Many come just for the wide variety of tasty brews, including the renowned Sierra Nevada Pale Ale as well as some Sierra Nevada brews available only on draft. Check the Big Room's full-calendar of rock and blues concerts.

Taproom and Restaurant: Tuesday-Thursday 11 a.m.-9 p.m., Friday-Saturday 11 a.m.-10 p.m., Sunday 11 a.m.-9 p.m. Guided Brewery Tours: Monday-Friday 2:30 p.m., Saturday noon-3 p.m., Sunday 2:30 p.m. Gift Shop: Daily 10 a.m.-6 p.m.

WILLIAM LAND PARK

3800 Land Park Drive, Sacramento, 916-277-6060; www.cityofsacramento.org

This downtown park is full of beautiful trees and picnic areas. There is a wading pool, basketball court, playground, softball fields, soccer fields, lakes, a rock garden, jogging path and more. William Land Golf Course, the city's oldest golf course, is also located here. The course has nine holes and a café. Take the kids to the onsite amusement park, Funderland (admission is free but you have to buy tickets for rides individually).

WHERE TO STAY

★★★HILTON SACRAMENTO ARDEN WEST

2200 Harvard St., Sacramento, 916-922-4700; www.sacramentoardenwest.hilton.com

This contemporary hotel in Sacramento's Point West area is close to the Cal Expo State Fairgrounds and minutes from the Capitol Rotunda. The guest rooms' soft camel-colored walls, earth-tone bedding and country pine furniture create a cozy atmosphere. Amenities include flat-screen televisions and pillow-top beds. Enjoy comfort foods at the onsite Harvard Street Grille and martinis at the Cameo Lounge.

331 rooms. Restaurant, bar. Business center. Fitness center. Pool. $151-250

★★★HYATT REGENCY SACRAMENTO

1209 L St., Sacramento, 916-443-1234, 800-633-7313; www.sacramento.hyatt.com

Directly across from the State Capitol and Capitol Park, this hotel is adjacent to the Sacramento Convention Center and Community Theater. Rooms have large working desks, leather ergonomic chairs, marble bathrooms and black-and-white photography. Dawson's steakhouse features creative dishes such as grilled salmon with fennel and leak ragout; and pan-roasted Muscovy duck with madeira and orange glaze. Enjoy a drink at one of two bars, Dawson's Bar or Amourath 1819 bar, which also has an outdoor patio.

503 rooms. Restaurant, bar. Business center. Fitness center. Pool. $251-350

★★★SHERATON GRAND SACRAMENTO HOTEL

1230 J St., Sacramento, 916-447-1700, 800-325-3535;
www.sheraton.com

Just a block from the State Capitol, this hotel has a historic setting in the restored 1923 Public Market Building. The modern guest rooms offer the Sheraton Sweet Sleeper bed, flat-screen TVs, Internet access, oversized desks and views of the skyline or city. There's a large 24-hour fitness center, a heated outdoor pool and nearby golf course. The three restaurants include Morgan's Central Valley Bistro, the more casual Glides Market and the Public Market Bar.

503 rooms. Restaurant, bar. Business center. Fitness center. Pool. Pets accepted. $151-250

★★★THE STERLING HOTEL

1300 H St., Sacramento, 916-448-1300, 800-365-7660;
www.sterlinghotel.com

This charming Victorian mansion set on landscaped gardens feels like a countryside retreat, yet it is only a few blocks from the city's downtown shopping plaza, the State Capitol and the convention center. The rooms have period furnishings, Italian marble bathrooms and Jacuzzi tubs. Enjoy a gourmet lunch and dinner at the hotel's Chanterelle restaurant, which features steaks, chicken, seafood, and vegetarian and vegan dishes. The restaurant has an outdoor patio where you can sample dishes such as butternut squash ravioli, a peppercorn-crusted filet or a Black Angus burger with chanterelles.

17 rooms. Restaurant. Complimentary breakfast. Business center. $151-250

RECOMMENDED

THE CITIZEN HOTEL

926 J St., Sacramento, 916-447-2700, 800-365-7660;
www.jdvhotesl.com

Only blocks away from the State Capitol, the Citizen caters to wheelers and dealers in this political city. The Governor's Suite overlooks the Capitol and the Mayor's Suite faces City Hall. All of the rooms have a political bent, with framed editorial cartoons adorning the walls and lampshades printed with text from the state constitution. If you want to meet some politicos, try mingling at the complimentary wine hour with local bottles (Monday-Thursday

---

WHICH SACRAMENTO HOTEL HAS THE MOST UNIQUE DÉCOR?

The Citizen Hotel embraces Sacramento's political scene with government-inspired décor. The lobby looks like a law library, with towering stacks of leather-bound books, and rooms have framed political cartoons and lampshades made of text from the California constitution.

WHAT IS THE MOST CLASSIC RESTAURANT IN SACRAMENTO?

The Firehouse is a Sacramento institution. Inside the fine dining restaurant, you'll find chandeliers, fine art and food that's equally elegant. Try the steak Delmonico, a center-cut rib-eye with caramelized shallot-tomato and house-cured pork belly.

5:30-6:30 p.m.) or grab dinner and a glass of wine from the all-California list from the onsite Grange Restaurant.

198 rooms. Restaurant, bar. Business center. Fitness center. $151-250

WHERE TO EAT

★★★BIBA
2801 Capitol Ave., Sacramento, 916-455-2422;
www.biba-restaurant.com

Since it opened in 1986, chef and owner Biba Caggiano's restaurant has offered a carefully crafted menu of Italian cuisine, an impressive wine list and a relaxed, contemporary atmosphere. Dishes include housemade pasta, grilled lamb chops and steak, veal cutlets and seared tuna. A prix fixe menu is also available during the week. Desserts feature a daily homemade gelato, cherry tarts, tiramisu and rich Italian chocolate mousse.

Italian. Lunch (Monday-Friday), dinner. Closed Sunday. Bar. $36-85

★★★CHANTERELLE
The Sterling Hotel, 1300 H St., Sacramento, 916-442-0451;
www.sterlinghotel.com

This 35-seat restaurant in the Sterling Hotel's four-story Victorian mansion is known for its regional organic California cuisine and quaint setting. Lunch and dinner entrées include grilled Australian lamb rack with pear-pearl onion and bacon mushroom hash, fig and apricot chutney; and porcini-crusted veal medallions with roasted mushrooms, mashed potatoes and veal demi-glace. There are options for vegetarians and vegans as well, such as the butternut squash ravioli with brown butter sage sauce, pine nuts and sautéed spinach or three cheese lasagna with eggplant, wild mushroom, spinach, zucchini, yellow squash and marinara sauce. Sunday brunch is served in the hotel's stunning ballroom.

American. Lunch, dinner, Sunday brunch. Outdoor seating. $36-85

★★★THE FIREHOUSE
1112 Second St., Sacramento, 916-442-4772;
www.firehouseoldsac.com

A Sacramento institution, this fine-dining destination has been in business since 1960. With fine artwork, chandeliers and formally attired waitstaff, this restored

1853 firehouse is a good choice for celebratory dinners. Entrées include a Tuscan pork shank braised with tomatoes, white wine and herbs, garlic mashed potatoes, rainbow chard, wild mushrooms and lemon gremolata; pancetta-wrapped sea scallops with fennel-pear chutney and walnut-arugula risotto croquette. There is also a changing monthly tasting menu.
American. Lunch (Monday-Friday), dinner. Bar. Reservations recommended. Outdoor seating. Bar. $36-85

★★★LEMON GRASS ASIAN GRILL & NOODLE BAR
601 Munroe St., Sacramento, 916-486-4891; www.lemongrassrestaurant.com
Chef and owner Mai Pham's food is inspired by that found on the streets and in the markets of Asia. Sample dishes include Bangkok beef with broccoli, mushrooms, onions and tomatoes stir fried with garlic, Thai basil and chilies; and monk's curry which includes tofu, broccoli, tomatoes, kabocha squash and seasonal vegetables simmering in a yellow curry-coconut milk.
Asian. Lunch (Monday-Friday), dinner. Closed Sunday. Reservations recommended. Outdoor seating. Bar $16-35

★★★MORTON'S, THE STEAKHOUSE
621 Capitol Mall, Sacramento, 916-442-5091; www.mortons.com
This steakhouse chain, which originated in Chicago in 1978, calls out to serious meat-lovers. The 24-ounce porterhouse is the house specialty, but any cut you get here is sure to be tender and juicy. There's also a good selection of fresh fish, lobster or chicken entrées. Desserts include double chocolate mousse, carrot cake and a rich hot chocolate cake.
American. Lunch (Monday-Friday), dinner. Reservations recommended. Bar. $36-85

WHERE TO SHOP

MIDTOWN SACRAMENTO SHOPPING DISTRICT
Alhambra Boulevard and C Street, Sacramento
Similar to shopping districts in San Francisco and Seattle, Midtown's J and K streets have independently-owned sidewalk cafés, coffee shops, boutiques, art galleries and interesting home and garden merchants. Among the area's stalwarts are **Mixed Bag** *(2405 K St.)*, which is jam-packed with a diverse inventory of jewelry, kitchenware and gifts; and **Tasha's the Uncommon Shop** *(1005 22nd St. at J Street)*, specializing in imports ranging from batik dresses to Middle Eastern décor.

HIGH SIERRA

This rustic portion of Northern California is where you'll find all of the great parks and ski spots. One of the most magnificent mountain lakes in the world, Lake Tahoe straddles two states and offers an abundance of wildlife and recreational opportunities. For a spectacular view, drive to the lake's southwestern part where Eagle Creek, one of the thousands of mountain streams that feed the lake, cascades 1,500 feet into Emerald Bay. The curved roads circling North America's largest alpine lake require some effort to navigate, but the shoreline's varied activities—historic sites, hiking, skiing and casinos—make Tahoe a good bet.

Volcanoes and glaciers took their time creating Mammoth Lakes, an outdoor paradise of rugged peaks, plentiful lakes, streams, waterfalls, alpine meadows and extensive forests. See the spectacular scenery in summer, then come back in winter to ski the slopes and soak in the hot springs.

Near the south entrance of Yosemite National Park, Oakhurst derives much of its economy from tourists who come to explore the park. Located along Highway 49, the Gold Chain Highway, the area is filled with historic structures dating to the Gold Rush and is home to the lovely Chateau du Sureau inn and Erna's Elderberry House restaurant.

Of course, Yosemite is one of the most popular and best-known national parks in the world. John Muir, the naturalist instrumental in the founding of this national park, wrote that here are "the most songful streams in the world, the noblest forests, the loftiest granite domes, the deepest ice sculptured canyons." Within 1,169 square miles, there are sheer cliffs, high-wilderness country, alpine meadows, lakes, snowfields, trails, streams and river beaches. Waterfalls are particularly magnificent during spring and early summer. More than 3 million people visit each year, but the views tend to distract from the crowds.

WHAT TO SEE

LAKE TAHOE AREA
ALPINE MEADOWS
2600 Alpine Meadows Road, Tahoe city, 530-583-4232; www.skialpine.com

Best known for its varied terrain, Alpine Meadows consists of 2,400 acres split between six bowls, steep chutes and wide-open glades (25 percent beginner, 40 percent intermediate and 35 percent advanced). The resort—13 miles south of I-80 at Truckee—has 13 lifts, a pair of snowboarding-oriented terrain parks, and a 600-foot superpipe for serious carvers. The nearest accommodations are in Tahoe City.
Mid-November-late May. Lifts: Daily 9 a.m.-4 p.m. Lodge: Daily 8 a.m.-4 p.m.

DESOLATION WILDERNESS AREA
Eldorado National Forest, 100 Forni Road, Placerville, 530-622-5061; www.fs.fed.us

Desolation has Yosemite's natural beauty without the roads and, by extension, traffic. The granite peaks and 130 alpine lakes in this 64,000-acre wilderness southwest of Lake Tahoe still attract backpackers and anglers, but the need for foot and horse travel helps keep crowds out. Glaciers carved and polished the rock here 200,000 years ago. Tree cover and vegetation are limited, but the animal life—including mule deer, black bears, porcupines, badgers and coyotes—is diverse. Fishermen come for the lakes' and streams' steady supply of rainbow and brook trout. Daily fees for campers are collected in order to increase the level of wilderness ranger patrol, maintenance and restoration among other things, and there are zone quotas as to how many people can be in each zone at a time. Reservations are required.

BEST ATTRACTIONS

WHAT ARE THE BEST PLACES FOR OUTDOOR FUN IN THE HIGH SIERRA?

BADGER PASS SKI AREA

Badger Pass is a great ski spot for families, and novices, because most of the mountain is dedicated to beginner and intermediate trails.

HEAVENLY MOUNTAIN RESORT

Fearless skiers and snowboarders tackle this mountain because it boasts the state's longest vertical drop at 3,500 feet.

SIERRA-AT-TAHOE

Sierra-at-Tahoe is a favorite spot for snowboarders. It offers six terrain parks, one half-pipe and a superpipe.

EMERALD BAY STATE PARK

Highway 89, Tahoe City, 530-541-3030; www.parks.ca.gov

Centered on the glacially carved inlet of its name, this park is surrounded by granite peaks and cliffs on the west side of Lake Tahoe. It is home to tiny Fanette Island, a lone chunk of granite that survived the glacial period, and Vikingsholm, a Scandinavian-style castle. Underwater Park is a scuba-diving hotspot, thanks to the presence of numerous shipwrecks dating from the late 1800s, the heyday of the long-gone Emerald Bay Resort. The park also features several nature trails, a 70-site campground, and a beach with swimming access.

HEAVENLY MOUNTAIN RESORT

3860 Saddle Road, South Lake Tahoe, 775-586-7000; www.skiheavenly.com

Straddling the Nevada-California border just south of Lake Tahoe, this resort has a distinct ski area on each side of the line. In California, Heavenly West offers 15 lifts, which take skiers and snowboarders to trails with the state's longest vertical drop—3,500 feet—and a snowboarding half-pipe. On the Nevada side of the mountain, Heavenly North also has 15 lifts, a snowboard cross-trail and a terrain park. Whichever you choose, the snow is clean and plentiful: 360 inches is the average annual snowfall, bolstered by one of the biggest snowmaking operations in the world. A redeveloped village opened in 2002 with a movie multiplex, an ice-skating rink and a host of eateries, night-spots, shops and hotel rooms.

LAKE TAHOE CRUISES

900 Ski Run Blvd., South Lake Tahoe, 775-589-4906, 800-238-2463; www.laketahoecruises.com

This long-standing operation offers a full slate of cruises—breakfast, brunch, lunch, dinner/dance and sightseeing. The fleet includes a pair of Mississippi River-style paddle wheelers. Cruise year-round on the 151-foot *M.S. Dixie II,* ported in Zephyr Cove. The Tahoe Queen, based out of South Lake Tahoe, becomes a ski shuttle/charter vessel during winter.

Daily. Reservations required.

SIERRA-AT-TAHOE

1111 Sierra-at-Tahoe Road, Twin Bridges, 530-659-7453; www.sierraattahoe.com

This large but low-key resort has 2,000 acres set against a 2,212-foot vertical rise, with 25 percent beginner, 50 percent intermediate and 25 percent expert slopes. A favorite of snowboarders, the resort features six terrain parks, one half-pipe and a superpipe. There is also a popular tubing hill but no on-mountain lodging. Shuttle bus service is available.

Mid-November-mid-April. Monday-Friday 9 a.m.-4 p.m., Saturday-Sunday 8:30 a.m.-4 p.m.

SQUAW VALLEY USA

1960 Squaw Valley Road, Olympic Valley, 530-583-6955; www.squaw.com

This ski resort hosted the 1960 Winter Olympics. Today, it has five high-speed quad chairlifts, eight triple chairlifts, eight double chairlifts, an aerial cable car, a gondola, five surface lifts, and a ski school. The longest run is 3.2 miles with the largest vertical drop being 2,850 feet. There are 25 miles of cross-country skiing for those interested in something more tame. Take an aerial cable car to the upper mountain where you'll find the Olympic Ice Pavilion for ice skating and amazing panoramic views. Surrounded by the Sierra Mountains, Squaw Valley's swimming lagoon and whirlpool help skiers relax after a long day. There are plenty of restaurants and bars here to visit when you're not on the slopes. Mid-November-mid-May, daily.

VIKINGSHOLM

Emerald Bay State Park, Tahoe City, 530-525-7277; www.vikingsholm.com

Amid cedar groves at the base of granite cliffs in Emerald Bay State Park stands the Scandinavian-style castle, Vikingsholm. Landowner Lora Knight commissioned her nephew, a Swedish architect, to design the place, and he drew inspiration from Norwegian churches, Swedish castles and traditional wooden homes in both countries. Tours are available in summer. Note that you have to hike a steep one-mile trail from the parking lot to get to the castle's doors.

Admission: adults $5, children 6-17 $3, children under 6 are free. Late-May-late September, daily 10 a.m.-4 p.m.

MAMMOTH LAKES

DEVILS POSTPILE NATIONAL MONUMENT

Mammoth Lakes, 760-934-2289; www.nps.gov

Southeast of Yosemite National Park and surrounded by Inyo National Forest, this monument is among the finest examples of columnar basalt in the world, formed approximately 100,000 years ago when basalt lava erupted in the area.

These columns, which stand 40 to 60 feet high, are a mile hike from the ranger station where you begin your tour. A short, steep trail leads to the top of the formation for a view of the ends of the columns, which have been polished by glaciers. Pumice, porous lava and nearby bubbling soda springs are evidence of recent volcanic activity. At Rainbow Falls, about two miles down the river trail from the Postpile, the San Joaquin River drops 101 feet, where the foam-white water starkly contrasts with the dark cliffs. Look for rainbows in the afternoon. *Mid-June-mid-October, daily.*

HOT CREEK GEOLOGIC SITE
Owens River Road, Mammoth Lakes, 760-924-5500; www.visitmammoth.com
Boiling hot springs warm the waters in Mammoth Creek as geysers gush upwards and fumaroles send up plenty of steam in this river setting surrounded by mountains. For a view of varied volcanic formations, make your way to boardwalks leading through a steep canyon. Fly-fish for trout upstream in the hot springs. Swimming is not recommended here. Pets are allowed.

INYO NATIONAL FOREST
760-873-2400; www.fs.fed.us/r5/inyo
With seven wilderness areas on 2 million acres of protected land, the Inyo National Forest is distinct for its variety of natural features, including Mount Whitney and the famous Minarets, a series of jagged, uniquely weathered peaks in the Sierra Nevadas. The Ancient Bristlecone Pine Forest, which is 4,600 years old and has 600-million-year-old fossils and a unique high-elevation alpine desert at 10,000-14,000 feet, is another interesting sight. Whether you're coming to enjoy a little nature or to play (swimming, boating, riding, pack trips, Nordic skiing and snowmobiling are all available), you're sure to enjoy a visit to this rich forest.

MAMMOTH MOUNTAIN SKI AREA
1 Minaret Road, Mammoth Lakes, 760-934-2571; www.mammothmountain.com
Blanketed by over 400 inches of snow each year, Mammoth's 3,500 skiable acres culminate much of that snow on the 11,053-foot peak of the mountain itself. The resort encompasses 28 lifts, three terrain parks and three half-pipes popular with snowboarders, a multitude of lodging and dining options, a golf course, cross-country ski area and a summertime mountain biking park. Fly-fishermen also love the area's snowmelt-fed streams and lakes.

YOSEMITE NATIONAL PARK
ANSEL ADAMS GALLERY
9031 Village Drive, Yosemite National Park, 209-372-4413; www.anseladams.com
Within Yosemite Village, you'll find the Ansel Adams Gallery, formerly known as Best's Studio, featuring the photography that made the park's landmarks recognizable to people across the country. Prints of Adams' work are available here along with contemporary photography and other fine art, handicrafts, books and souvenirs.
Daily 10 a.m.-5 p.m.

BADGER PASS SKI AREA

Glacier Point Road, Yosemite National Park, 559-253-5635; www.badgerpass.com

If you visit the park in winter, you'll have the opportunity to cross-country ski, ice skate in Yosemite Valley and snowshoe in the Badger Pass area. Badger Pass makes a good family ski destination with 85 percent of the mountain devoted to beginner and intermediate trails. The area is equipped with one triple, three double and one cable tow lift, ski patrol and rentals. There is an ice skating rink, ski tours, snow tubing and snowshoeing among other activities.

Mid-December-late March, daily 9 a.m.-4 p.m.; depending on conditions.

CAMPING

www.nps.gov

According to his good friend Teddy Roosevelt, John Muir said that camping is "the only way in which to see at their best the majesty and charm of the Sierras." Yosemite has 13 campgrounds, including accommodations for traditional tent camping, RVs and canvas tents, and of course, an extensive backcountry for the more adventurous. Camping is limited to 30 days in a calendar year; May to mid-September, camping is limited to seven days in Yosemite Valley, and in the rest of the park to 14 days. Campsites in the valley campgrounds, Hodgdon Meadow, Crane Flat, Wawona and half of Tuolumne Meadows campgrounds may be reserved in advance *(877-444-6777; www.recreation.gov)*. Reservations are highly recommended, as these sites are routinely booked solid in the summer. Other park campgrounds are on a first-come, first-served basis and typically fill very early in the day. Winter camping is permitted in the Valley, Hodgdon Meadow and Wawona only.

GLACIER POINT

The exquisite panorama at Glacier Point from the rim 3,214 feet above Yosemite Valley captures views of the high Sierra and the valley below and faces Half Dome head-on in all its glory. Across the valley from here are Yosemite Falls, the Royal Arches, North Dome, Basket Dome, Mount Watkins and Washington Column. Up the Merced Canyon are Vernal and Nevada falls. Grizzly Peak, Liberty Cap, and the towering peaks along the Sierras' crest and the Clark Range mark the skyline. The road is closed to vehicles in winter but open to skiers and snowshoers.

MARIPOSA GROVE

This is the largest and most visited of Yosemite's three groves of giant sequoia trees. The two-mile road to the grove is closed to cars from November to April, depending on conditions, but can be walked, skied or snowshoed anytime. Merced and Tuolumne groves are near Crane Flat, northwest of Yosemite Valley. The Grizzly Giant in Mariposa Grove, 209 feet high and 34.7 feet in diameter at its base, is estimated to be 2,700 years old.

MONO LAKE

Highway 395 and Third Street, Lee Vining, 760-647-6595; www.monolake.org

Located in the Mono Basin National Forest Scenic Area, one of North America's

oldest lakes contains 250 percent more salt than the Pacific Ocean. Millions of migratory waterfowl feed here on brine shrimp, but there are no fish. Come to explore and bird-watch, bike and picnic at the Mono Lake Country Park (only 5 miles north of Lee Vining). Mark Twain wrote about the lake and its islands, volcanoes and gulls in *Roughing It.*
Daily.

YOSEMITE MUSEUM

209-372-0200; www.nps.gov

Next to the visitor center, this museum has displays that explore the cultural history of the indigenous Miwok and Paiute peoples and an art gallery. Just behind the museum is the Indian Village of Ahwahnee, a reconstructed Miwok-Paiute village with a self-guided trail, which is always open.
Daily 9 a.m.-4:30 p.m.

YOSEMITE MOUNTAIN SUGAR PINE RAILROAD

Fish Camp, 56001 Highway 41, Yosemite National Park, 559-683-7273; www.ymsprr.com

Take a four-mile historic narrow-gauge steam train excursion through scenic Sierra National Forest, which is south of Yosemite. These locomotives were used to haul log trains through the mountains. Take either the Logger steam train, Jenny Railcars—which are narrated—or the moonlight special, which includes a barbecue and live entertainment.
See website for schedule and pricing.

YOSEMITE VALLEY

209-372-0200; www.nps.gov

A must-see, and the main reason most people come to this park, the valley lies at the foot of such wonders as the 5,000-foot Half Dome, the 3,000-foot sheer granite wall of El Capitan and the roaring Yosemite and Bridalveil Falls. One of the most famous views is of the Tunnel View, in which you gaze up at Cloud's Rest, with El Capitan on the left and Bridal Veil Falls on the right. Follow signs for Yosemite Village to reach the **Yosemite Valley Visitor Center** *(www.yosemite.org)*, the largest information station in the park, where you'll find details on all there is to see and do during your stay.

WHERE TO STAY

LAKE TAHOE AREA

★★★CHALET VIEW LODGE

72056 Highway 70, Portola, 530-832-5528; www.chaletviewlodge.com

Staying at this country lodge, located north of Lake Tahoe in the Mohawk Valley, feels like a weekend away at the home of a stylish friend. The cozy lobby has deep leather couches and a fireplace. Rooms feature luxury bedding, Jacuzzi tubs, flat-screen TVs and Starbucks coffee for the coffeemaker. The restaurant serves breakfast and dinner.
45 rooms. Restaurant, bar. Fitness center. Pool. Spa. $151-250

WHICH HIGH SIERRA HOTELS ARE BEST FOR A QUIET ESCAPE?

Chateau Du Sureau: Hidden away in the Sierra Nevada forest, this hotel offers a soothing nature retreat. Plus, the rooms don't have TVs, so the only noise you'll hear is the chirping birds.

The Ahwahnee Hotel: If you are looking to get away from it all, hide out in this hotel, which sits in Yosemite National Park.

★★★EMBASSY SUITES LAKE TAHOE HOTEL & SKI RESORT

4130 Lake Tahoe Blvd., South Lake Tahoe, 530-544-5400, 877-497-8483; www.embassytahoe.com

This hotel is designed with the guest rooms all facing a landscaped inner atrium. Amenities include a restaurant, lounges, several patios, a swimming pool, fitness center, sauna and meeting and banquet facilities. The lodge is within walking distance of all the major casinos and the lake. A free shuttle takes you to the Heavenly and Sierra-at-Tahoe ski resorts.

400 rooms. Restaurant, bar. Complimentary breakfast. Business center. Fitness center. Pool.

★★★RESORT AT SQUAW CREEK

400 Squaw Creek Road, Olympic Valley, 530-583-6300, 800-327-3353; www.squawcreek.com

This full-service resort is just minutes by a private chairlift from the challenging peaks and scenic trails of Squaw Valley, site of the 1960 Winter Olympics. The resort is well-known for its terrific 18-hole golf course (designed by Robert Trent Jones, Jr.), spa, tennis courts and hiking and biking trails, as well as its outdoor skating rink, heated pools, hot tubs and multitude of snowbound activities. This family-friendly mountain getaway also has comfortable rooms and suites and five dining outlets.

405 rooms. Restaurant, bar. Spa. $151-250

★★★THE RITZ-CARLTON, LAKE TAHOE

13031 Ritz-Carlton Highlands Court, Truckee, 530-562-3000; www.ritzcarlton.com

This newly opened Ritz-Carlton is located a short distance from famous Lake Tahoe. Exciting adventures on the lake or lounging on the beach are available all summer long. If you visit in the winter, the resort has enticing ski-in access. The hotel offers all the amenities you'd expect from a Ritz-Carlton as well as luxurious rooms with a sophisticated mountain retreat decor. The signature restaurant Manzanita, from famed San Francisco chef Traci Des Jardins, offers local and organic cuisine in the chef's noteworthy French style but with mountain influences. Be sure to grab a drink by the cozy Living Room lounge. The 17,000-square-foot Highlands Spa is the ultimate respite from the boundless activities offered in and around Lake Tahoe. After a hard day on the slopes, you may want to indulge in the Pinyon Pine Nut Warm Stone massage, a deep pressure treatment that uses essential oils of the pinyon pine nut. These oils are prized for their ability to soothe achy muscles.

170 rooms. Restaurant, bar. Fitness center. Spa. $351 and up

MAMMOTH LAKES

★★★MAMMOTH MOUNTAIN INN

1 Minaret Road, Mammoth Lakes, 760-934-2581, 800-626-6684;
www.mammothmountain.com

The Mammoth Mountain Inn is a great place to base your vacation if you want to wake up on the mountain itself. Steps away from the gondola and Main Lodge, this Inn is the perfect location for those who want to get on the slopes as soon as possible. Choose from basic rooms to condos or suites; condo units are equipped with a kitchen and dining area and suites come with a refrigerator. All rooms offer Internet access, a telephone and TV/DVD. Head to the Mountainside Grill for California cuisine or to the Dry Creek Bar for cocktails.

213 rooms. Restaurant, bar. Business center. Fitness center. Pool. $251-350

OAKHURST

★★★★CHATEAU DU SUREAU

48688 Victoria Lane, Oakhurst, 559-683-6860; www.chateausureau.com

Tucked away in the heart of the Sierra Nevada forest is a lovely hideaway known as Chateau du Sureau. Foodies have been coming to the Elderberry House restaurant since 1984 for its haute cuisine, and the restaurant did so well that owner Erna Kubin-Clanin opened an inn to accommodate her guests. This charming Provençal castle features quaint balconies and a dramatic round fieldstone tower. The grounds are planted with manicured topiaries and the stucco walls are dotted with Elderberry bushes that cover the castle's rolling grounds. Inside, chambermaids wearing black with white-linen aprons deliver baskets of goodies and tea. There is no front desk, no check-in formalities. The 10 unique bedrooms, nearly all of which have fireplaces, include canopy and sleigh beds, cathedral ceilings and views of the Sierra Nevada Mountains and there are no televisions, so you can truly relax. There is a swimming pool, bocce ball court and life-size chess set to keep guests busy; or enjoy a spa treatment at the Spa Sureau.

10 rooms. Closed two weeks in January. Restaurant, bar. Complimentary breakfast. Pool. Spa. $351 and up

YOSEMITE NATIONAL PARK

★★★THE AHWAHNEE HOTEL

Yosemite Valley, Yosemite National Park, 801-559-4884; www.yosemitepark.com

Opened in 1927, this storied hotel, located within Yosemite National Park, is a celebration of Native American and colonial American designs. Its wooded, natural setting is perfectly complemented by the Native American décor, including artifacts and artwork created by the Yosemite Miwok. The rooms and suites may appear rustic, but the public spaces are glorious, with impressive stained-glass windows, intricate stonework and mosaics in the lobby, as well as a lounge, solarium and dining room.

123 rooms. Restaurant, bar. $351 and up

★★★TENAYA LODGE AT YOSEMITE

1122 Highway 41, Fish Camp, 559-683-6555, 888-514-2167; www.tenayalodge.com

Situated on 35 acres adjacent to the Sierra National Forest and just two miles from Yosemite, this elegant mountain retreat is just the place to see the sights without forsaking the comforts of home. The newly renovated guest rooms and suites share an upscale yet rustic appeal. Guests are supplied with all-natural, eco-friendly bath amenities. Activities are plentiful, both on the property and off, including a terrific children's program. Enjoy fine dining at Sierra, while Jackalopes Bar & Grill is ideal for the entire family.

244 rooms. Restaurant, bar. Fitness center. Pool. Spa. $151-250

WHERE TO EAT

LAKE TAHOE AREA

★★★EVANS AMERICAN GOURMET CAFÉ

536 Emerald Bay Road, South Lake Tahoe, 530-542-1990; www.evanstahoe.com

This café has a creative menu that includes options such as roast venison loin with pinot noir-dried cherry demi-glace and parsnip mashed potatoes. The extensive wine list emphasizes selections from California and the Northwest. Desserts, including butter pecan bananas foster, crème brûlée and frozen white chocolate mousse, are made fresh daily.

American. Dinner. $16-35

★★★MANZANITA

The Ritz-Carlton, Lake Tahoe, 13031 Ritz-Carlton Highlands Court, Truckee, 530-562-3000; www.ritzcarlton.com

Famed San Francisco chef Traci Des Jardins is at the helm of this mountainside restaurant within the Ritz-Carlton, Lake Tahoe. The restaurant appeals to guests and locals alike, thanks to guaranteed crowd pleasers such as fried olives, duck meatballs and a grass-fed hamburger with pommes frites. Entrees include Mystic River salmon and red wine braised short ribs with horseradish potato purée and an herb salad. The restaurant bustles with energy from the open kitchen and a spacious lounge. Open for breakfast, lunch and dinner, it's always a good time to visit this innovative yet comforting restaurant.

American, French. Breakfast, lunch, dinner. Reservations recommended. $36-85

★★★SWISS CHALETS

2544 Lake Tahoe Blvd., South Lake Tahoe, 530-544-3304; www.tahoeswisschalet.com

This restaurant, which resembles a chalet you would expect to find among the Swiss Alps, has been chef-owned and operated since 1957. Swiss specialties are the focus of the menu. Enjoy fondue as they do in Switzerland, or try one of the specialty dishes such as authentic wienerschnitzel.

Swiss. Dinner. Closed Monday. Children's menu. Bar. $16-35

OAKHURST

★★★★ERNA'S ELDERBERRY HOUSE

Chateau Du Sureau, 48688 Victoria Lane, Oakhurst, 559-683-6800; www.chateausureau.com

This charming restaurant, with three dining areas, offers an exquisite seasonal menu of California cuisine served in a setting decorated with antique French provincial furnishings, brocade tapestries and original oil paintings. Since 1984, Erna Kubin-Clanin has guided the kitchen toward farm-raised meats and local produce. Prix fixe menus change daily and consist of five courses paired with three or four California or international wines; or choose a meal off the à la carte menu with options such as wienerschnitzel or braised rabbit. The 725-bottle wine list is overseen by Erna's daughter Renee and includes several rare and cult California wines as well as many Austrian selections, in honor of Erna's birthplace.

American, French. Dinner, Sunday brunch. Closed first two weeks in January. Reservations recommended. Outdoor seating. Bar. $86 and up

---

WHAT IS THE MOST CLASSIC RESTAURANT IN THE HIGH SIERRAS?

The success of fine dining eatery **Erna's Elderberry House** spawned Chateau Du Sureau. Foodies flock to this eatery in the forest for superb Californian cuisine, such as grilled Monterey king salmon with horseradish sabayon and glazed celeriac.

RECOMMENDED

YOSEMITE NATIONAL PARK
THE AHWAHNEE DINING ROOM
The Ahwahnee Hotel, Yosemite National Park, Yosemite Valley, 209-372-1489, 801-559-4884; www.yosemitepark.com

The architecture is enough to make a meal here worthwhile, with a grand 34-foot-high beamed ceiling and floor-to-ceiling windows exposing the beauty beyond the glass. But the gourmet California cuisine, including organic, sustainable and locally grown ingredients, could easily stand alone. Try a specialty such as the roast prime rib of California grass-fed beef au jus or the spinach and chickpea crêpes.

American. Breakfast, lunch, dinner, Sunday brunch. Reservations recommended. $35-86

SPAS

OAKHURST
★★★★SPA DU SUREAU
48688 Victoria Lane, Oakhurst, 559-683-6193; www.chateausureau.com

Decorated throughout in charming Art Deco style, there are only three treatment rooms (all with iPod docks) and one wet room at this petite spa. The focal point, however, is the decadent double treatment room with its black marble fireplace, two massage tables separated by translucent drapes, lounge chairs and Jacuzzi. The spa also features a Hydrostorm shower system—one of only a handful in the country—that uses aroma and color therapy aquatics. The treatment menu includes European Kur baths, which feature marine hydrotherapy and use only top-notch ingredients, such as moor mud from the Czech Republic, touted for its high concentration of vitamins and minerals.

NORTHERN CALIFORNIA

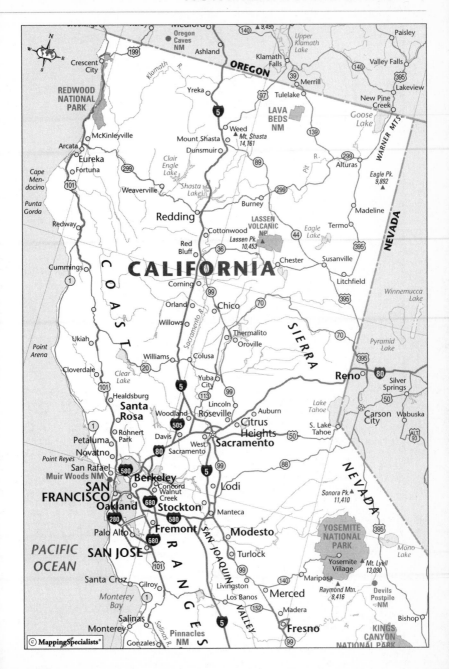

NORTHERN CALIFORNIA

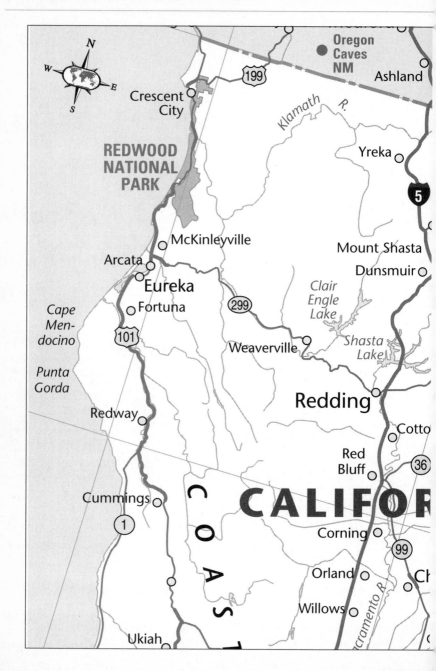

N
W E
S

Oregon
Caves
NM

Ashland

199

Klamath R.

Crescent
City

REDWOOD
NATIONAL
PARK

Yreka

5

McKinleyville

Mount Shasta

Arcata

Dunsmuir

Eureka

Clair
Engle
Lake

Fortuna

299

Cape
Men-
docino

101

Weaverville

Shasta
Lake

Punta
Gorda

Redway

Redding

Cotto

Red
Bluff

36

Cummings

CALIFOR

1

Corning

99

Orland

Ch

Willows

Sacramento R.

Ukiah

C O A S T

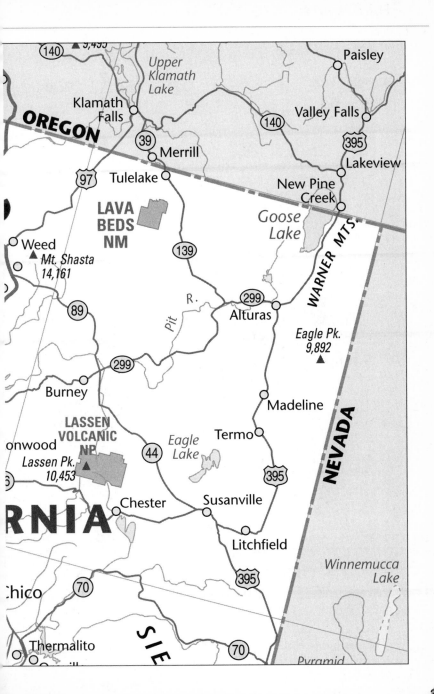

BAY AREA

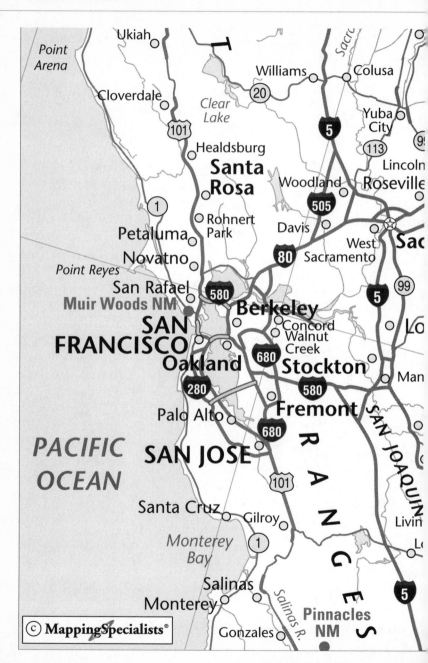

Point
Arena

Ukiah

T

Sacr

Williams

Colusa

Cloverdale

Clear
Lake

20

Yuba
City

5

101

Healdsburg

113

99

Lincoln

**Santa
Rosa**

Woodland

Roseville

1

505

Rohnert
Park

Davis

West
Sacramento

Sac

Petaluma

80

Novatno

Point Reyes

San Rafael

580

99

5

Muir Woods NM

**SAN
FRANCISCO**

Berkeley

Concord
Walnut
Creek

Lo

Oakland

680

Stockton

280

580

Man

Palo Alto

Fremont

680

SAN JOAQUIN

*PACIFIC
OCEAN*

SAN JOSE

R
A
N
G
E
S

101

Santa Cruz

Gilroy

Livin

Lo

*Monterey
Bay*

1

Salinas

5

Monterey

Salinas R.

© **Mapping**Specialists®

Gonzales

**Pinnacles
NM**

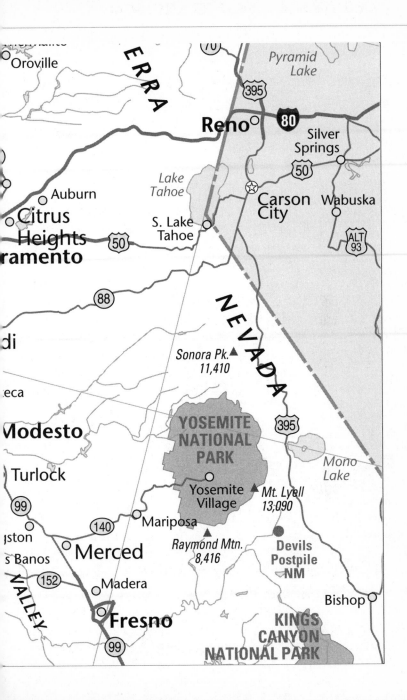

Oroville

ERRA

Pyramid
Lake

70

395

Reno

80

Silver
Springs

Auburn

50

Lake
Tahoe

Carson
City

Wabuska

Citrus

Heights

S. Lake
Tahoe

ramento

50

ALT
93

88

NEVADA

di

Sonora Pk.
11,410

eca

Modesto

YOSEMITE
NATIONAL
PARK

395

Turlock

Mono
Lake

99

Yosemite
Village

Mt. Lyell
13,090

140

Mariposa

ston

Merced

Raymond Mtn.
8,416

Devils
Postpile
NM

s Banos

152

Madera

Bishop

VALLEY

Fresno

KINGS
CANYON
NATIONAL PARK

99

OVERVIEW OF SAN FRANCISCO

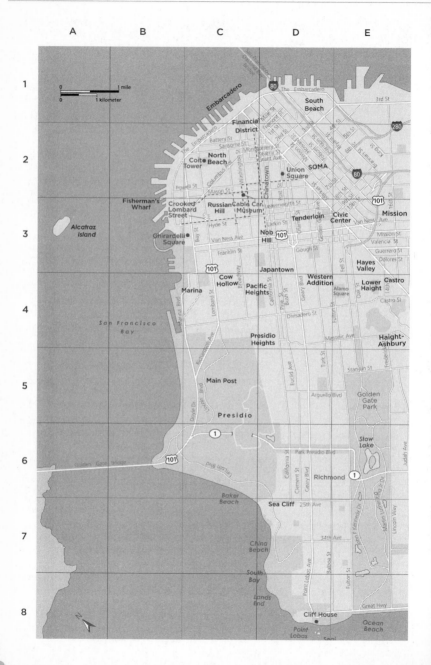

SAN FRANCISCO CABLE CARS

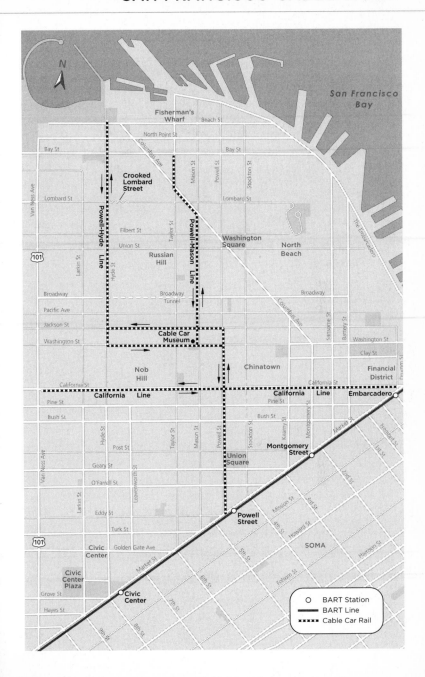

WEST SAN FRANCISCO

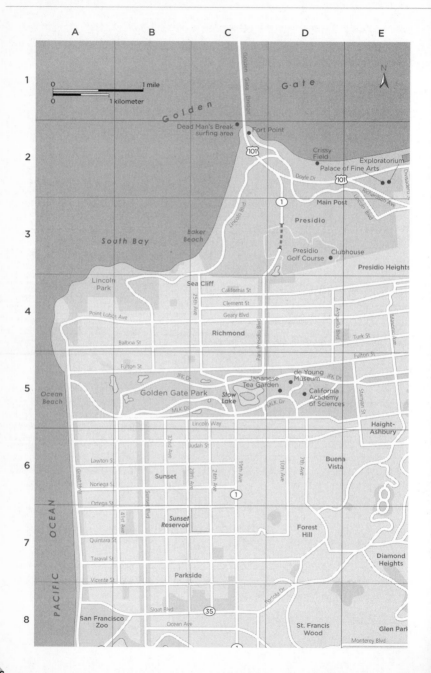

EAST SAN FRANCISCO

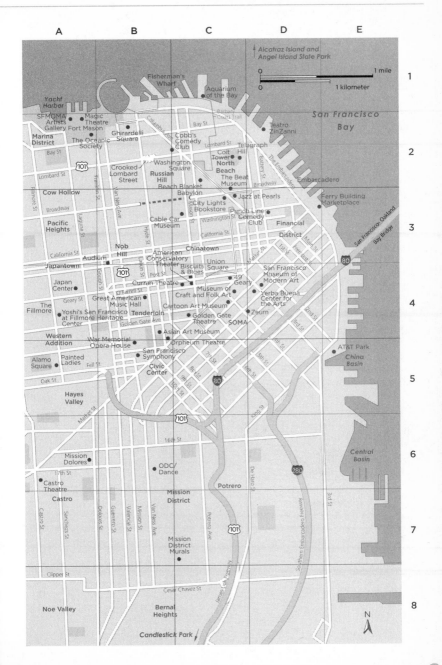

Alcatraz Island and Angel Island State Park

0 —— 1 mile
0 —— 1 kilometer

San Francisco Bay

Fisherman's Wharf

Aquarium of the Bay

Yacht Harbor

SFMOMA Artists Gallery Fort Mason
Magic Theatre
The Oceanic Society
Ghirardelli Square

Marina District

Teatro ZinZanni

Cobb's Comedy Club

Bay St
Lombard St

Coit Tower
North Beach
Telegraph Hill

Embarcadero

Crooked Lombard Street
Washington Square
Russian Hill
The Beat Museum

Beach Blanket Babylon

Ferry Building Marketplace

Cow Hollow

City Lights Bookstore

Jazz at Pearls

Broadway

Cable Car Museum
Punch Line Comedy Club

Pacific Heights

Washington St

California St

Financial District

San Francisco-Oakland Bay Bridge

Nob Hill

Chinatown

Audium
Japantown

American Conservatory Theater

Union Square

San Francisco Museum of Modern Art

Japan Center

Biscuits & Blues

Curran Theatre

Geary
49

Great American Music Hall

Museum of Craft and Folk Art

Yerba Buena Center for the Arts

The Fillmore

O'Farrell St

Cartoon Art Museum

Zeum

Yoshi's San Francisco at Fillmore Heritage Center

Tenderloin

Golden Gate Theatre

SOMA

Western Addition

War Memorial Opera House

Asian Art Museum

Orpheum Theatre

Alamo Square
Painted Ladies

San Francisco Symphony

AT&T Park
China Basin

Civic Center

Oak St

Hayes Valley

Central Basin

Market St

16th St

Mission Dolores

ODC/ Dance

17th St

Potrero

Castro Theatre

Mission District

Castro

De Haro St

Mission District Murals

Clipper St

Cesar Chavez St

Noe Valley

Bernal Heights

N

Candlestick Park

GOLDEN GATE PARK

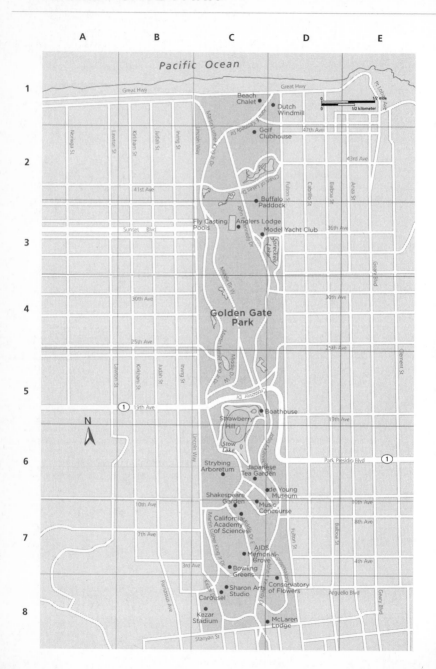

NOTES

NOTES

NOTES

NOTES

NOTES

NOTES